SUICIDE RISK™

VOLUME SIX • THE BREAKING OF SO GREAT A THING

ROSS RICHIE CEO & Founder • MATT GAGNON Editor-in-Chief • FILIP SABLIK President of Publishing & Marketing • STEPHEN CHRISTY President of Development • LANCE KREITER VP of Licensing & Merchandising
PHIL BARBARO VP of Finance • BRYCE CARLSON Managing Editor • MEL CAYLO Marketing Manager • SCOTT NEWMAN Production Design Manager • IRENE BRADISH Operations Manager • CHRISTINE DINH Brand Communications Manager
SIERRA HAHN Senior Editor • DAFNA PLEBAN Editor • SHANNON WATTERS Editor • ERIC HARBURN Editor • IAN BRILL Editor • WHITNEY LEOPARD Associate Editor • JASMINE AMIRI Associate Editor • CHRIS ROSA Associate Editor
ALEX GALER Assistant Editor • CAMERON CHITTOCK Assistant Editor • MARY GUMPORT Assistant Editor • KELSEY DIETERICH Production Designer • JILLIAN CRAB Production Designer • KARA LEOPARD Production Designer
MICHELLE ANKLEY Production Design Assistant • DEVIN FUNCHES E-Commerce & Inventory Coordinator • AARON FERRARA Operations Coordinator • ELIZABETH LOUGHRIDGE Accounting Coordinator • JOSÉ MEZA Sales Assistant
JAMES ARRIOLA Mailroom Assistant • STEPHANIE HOCUTT Marketing Assistant • SAM KUSEK Direct Market Representative • HILLARY LEVI Executive Assistant • KATE ALBIN Administrative Assistant

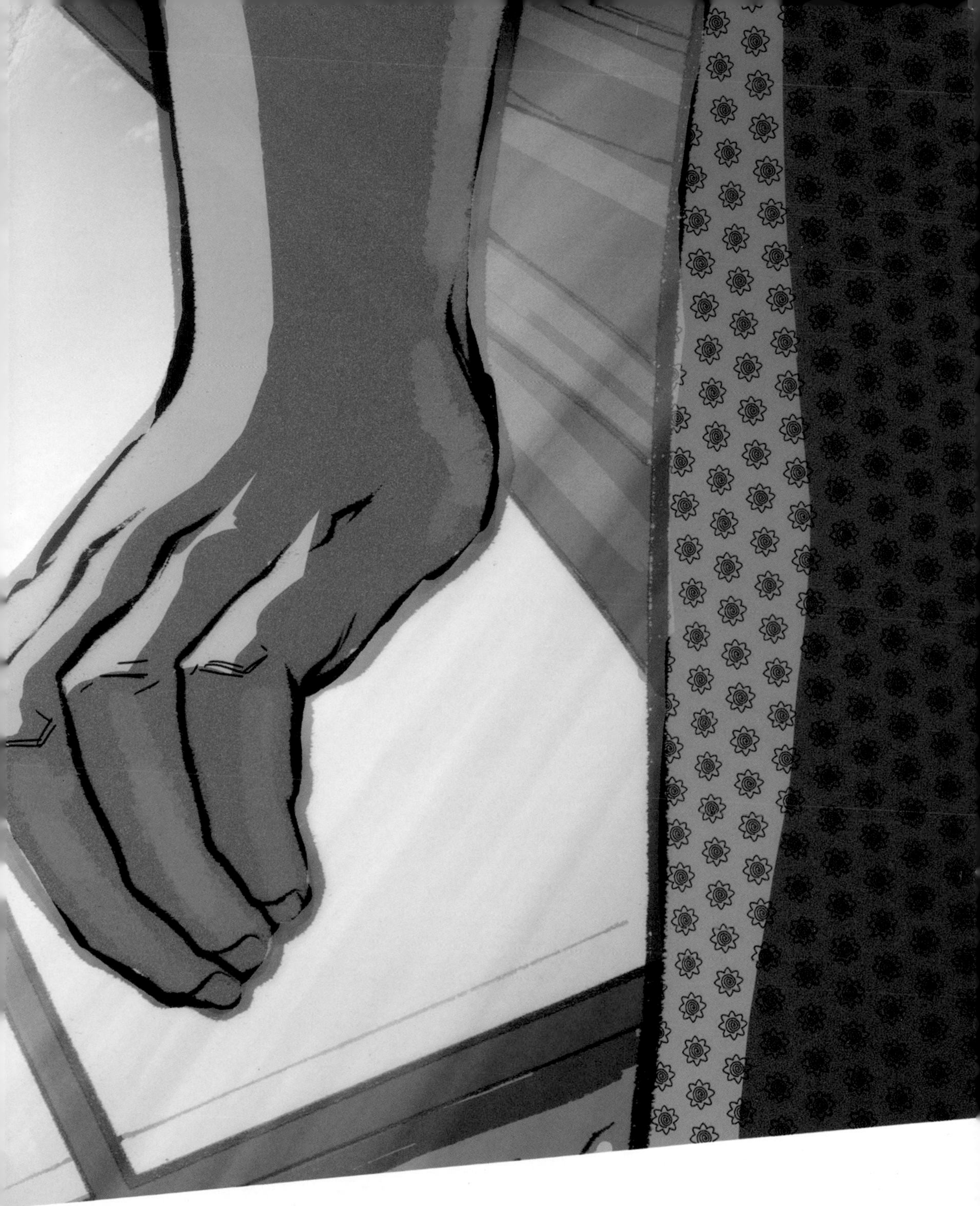

Created & Written By
MIKE CAREY

Art By
ELENA CASAGRANDE
with ink assists by MICHELE PASTA
and layout assists by GIORGIA SPOSITO

Colors By
ANDREW ELDER

Letters By
ED DUKESHIRE

Editors
DAFNA PLEBAN
MATT GAGNON

Cover By
STEPHANIE HANS

Trade Design By
KARA LEOPARD

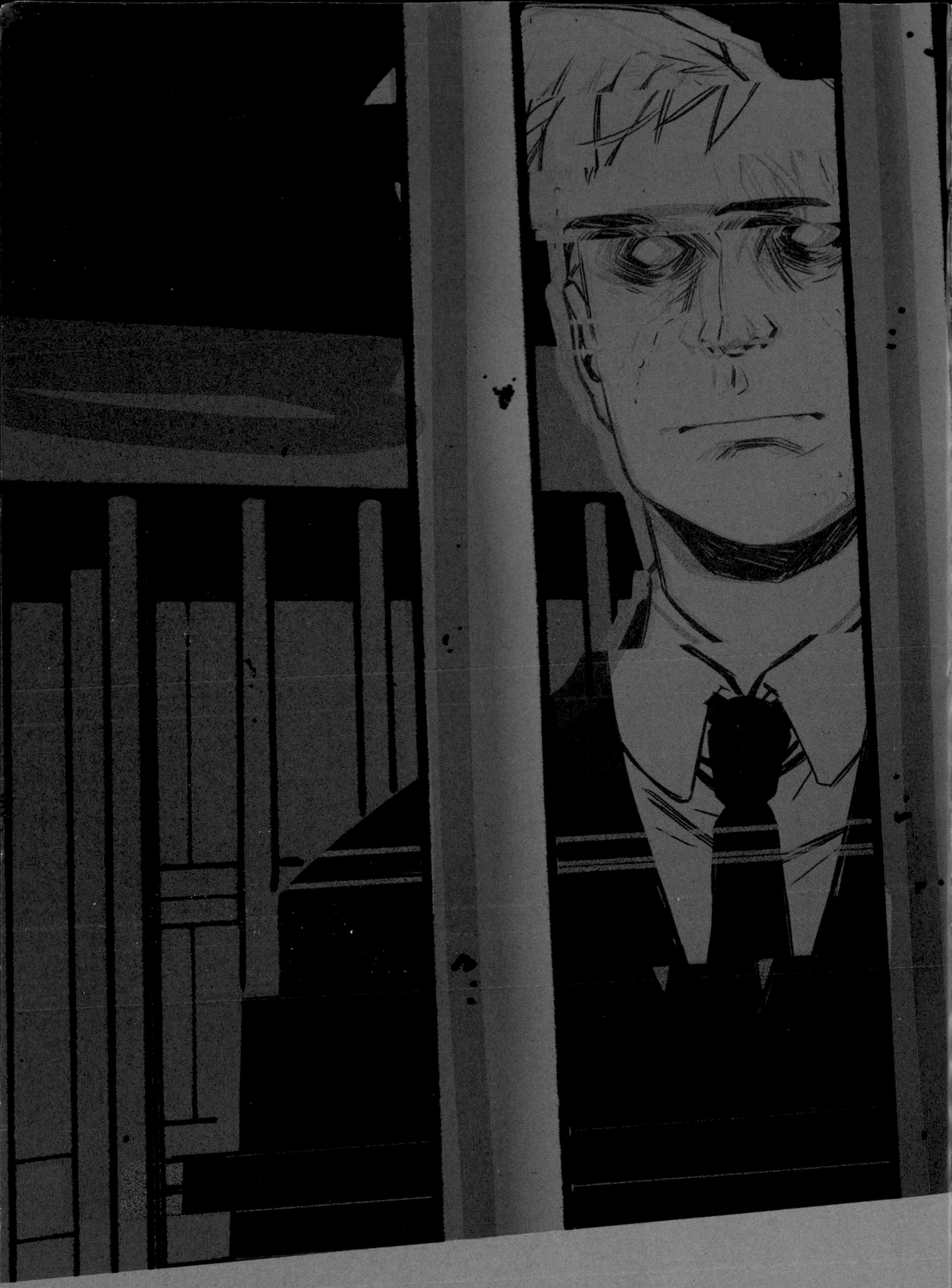

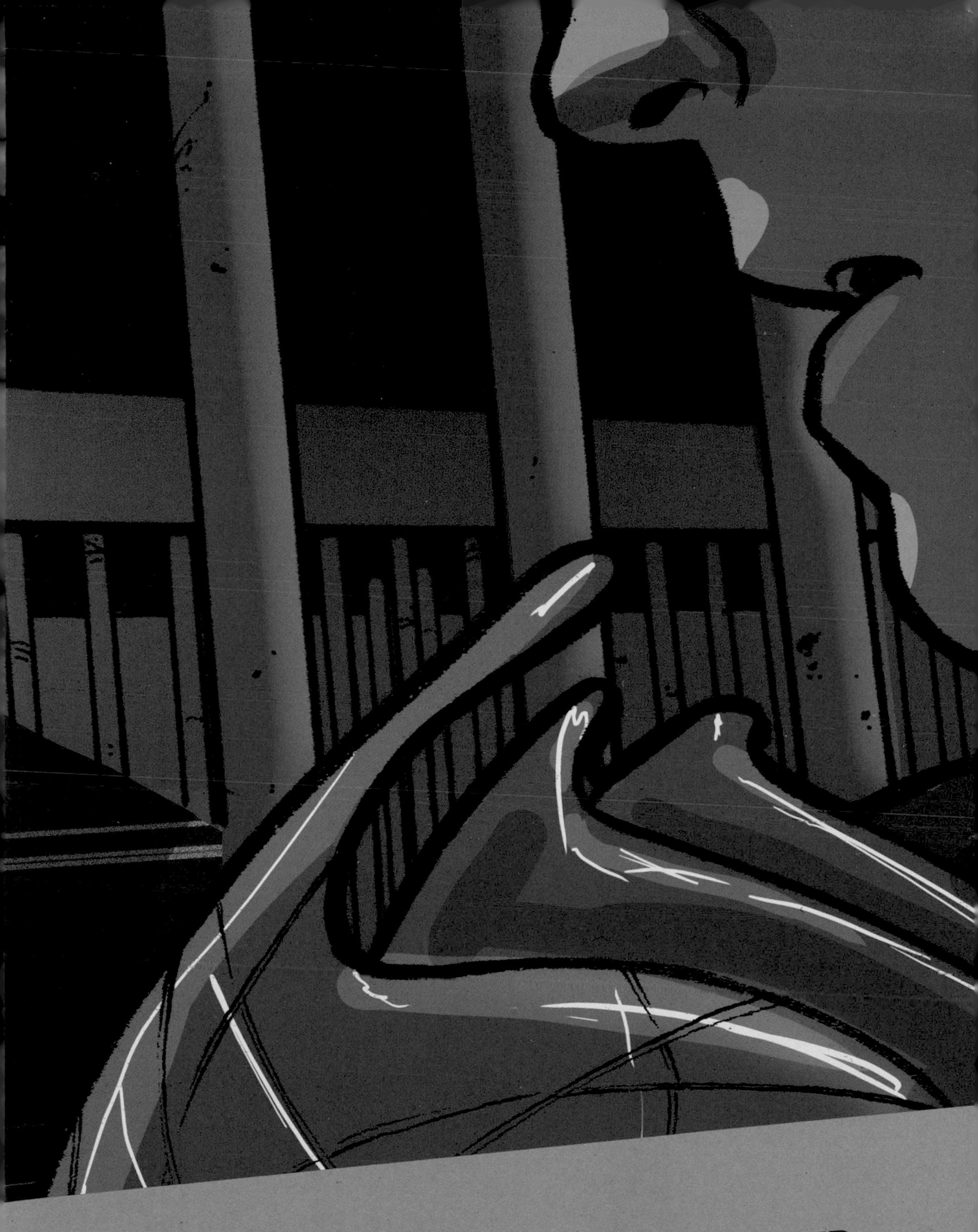

"BUT **THIS** IS WHAT YOU'VE EARNED.
AND IT **REJOICES** ME TO GIVE IT."
Chapter 22

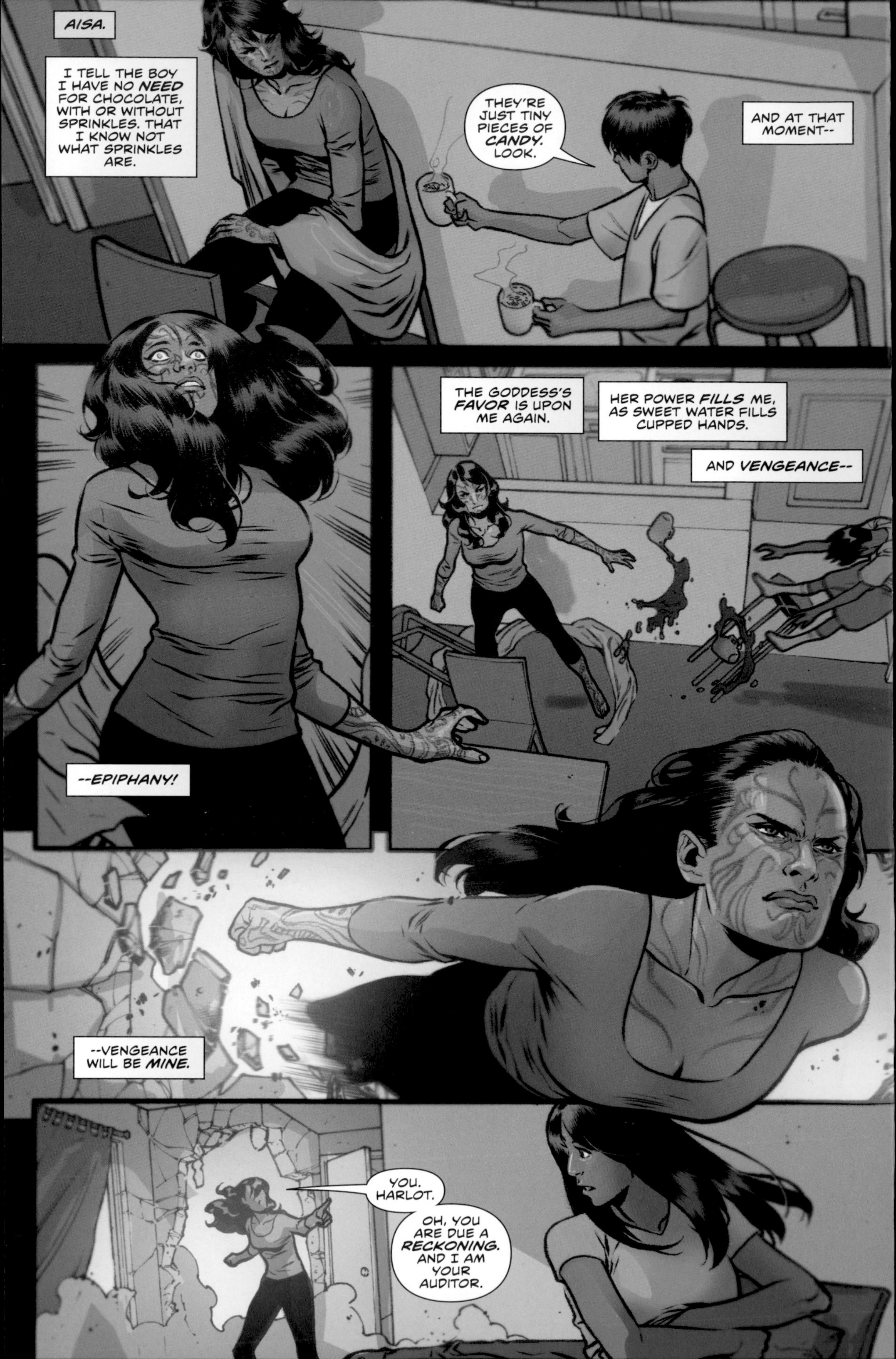
AISA.
I TELL THE BOY I HAVE NO NEED FOR CHOCOLATE, WITH OR WITHOUT SPRINKLES. THAT I KNOW NOT WHAT SPRINKLES ARE.
THEY'RE JUST TINY PIECES OF CANDY. LOOK.
AND AT THAT MOMENT--
--EPIPHANY!
THE GODDESS'S FAVOR IS UPON ME AGAIN.
HER POWER FILLS ME, AS SWEET WATER FILLS CUPPED HANDS.
AND VENGEANCE--
--VENGEANCE WILL BE MINE.
YOU. HARLOT.
OH, YOU ARE DUE A RECKONING. AND I AM YOUR AUDITOR.

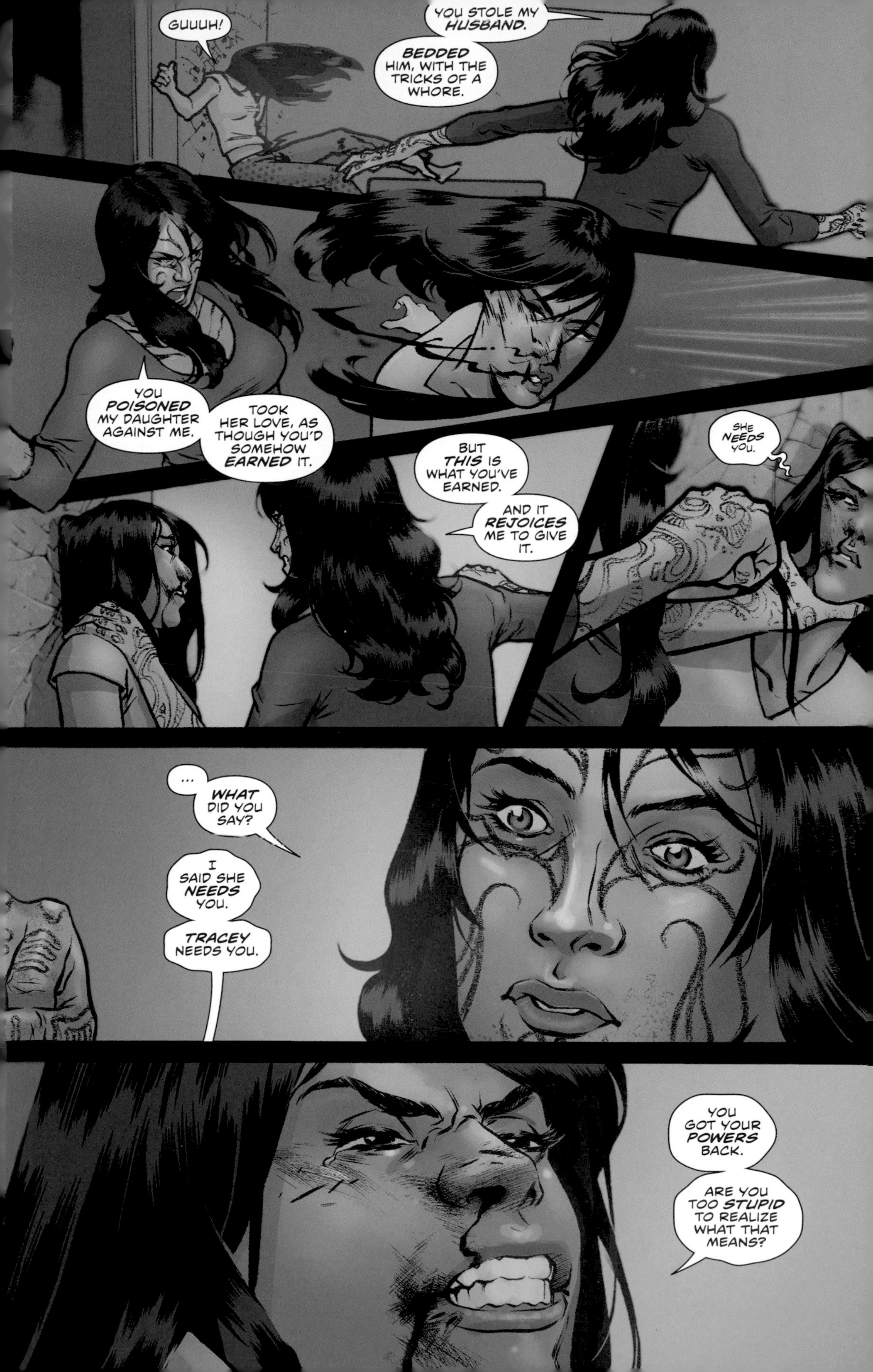
GUUUH!
YOU STOLE MY HUSBAND.
BEDDED HIM, WITH THE TRICKS OF A WHORE.
YOU POISONED MY DAUGHTER AGAINST ME.
TOOK HER LOVE, AS THOUGH YOU'D SOMEHOW EARNED IT.
BUT THIS IS WHAT YOU'VE EARNED.
AND IT REJOICES ME TO GIVE IT.
SHE NEEDS YOU.
... WHAT DID YOU SAY?
I SAID SHE NEEDS YOU.
TRACEY NEEDS YOU.
YOU GOT YOUR POWERS BACK.
ARE YOU TOO STUPID TO REALIZE WHAT THAT MEANS?

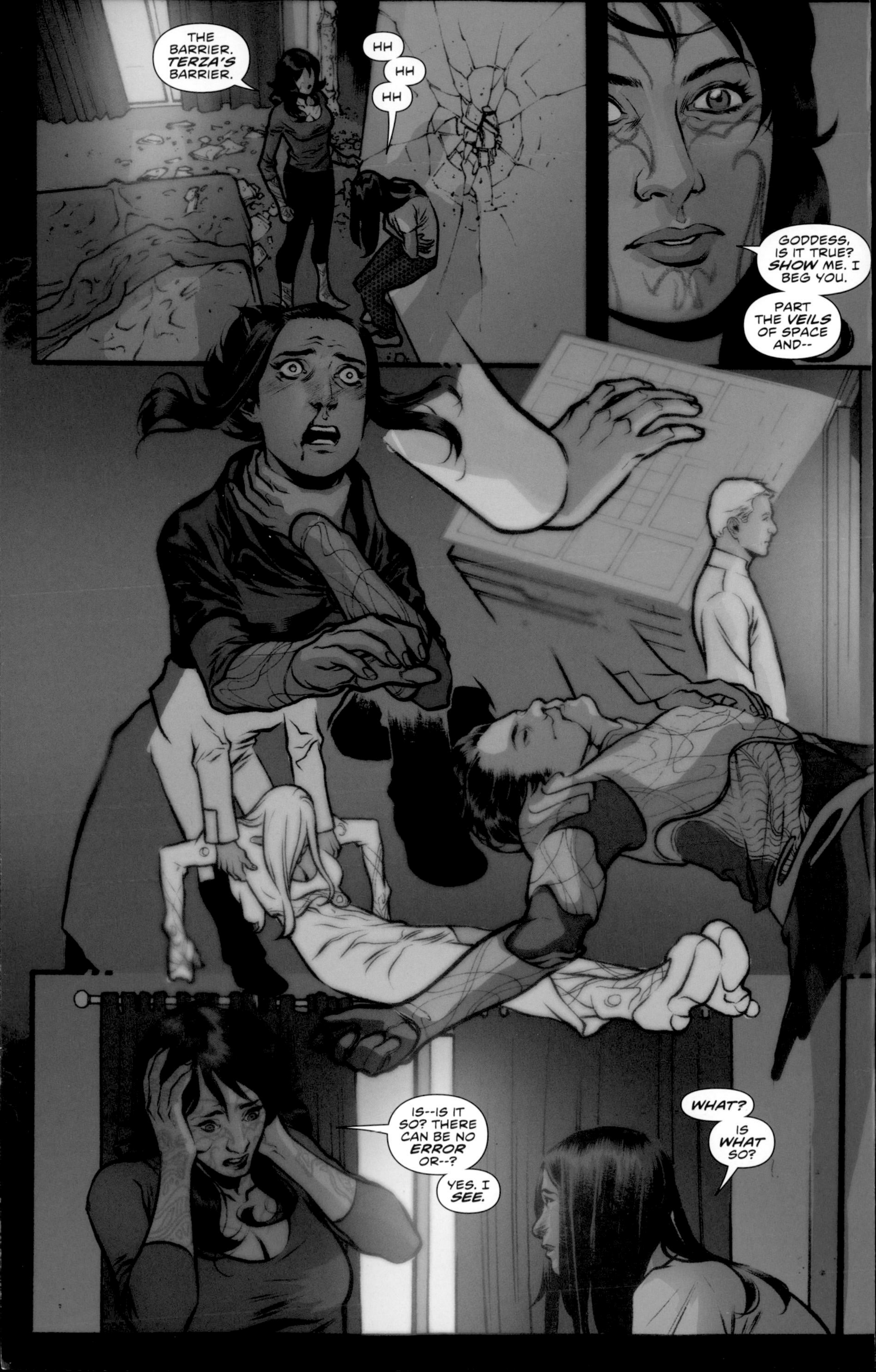
THE BARRIER. TERZA'S BARRIER.
HH
HH
HH
GODDESS, IS IT TRUE? SHOW ME. I BEG YOU.
PART THE VEILS OF SPACE AND--
IS--IS IT SO? THERE CAN BE NO ERROR OR--?
YES. I SEE.
WHAT?
IS WHAT SO?

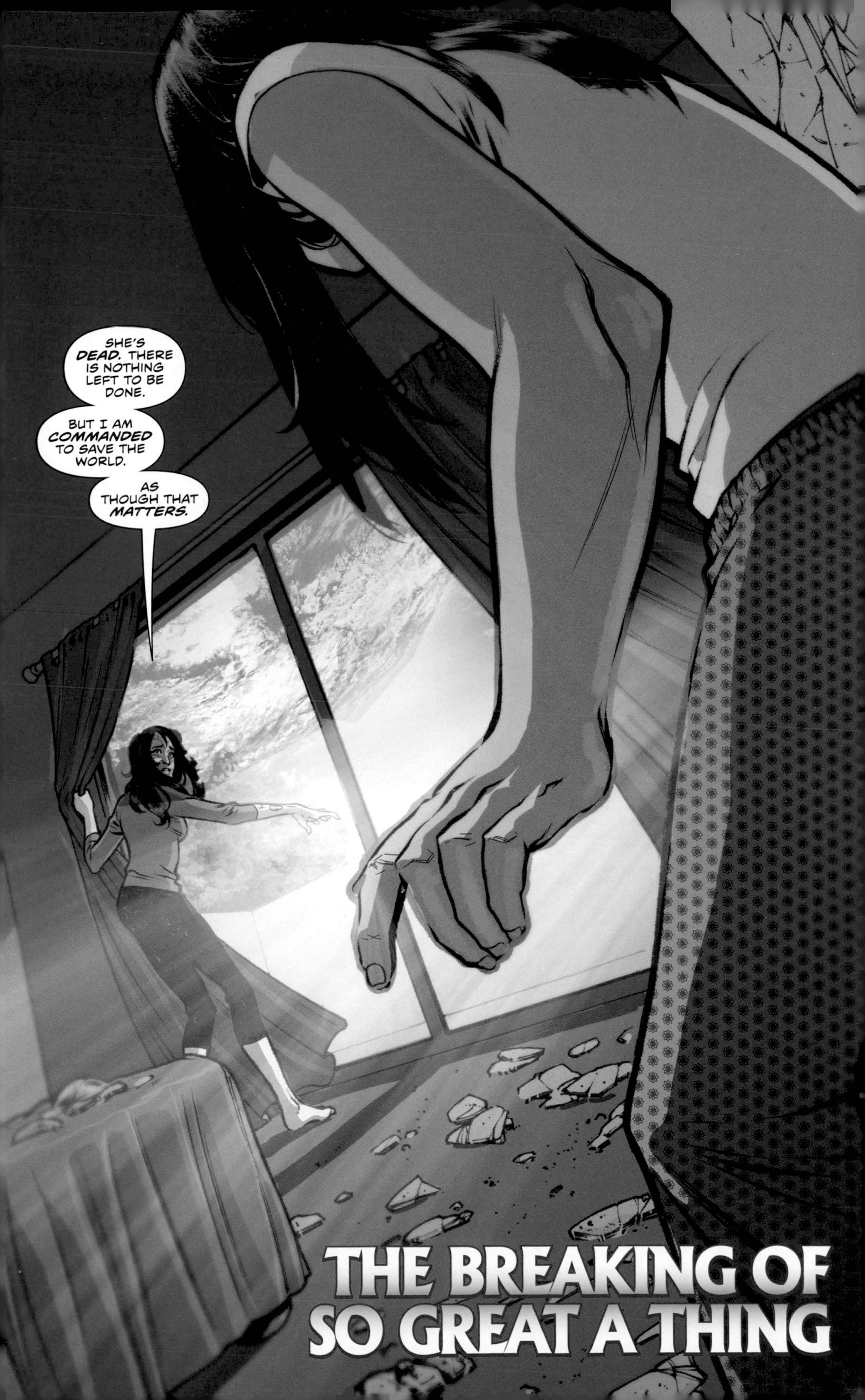
SHE'S DEAD. THERE IS NOTHING LEFT TO BE DONE.
BUT I AM COMMANDED TO SAVE THE WORLD.
AS THOUGH THAT MATTERS.
THE BREAKING OF SO GREAT A THING

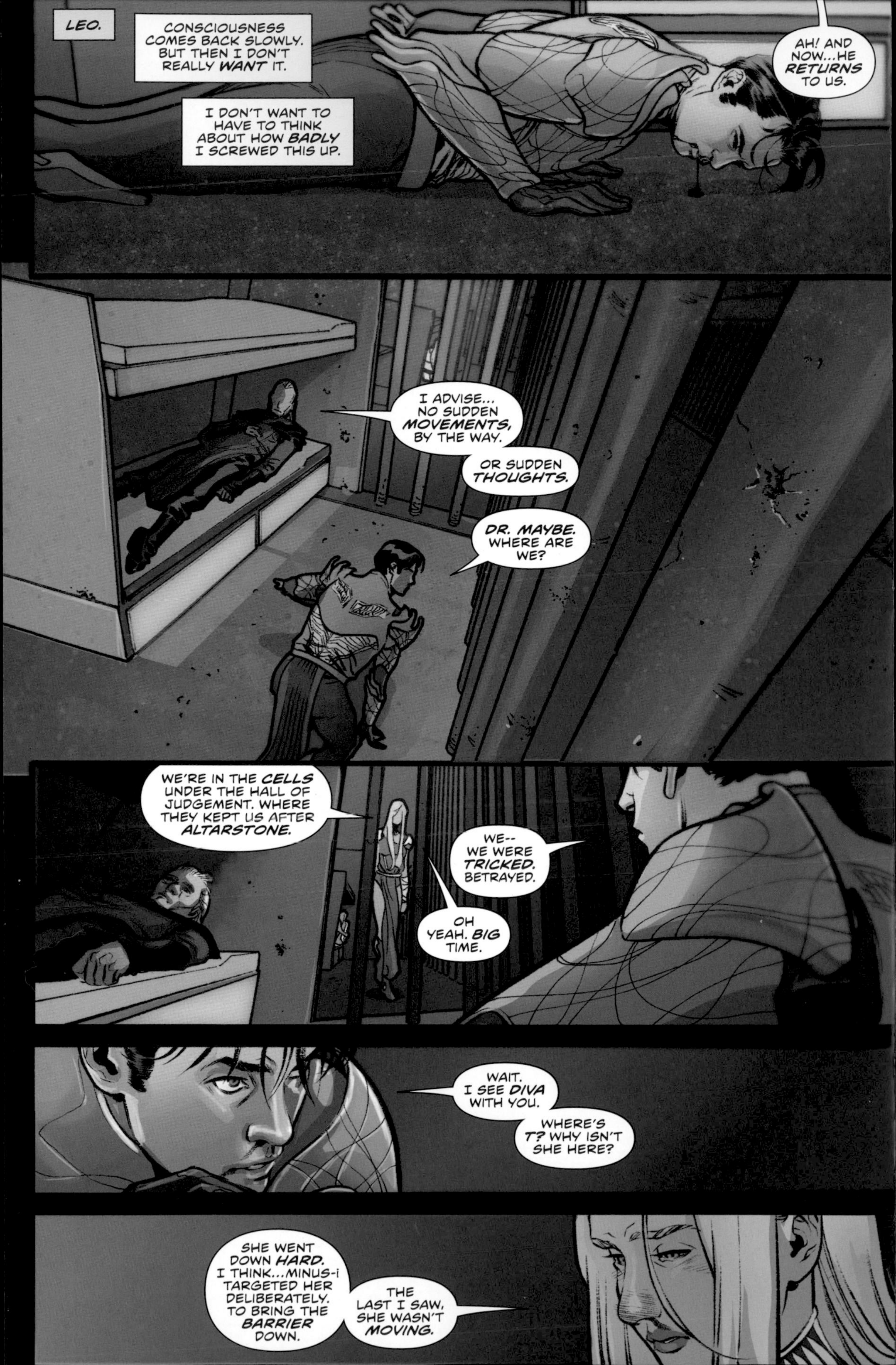
LEO.
CONSCIOUSNESS COMES BACK SLOWLY. BUT THEN I DON'T REALLY WANT IT.
I DON'T WANT TO HAVE TO THINK ABOUT HOW BADLY I SCREWED THIS UP.
AH! AND NOW...HE RETURNS TO US.
I ADVISE... NO SUDDEN MOVEMENTS, BY THE WAY.
OR SUDDEN THOUGHTS.
DR. MAYBE. WHERE ARE WE?
WE'RE IN THE CELLS UNDER THE HALL OF JUDGEMENT. WHERE THEY KEPT US AFTER ALTARSTONE.
WE-- WE WERE TRICKED. BETRAYED.
OH YEAH. BIG TIME.
WAIT. I SEE DIVA WITH YOU.
WHERE'S T? WHY ISN'T SHE HERE?
SHE WENT DOWN HARD. I THINK...MINUS-i TARGETED HER DELIBERATELY. TO BRING THE BARRIER DOWN.
THE LAST I SAW, SHE WASN'T MOVING.

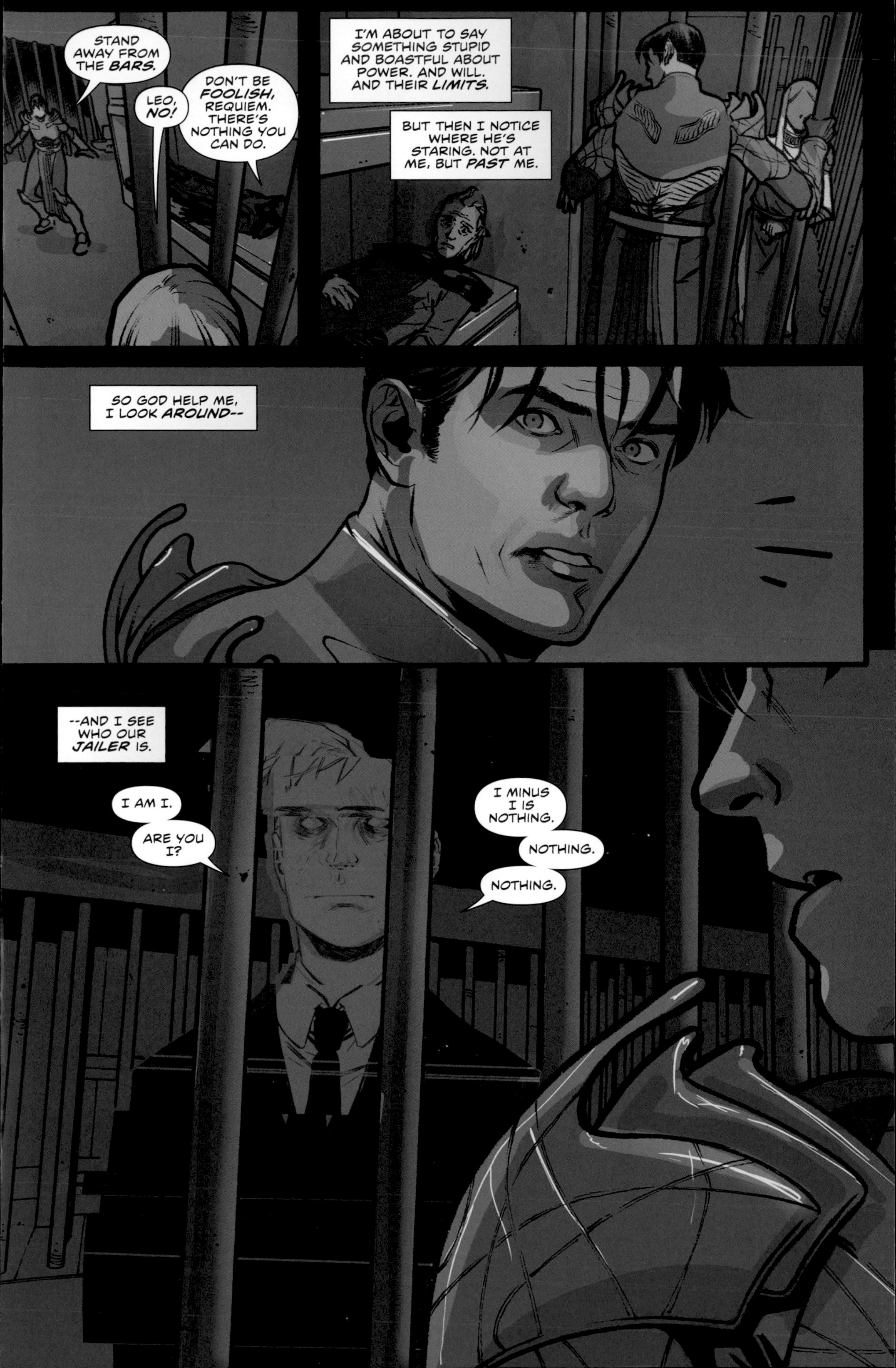
STAND AWAY FROM THE BARS.
LEO, NO!
DON'T BE FOOLISH, REQUIEM. THERE'S NOTHING YOU CAN DO.
I'M ABOUT TO SAY SOMETHING STUPID AND BOASTFUL ABOUT POWER. AND WILL. AND THEIR LIMITS.
BUT THEN I NOTICE WHERE HE'S STARING. NOT AT ME, BUT PAST ME.
SO GOD HELP ME, I LOOK AROUND--
--AND I SEE WHO OUR JAILER IS.
I AM I.
ARE YOU I?
I MINUS I IS NOTHING.
NOTHING.
NOTHING.

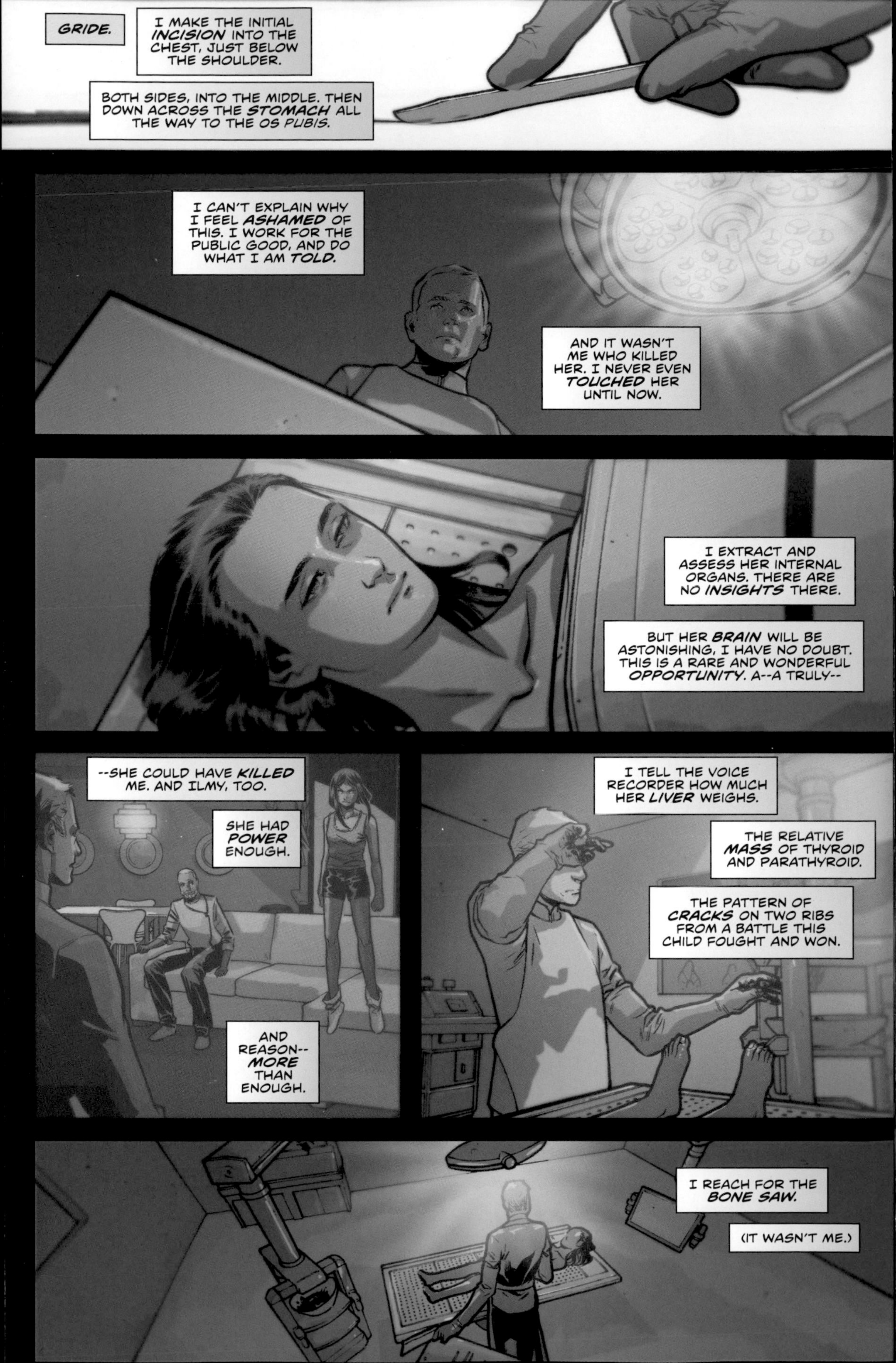
GRIDE.
I MAKE THE INITIAL INCISION INTO THE CHEST, JUST BELOW THE SHOULDER.
BOTH SIDES, INTO THE MIDDLE. THEN DOWN ACROSS THE STOMACH ALL THE WAY TO THE OS PUBIS.
I CAN'T EXPLAIN WHY I FEEL ASHAMED OF THIS. I WORK FOR THE PUBLIC GOOD, AND DO WHAT I AM TOLD.
AND IT WASN'T ME WHO KILLED HER. I NEVER EVEN TOUCHED HER UNTIL NOW.
I EXTRACT AND ASSESS HER INTERNAL ORGANS. THERE ARE NO INSIGHTS THERE.
BUT HER BRAIN WILL BE ASTONISHING, I HAVE NO DOUBT. THIS IS A RARE AND WONDERFUL OPPORTUNITY. A--A TRULY--
--SHE COULD HAVE KILLED ME. AND ILMY, TOO.
SHE HAD POWER ENOUGH.
AND REASON--MORE THAN ENOUGH.
I TELL THE VOICE RECORDER HOW MUCH HER LIVER WEIGHS.
THE RELATIVE MASS OF THYROID AND PARATHYROID.
THE PATTERN OF CRACKS ON TWO RIBS FROM A BATTLE THIS CHILD FOUGHT AND WON.
I REACH FOR THE BONE SAW.
(IT WASN'T ME.)

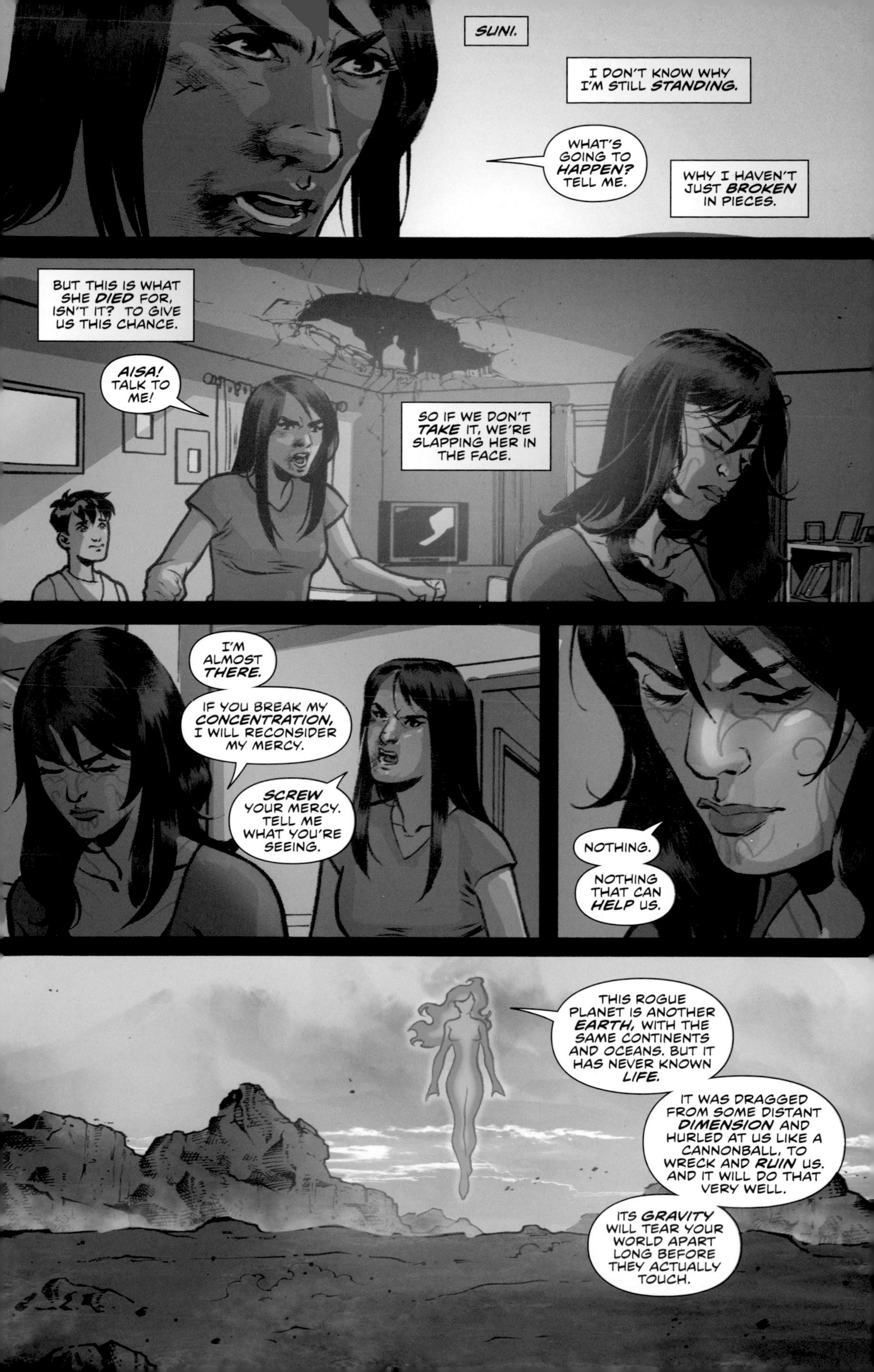
SUNI.
I DON'T KNOW WHY I'M STILL STANDING.
WHAT'S GOING TO HAPPEN? TELL ME.
WHY I HAVEN'T JUST BROKEN IN PIECES.
BUT THIS IS WHAT SHE DIED FOR, ISN'T IT? TO GIVE US THIS CHANCE.
AISA! TALK TO ME!
SO IF WE DON'T TAKE IT, WE'RE SLAPPING HER IN THE FACE.
I'M ALMOST THERE.
IF YOU BREAK MY CONCENTRATION, I WILL RECONSIDER MY MERCY.
SCREW YOUR MERCY. TELL ME WHAT YOU'RE SEEING.
NOTHING.
NOTHING THAT CAN HELP US.
THIS ROGUE PLANET IS ANOTHER EARTH, WITH THE SAME CONTINENTS AND OCEANS. BUT IT HAS NEVER KNOWN LIFE.
IT WAS DRAGGED FROM SOME DISTANT DIMENSION AND HURLED AT US LIKE A CANNONBALL, TO WRECK AND RUIN US. AND IT WILL DO THAT VERY WELL.
ITS GRAVITY WILL TEAR YOUR WORLD APART LONG BEFORE THEY ACTUALLY TOUCH.

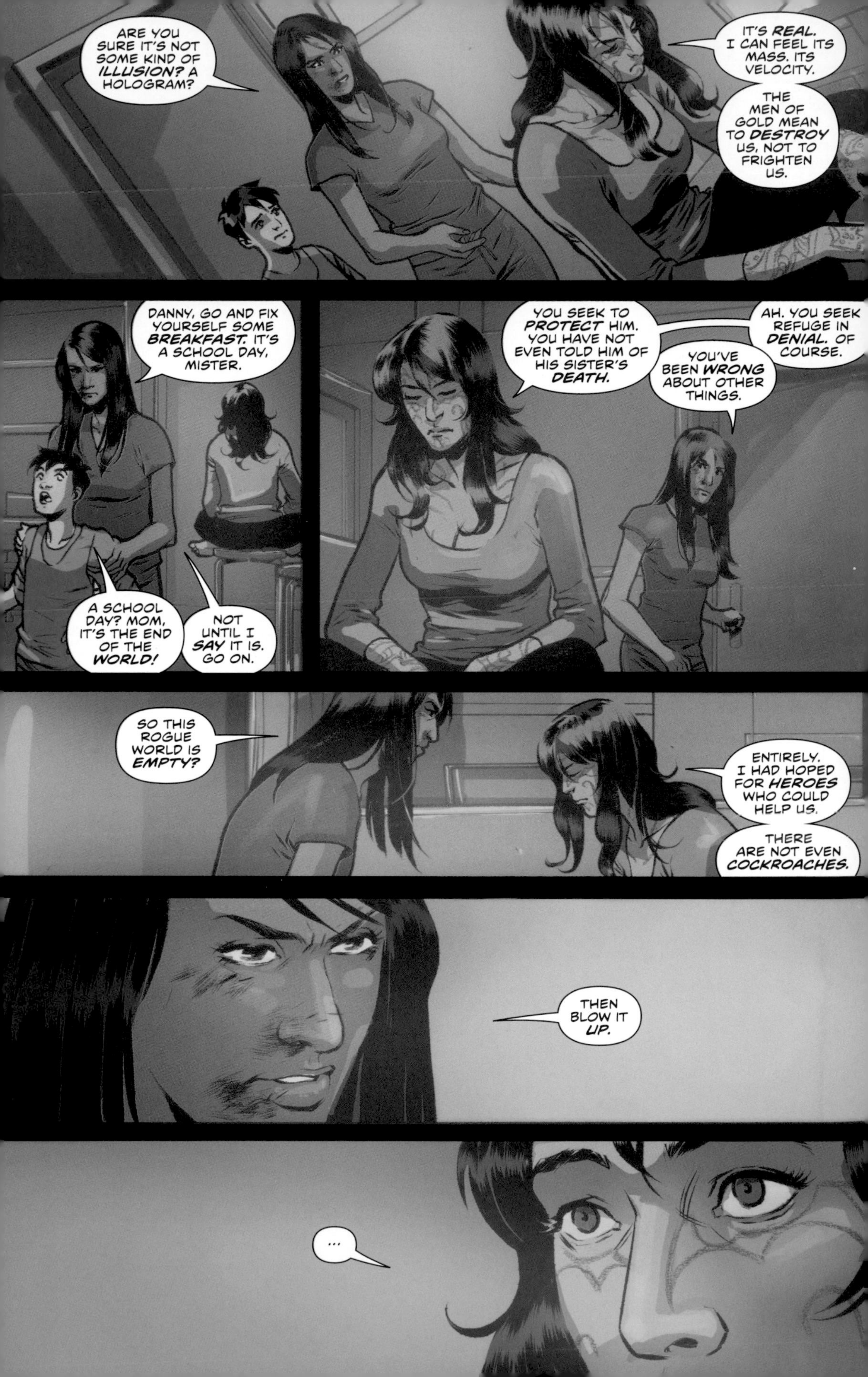
ARE YOU SURE IT'S NOT SOME KIND OF ILLUSION? A HOLOGRAM?
IT'S REAL. I CAN FEEL ITS MASS. ITS VELOCITY.
THE MEN OF GOLD MEAN TO DESTROY US, NOT TO FRIGHTEN US.
DANNY, GO AND FIX YOURSELF SOME BREAKFAST. IT'S A SCHOOL DAY, MISTER.
A SCHOOL DAY? MOM, IT'S THE END OF THE WORLD!
NOT UNTIL I SAY IT IS. GO ON.
YOU SEEK TO PROTECT HIM. YOU HAVE NOT EVEN TOLD HIM OF HIS SISTER'S DEATH.
YOU'VE BEEN WRONG ABOUT OTHER THINGS.
AH. YOU SEEK REFUGE IN DENIAL. OF COURSE.
SO THIS ROGUE WORLD IS EMPTY?
ENTIRELY. I HAD HOPED FOR HEROES WHO COULD HELP US.
THERE ARE NOT EVEN COCKROACHES.
THEN BLOW IT UP.
...

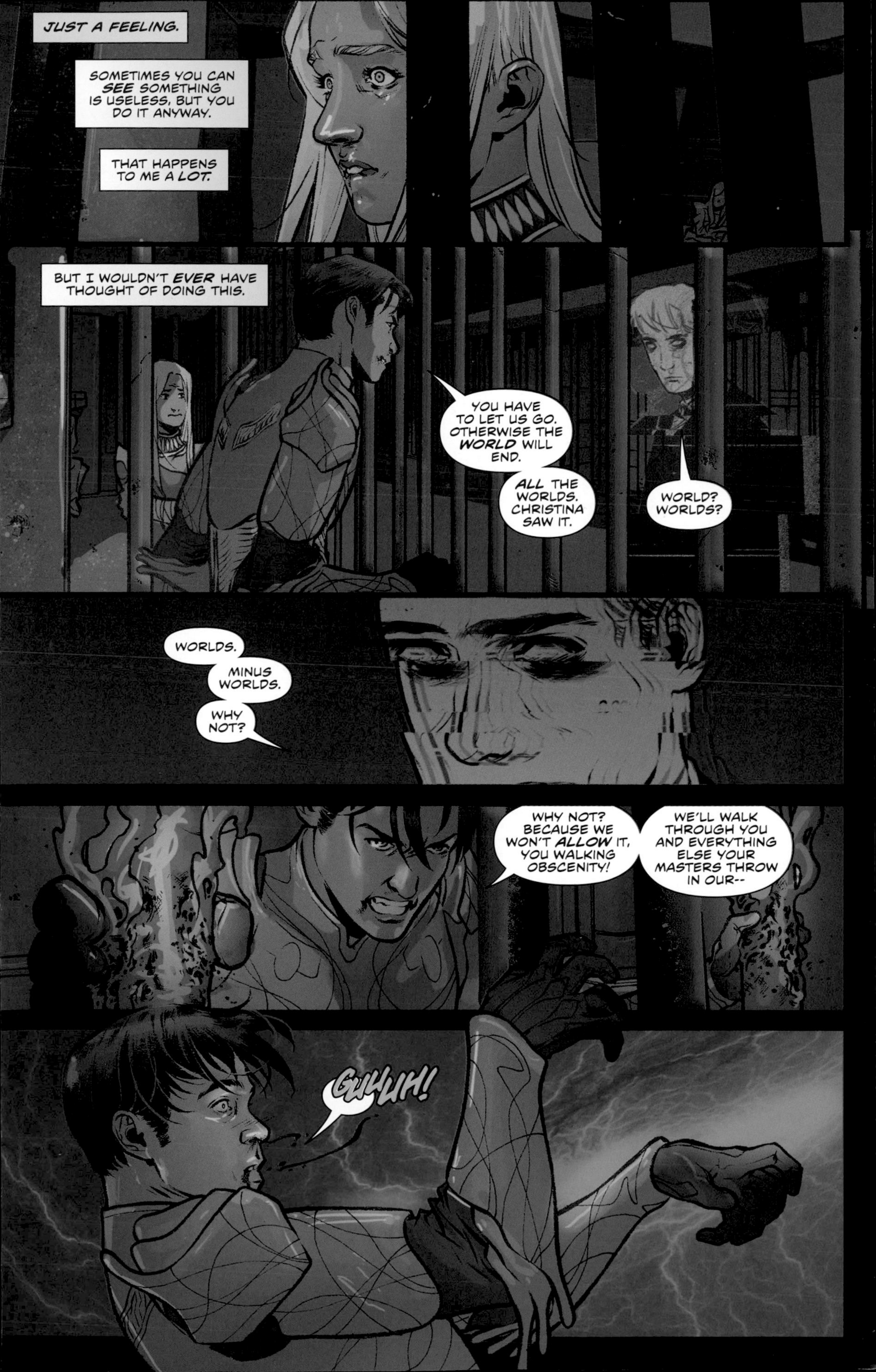
JUST A FEELING.
SOMETIMES YOU CAN SEE SOMETHING IS USELESS, BUT YOU DO IT ANYWAY.
THAT HAPPENS TO ME A LOT.
BUT I WOULDN'T EVER HAVE THOUGHT OF DOING THIS.
YOU HAVE TO LET US GO. OTHERWISE THE WORLD WILL END.
ALL THE WORLDS. CHRISTINA SAW IT.
WORLD? WORLDS?
WORLDS.
MINUS WORLDS.
WHY NOT?
WHY NOT? BECAUSE WE WON'T ALLOW IT, YOU WALKING OBSCENITY!
WE'LL WALK THROUGH YOU AND EVERYTHING ELSE YOUR MASTERS THROW IN OUR--
GUUUH!

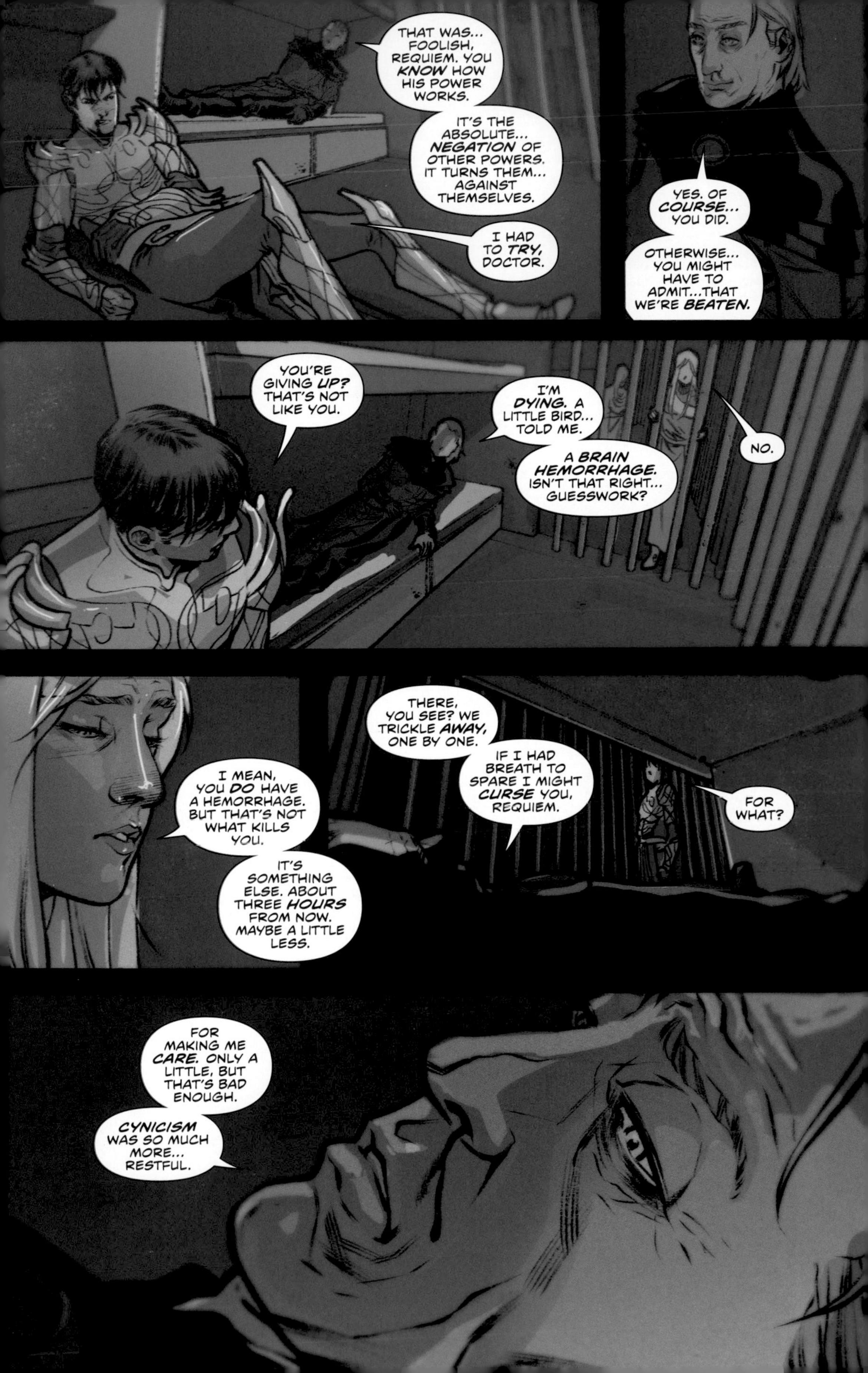
THAT WAS... FOOLISH, REQUIEM. YOU KNOW HOW HIS POWER WORKS.
IT'S THE ABSOLUTE... NEGATION OF OTHER POWERS. IT TURNS THEM... AGAINST THEMSELVES.
I HAD TO TRY, DOCTOR.
YES. OF COURSE... YOU DID.
OTHERWISE... YOU MIGHT HAVE TO ADMIT...THAT WE'RE BEATEN.
YOU'RE GIVING UP? THAT'S NOT LIKE YOU.
I'M DYING. A LITTLE BIRD... TOLD ME.
A BRAIN HEMORRHAGE. ISN'T THAT RIGHT... GUESSWORK?
NO.
I MEAN, YOU DO HAVE A HEMORRHAGE. BUT THAT'S NOT WHAT KILLS YOU.
IT'S SOMETHING ELSE. ABOUT THREE HOURS FROM NOW. MAYBE A LITTLE LESS.
THERE, YOU SEE? WE TRICKLE AWAY, ONE BY ONE.
IF I HAD BREATH TO SPARE I MIGHT CURSE YOU, REQUIEM.
FOR WHAT?
FOR MAKING ME CARE. ONLY A LITTLE, BUT THAT'S BAD ENOUGH.
CYNICISM WAS SO MUCH MORE... RESTFUL.

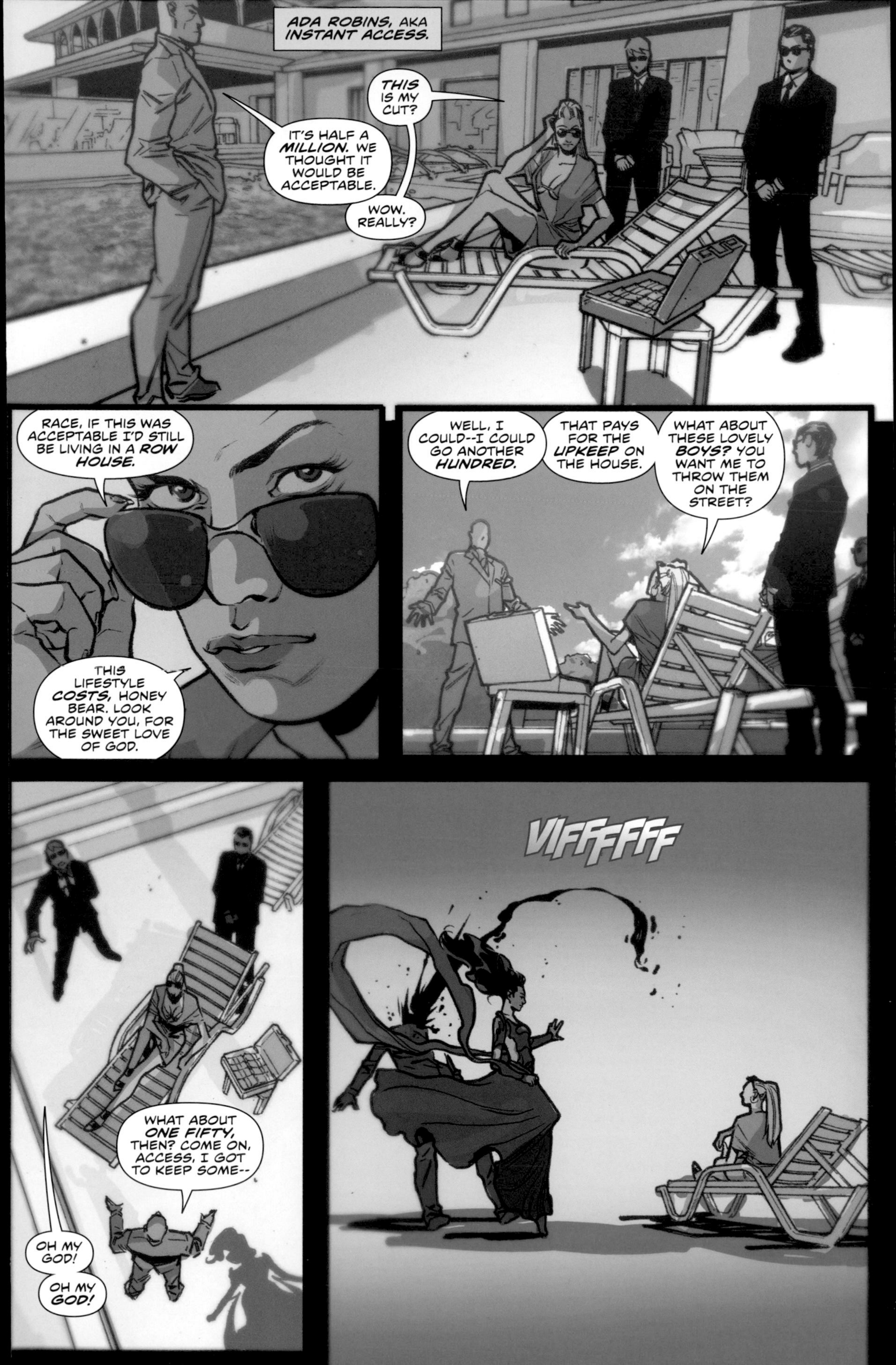
ADA ROBINS, AKA INSTANT ACCESS.
THIS IS MY CUT?
IT'S HALF A MILLION. WE THOUGHT IT WOULD BE ACCEPTABLE.
WOW. REALLY?
RACE, IF THIS WAS ACCEPTABLE I'D STILL BE LIVING IN A ROW HOUSE.
THIS LIFESTYLE COSTS, HONEY BEAR. LOOK AROUND YOU, FOR THE SWEET LOVE OF GOD.
WELL, I COULD--I COULD GO ANOTHER HUNDRED.
THAT PAYS FOR THE UPKEEP ON THE HOUSE.
WHAT ABOUT THESE LOVELY BOYS? YOU WANT ME TO THROW THEM ON THE STREET?
WHAT ABOUT ONE FIFTY, THEN? COME ON, ACCESS, I GOT TO KEEP SOME--
OH MY GOD!
OH MY GOD!
VIFFFFFF

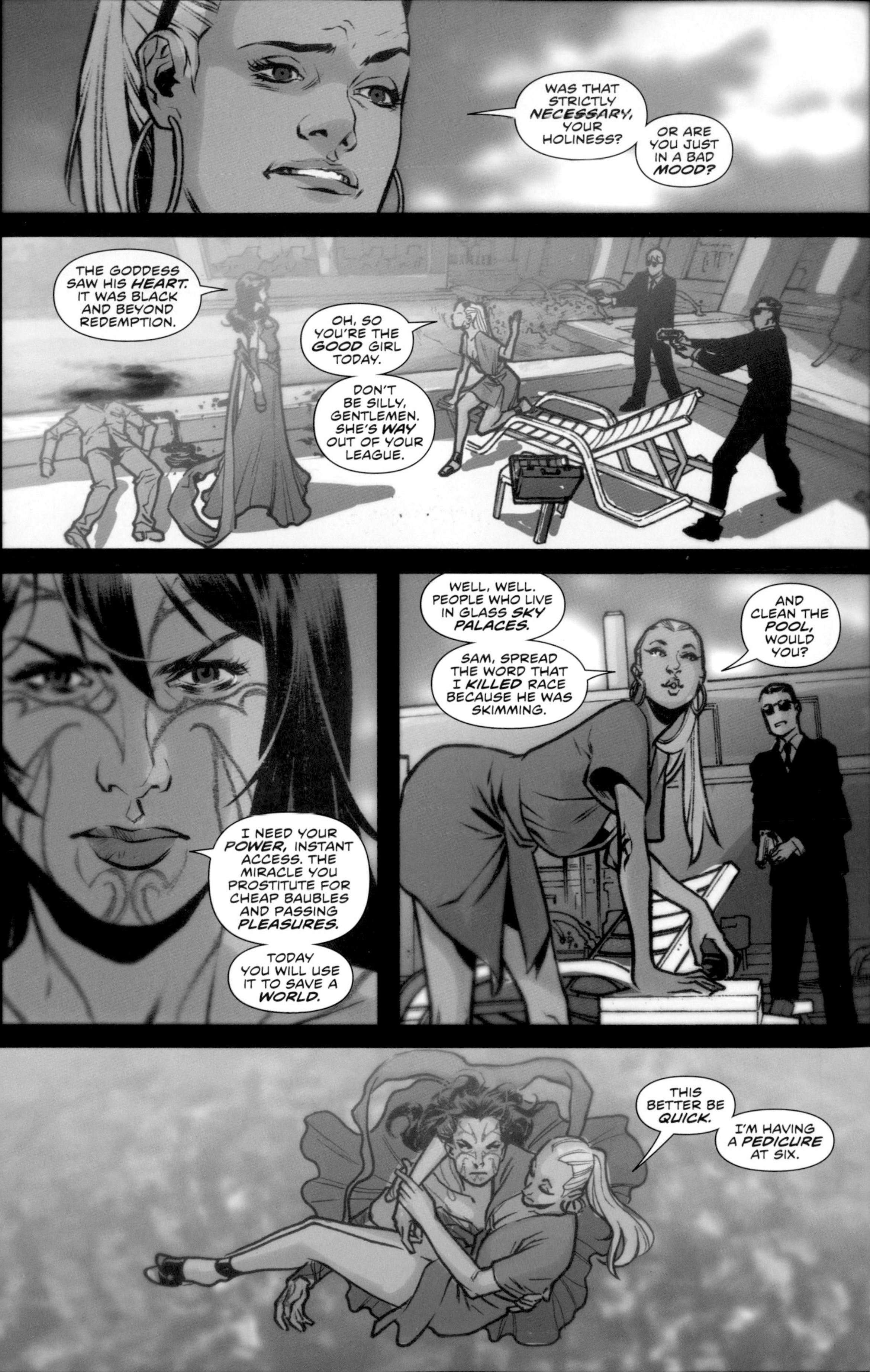
WAS THAT STRICTLY NECESSARY, YOUR HOLINESS?
OR ARE YOU JUST IN A BAD MOOD?
THE GODDESS SAW HIS HEART. IT WAS BLACK AND BEYOND REDEMPTION.
OH, SO YOU'RE THE GOOD GIRL TODAY.
DON'T BE SILLY, GENTLEMEN. SHE'S WAY OUT OF YOUR LEAGUE.
I NEED YOUR POWER, INSTANT ACCESS. THE MIRACLE YOU PROSTITUTE FOR CHEAP BAUBLES AND PASSING PLEASURES.
TODAY YOU WILL USE IT TO SAVE A WORLD.
WELL, WELL. PEOPLE WHO LIVE IN GLASS SKY PALACES.
SAM, SPREAD THE WORD THAT I KILLED RACE BECAUSE HE WAS SKIMMING.
AND CLEAN THE POOL, WOULD YOU?
THIS BETTER BE QUICK.
I'M HAVING A PEDICURE AT SIX.

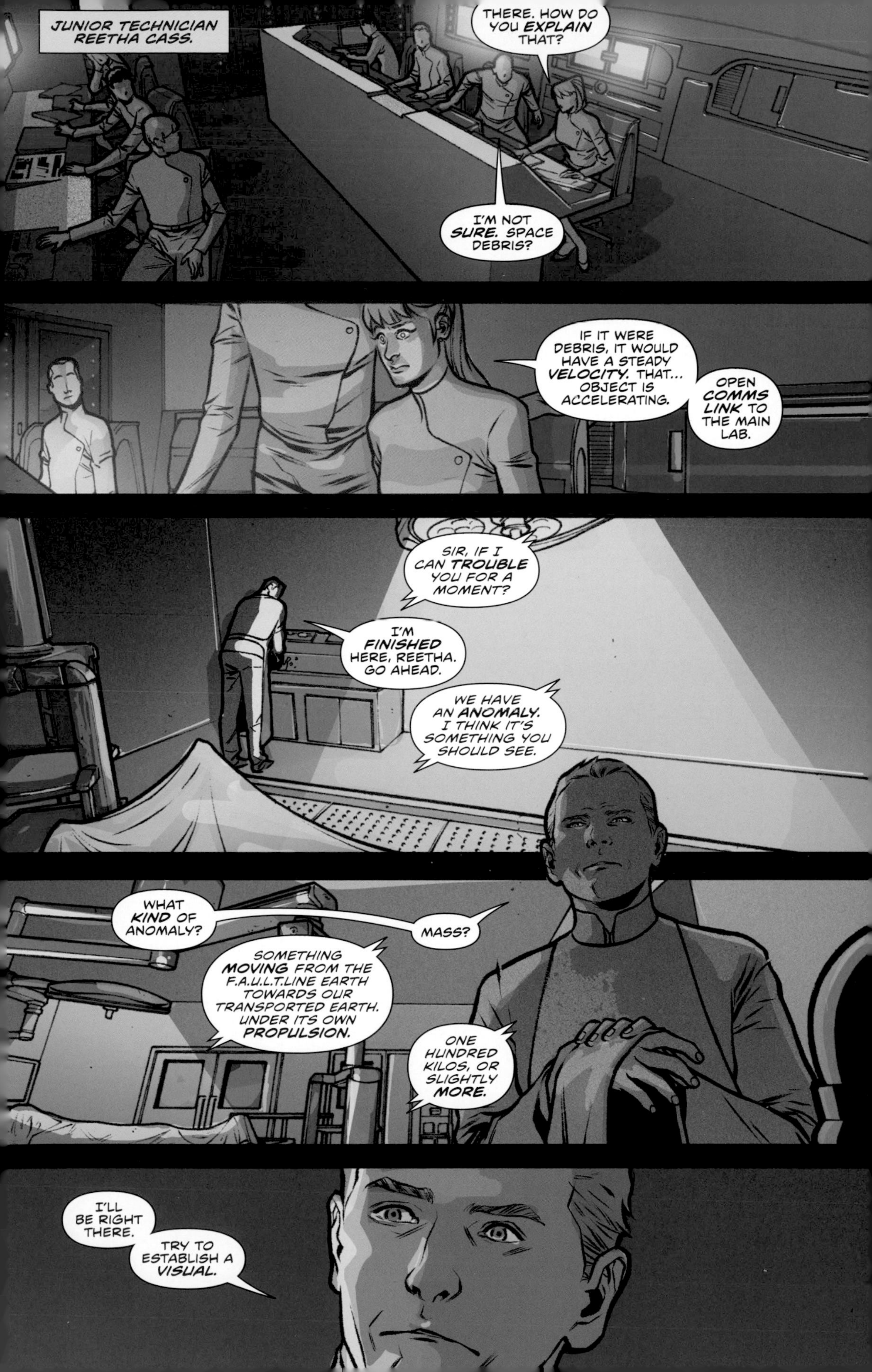
JUNIOR TECHNICIAN REETHA CASS.
THERE. HOW DO YOU EXPLAIN THAT?
I'M NOT SURE. SPACE DEBRIS?
IF IT WERE DEBRIS, IT WOULD HAVE A STEADY VELOCITY. THAT... OBJECT IS ACCELERATING.
OPEN COMMS LINK TO THE MAIN LAB.
SIR, IF I CAN TROUBLE YOU FOR A MOMENT?
I'M FINISHED HERE, REETHA. GO AHEAD.
WE HAVE AN ANOMALY. I THINK IT'S SOMETHING YOU SHOULD SEE.
WHAT KIND OF ANOMALY?
SOMETHING MOVING FROM THE F.A.U.L.T.LINE EARTH TOWARDS OUR TRANSPORTED EARTH. UNDER ITS OWN PROPULSION.
MASS?
ONE HUNDRED KILOS, OR SLIGHTLY MORE.
I'LL BE RIGHT THERE.
TRY TO ESTABLISH A VISUAL.

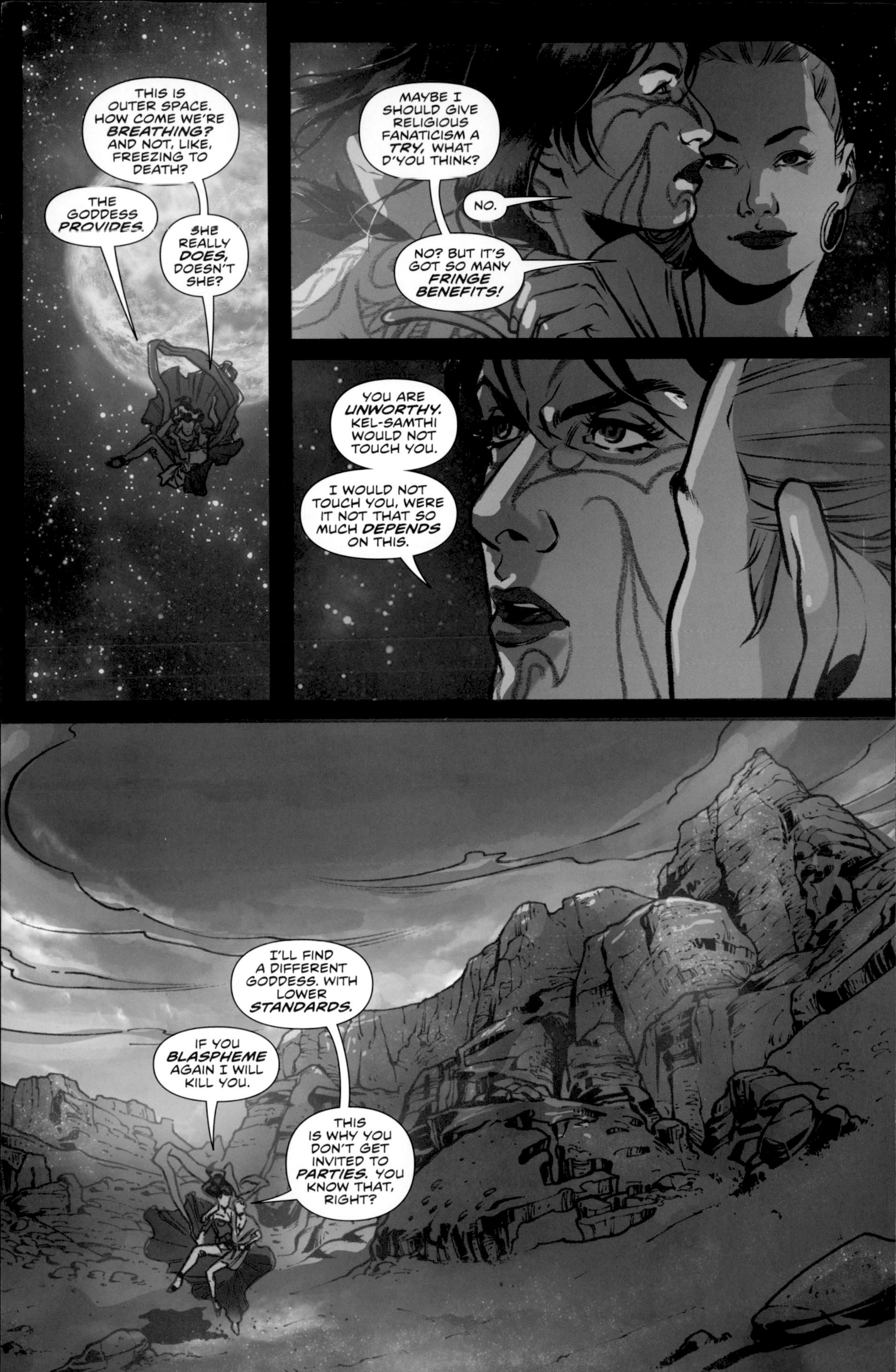
THIS IS OUTER SPACE. HOW COME WE'RE BREATHING? AND NOT, LIKE, FREEZING TO DEATH?
THE GODDESS PROVIDES.
SHE REALLY DOES, DOESN'T SHE?
MAYBE I SHOULD GIVE RELIGIOUS FANATICISM A TRY, WHAT D'YOU THINK?
NO.
NO? BUT IT'S GOT SO MANY FRINGE BENEFITS!
YOU ARE UNWORTHY. KEL-SAMTHI WOULD NOT TOUCH YOU.
I WOULD NOT TOUCH YOU, WERE IT NOT THAT SO MUCH DEPENDS ON THIS.
I'LL FIND A DIFFERENT GODDESS. WITH LOWER STANDARDS.
IF YOU BLASPHEME AGAIN I WILL KILL YOU.
THIS IS WHY YOU DON'T GET INVITED TO PARTIES. YOU KNOW THAT, RIGHT?

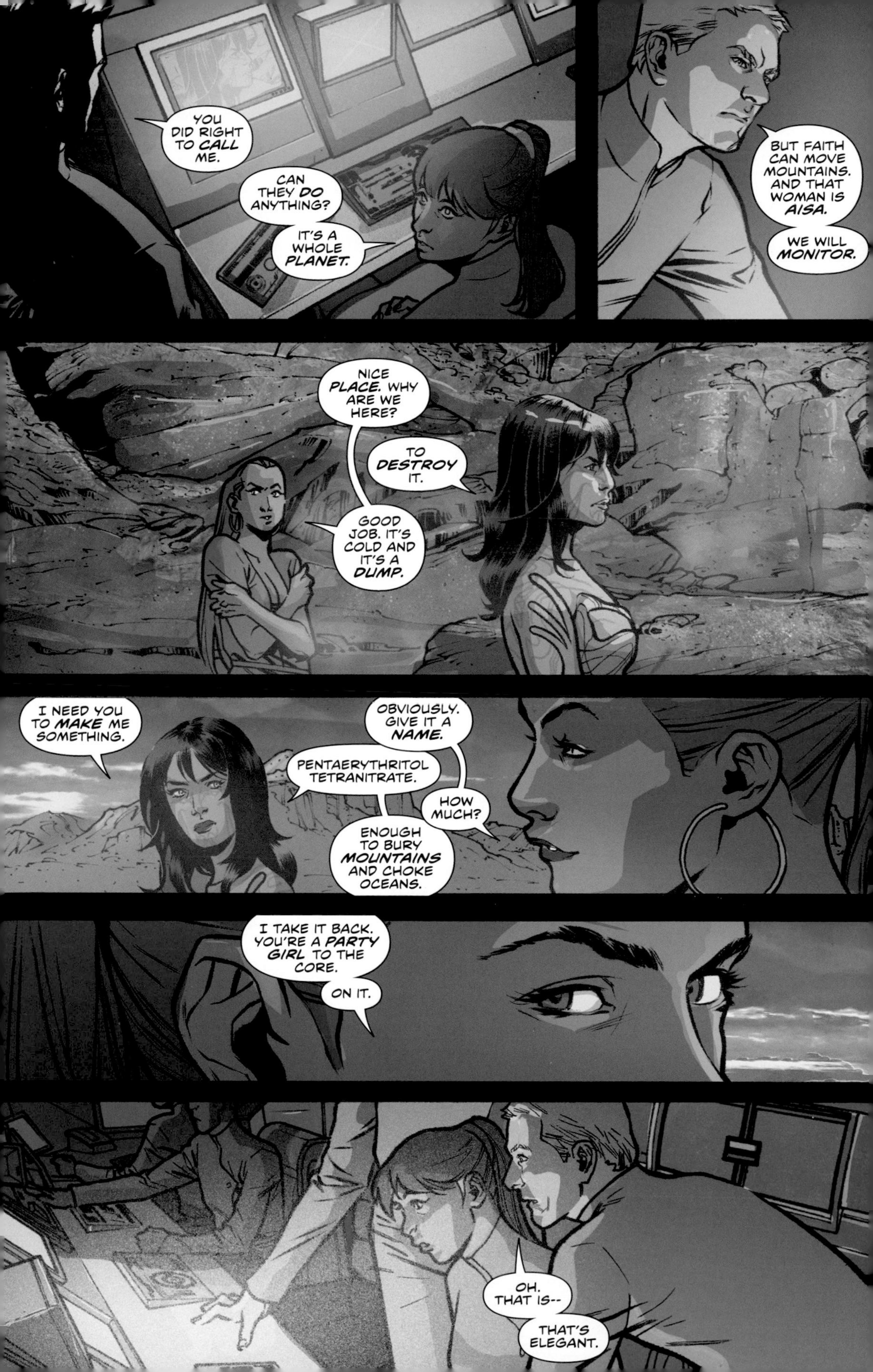
YOU DID RIGHT TO CALL ME.
CAN THEY DO ANYTHING?
IT'S A WHOLE PLANET.
BUT FAITH CAN MOVE MOUNTAINS. AND THAT WOMAN IS AISA.
WE WILL MONITOR.
NICE PLACE. WHY ARE WE HERE?
TO DESTROY IT.
GOOD JOB. IT'S COLD AND IT'S A DUMP.
I NEED YOU TO MAKE ME SOMETHING.
OBVIOUSLY. GIVE IT A NAME.
PENTAERYTHRITOL TETRANITRATE.
HOW MUCH?
ENOUGH TO BURY MOUNTAINS AND CHOKE OCEANS.
I TAKE IT BACK. YOU'RE A PARTY GIRL TO THE CORE.
ON IT.
OH. THAT IS--
THAT'S ELEGANT.

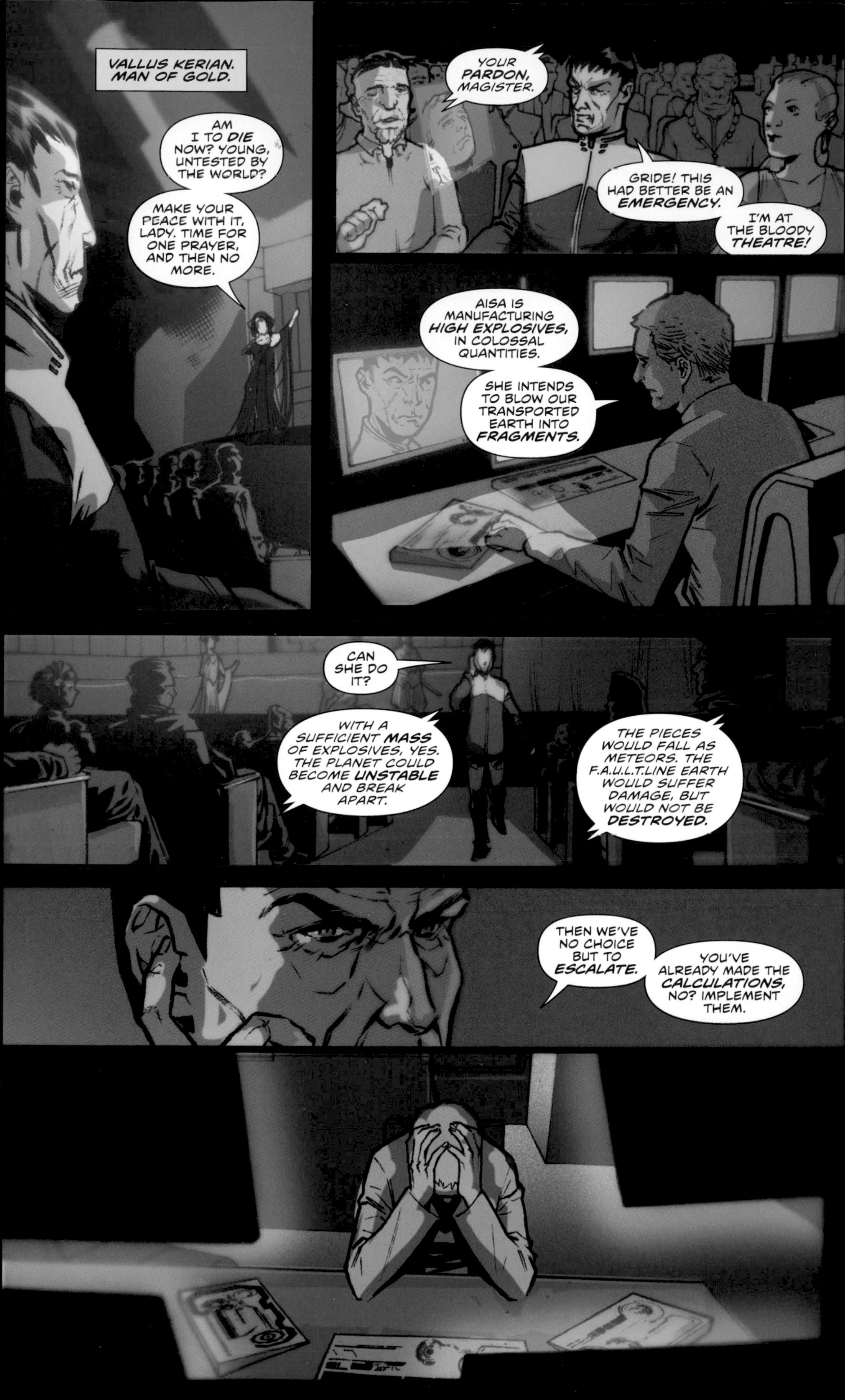
VALLUS KERIAN. MAN OF GOLD.
AM I TO DIE NOW? YOUNG, UNTESTED BY THE WORLD?
MAKE YOUR PEACE WITH IT, LADY. TIME FOR ONE PRAYER, AND THEN NO MORE.
YOUR PARDON, MAGISTER.
GRIDE! THIS HAD BETTER BE AN EMERGENCY.
I'M AT THE BLOODY THEATRE!
AISA IS MANUFACTURING HIGH EXPLOSIVES, IN COLOSSAL QUANTITIES.
SHE INTENDS TO BLOW OUR TRANSPORTED EARTH INTO FRAGMENTS.
CAN SHE DO IT?
WITH A SUFFICIENT MASS OF EXPLOSIVES, YES. THE PLANET COULD BECOME UNSTABLE AND BREAK APART.
THE PIECES WOULD FALL AS METEORS. THE F.A.U.L.T.LINE EARTH WOULD SUFFER DAMAGE, BUT WOULD NOT BE DESTROYED.
THEN WE'VE NO CHOICE BUT TO ESCALATE.
YOU'VE ALREADY MADE THE CALCULATIONS, NO? IMPLEMENT THEM.

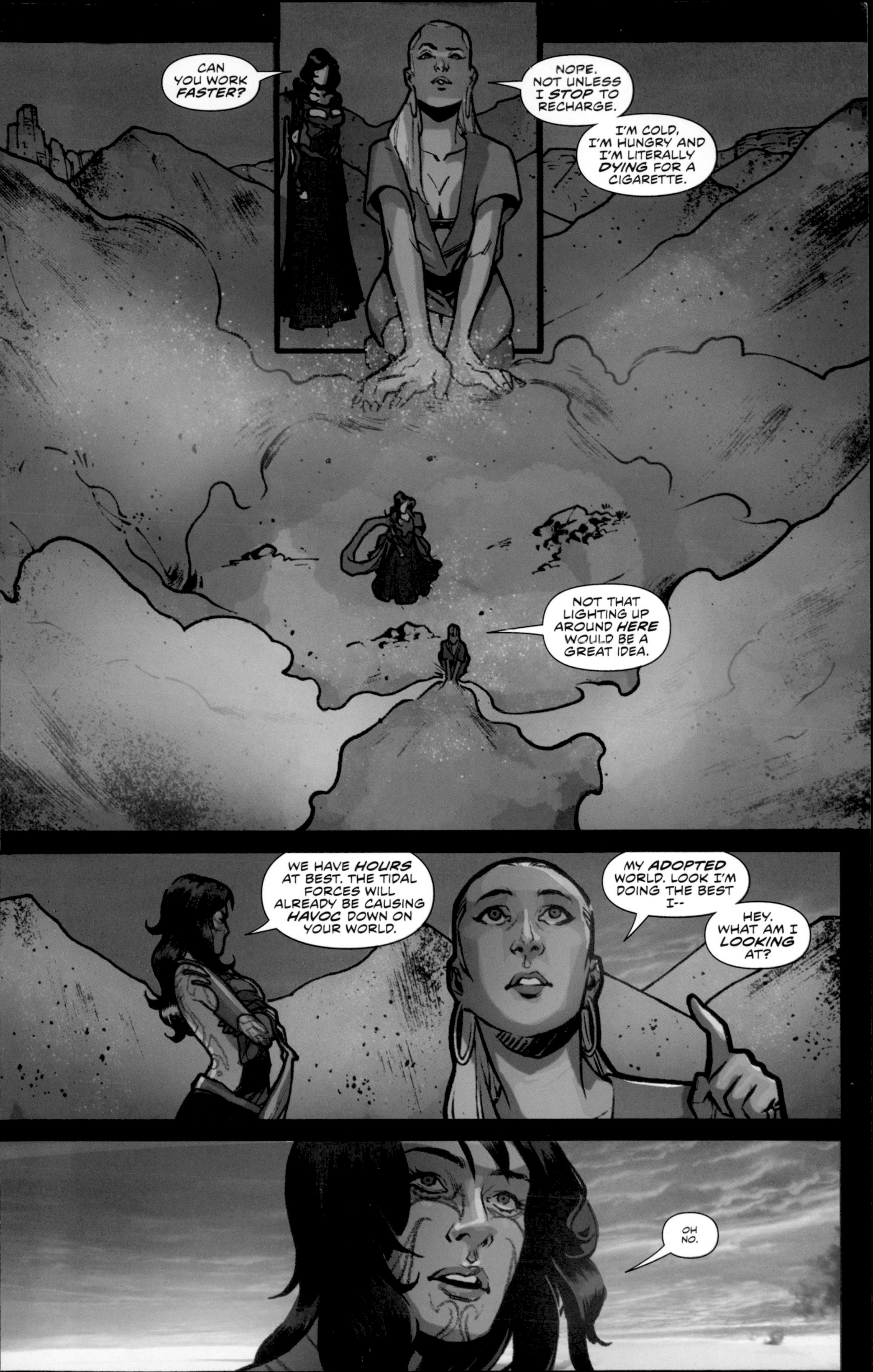
CAN YOU WORK *FASTER?*
NOPE. NOT UNLESS I *STOP* TO RECHARGE.
I'M COLD, I'M HUNGRY AND I'M LITERALLY *DYING* FOR A CIGARETTE.
NOT THAT LIGHTING UP AROUND *HERE* WOULD BE A GREAT IDEA.
WE HAVE *HOURS* AT BEST. THE TIDAL FORCES WILL ALREADY BE CAUSING *HAVOC* DOWN ON YOUR WORLD.
MY *ADOPTED* WORLD. LOOK I'M DOING THE BEST I--
HEY. WHAT AM I *LOOKING* AT?
OH NO.

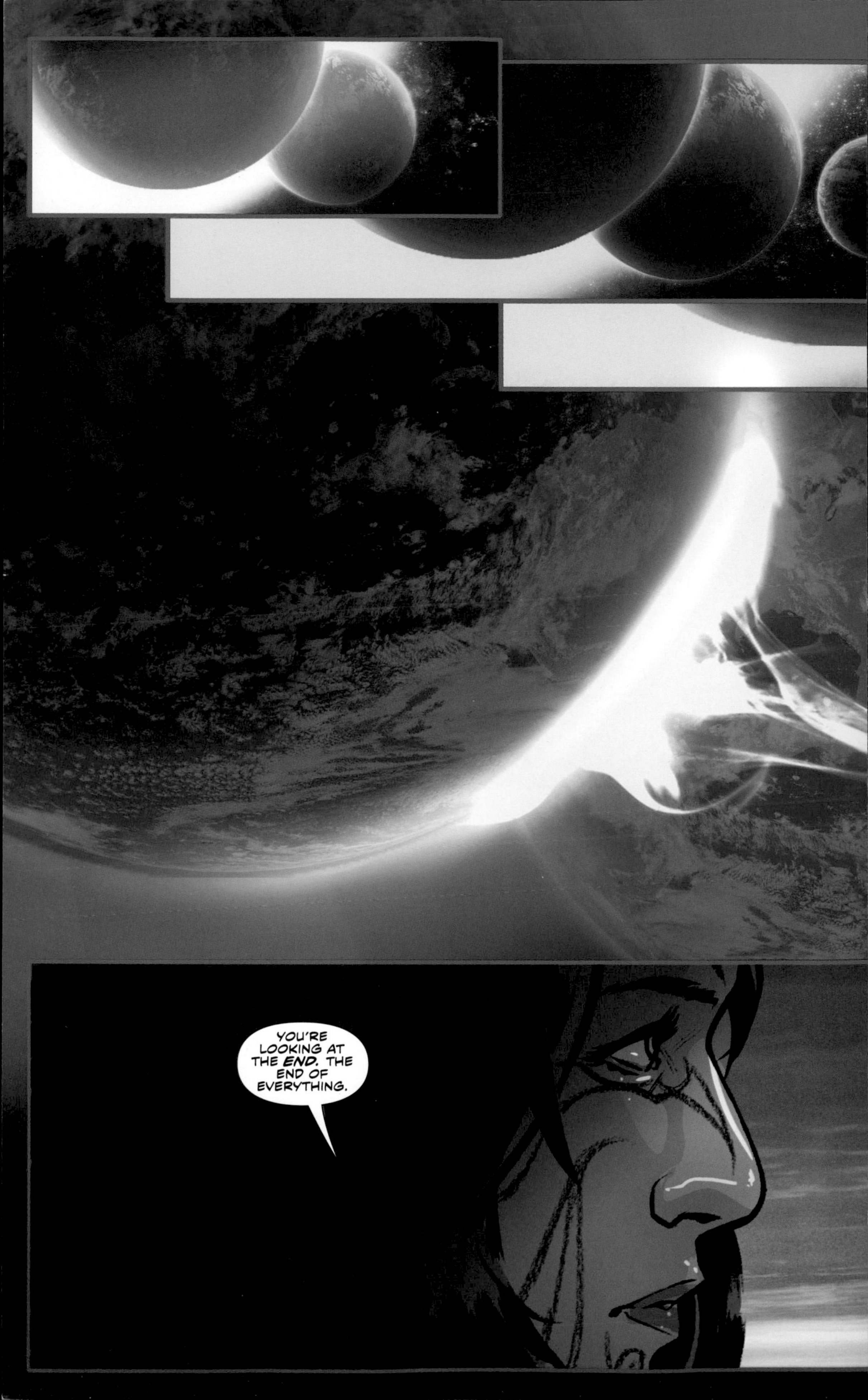
YOU'RE LOOKING AT THE END. THE END OF EVERYTHING.

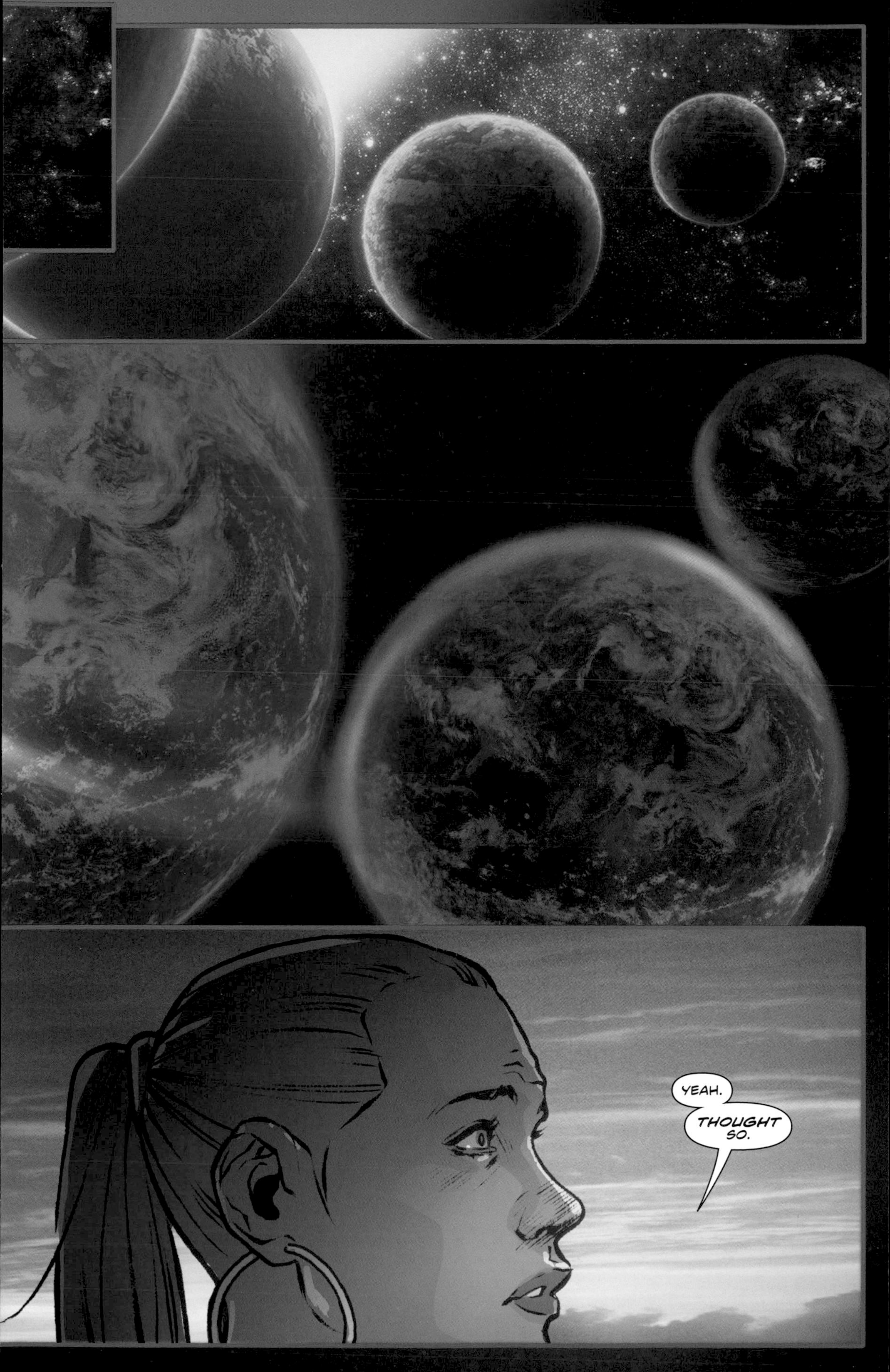
YEAH.
THOUGHT SO.

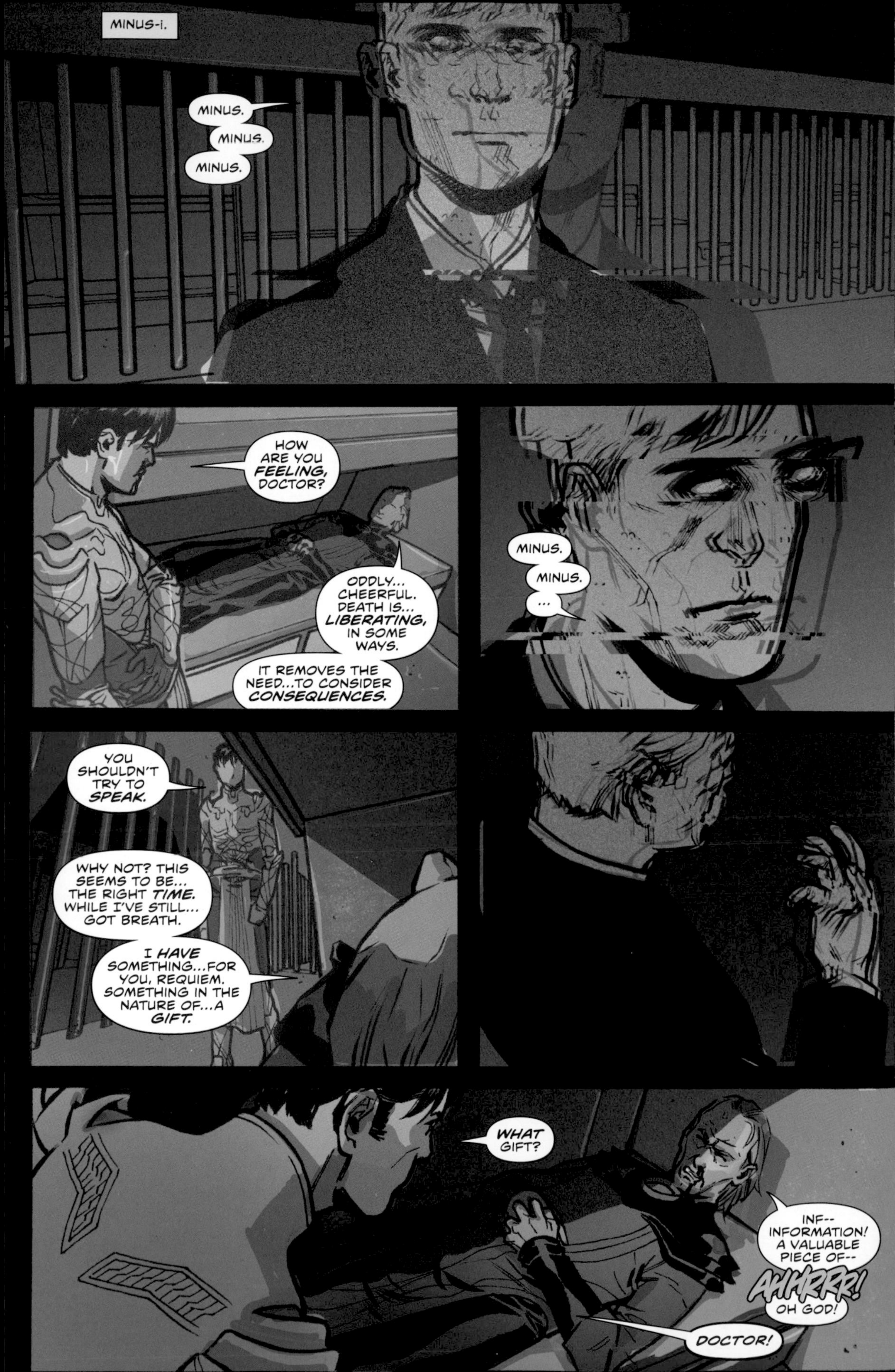
MINUS-i.
MINUS.
MINUS.
MINUS.
HOW ARE YOU FEELING, DOCTOR?
ODDLY... CHEERFUL. DEATH IS... LIBERATING, IN SOME WAYS.
IT REMOVES THE NEED...TO CONSIDER CONSEQUENCES.
MINUS.
MINUS.
...
YOU SHOULDN'T TRY TO SPEAK.
WHY NOT? THIS SEEMS TO BE... THE RIGHT TIME. WHILE I'VE STILL... GOT BREATH.
I HAVE SOMETHING...FOR YOU, REQUIEM. SOMETHING IN THE NATURE OF...A GIFT.
WHAT GIFT?
INF-- INFORMATION! A VALUABLE PIECE OF--
AHHRRR!
OH GOD!
DOCTOR!

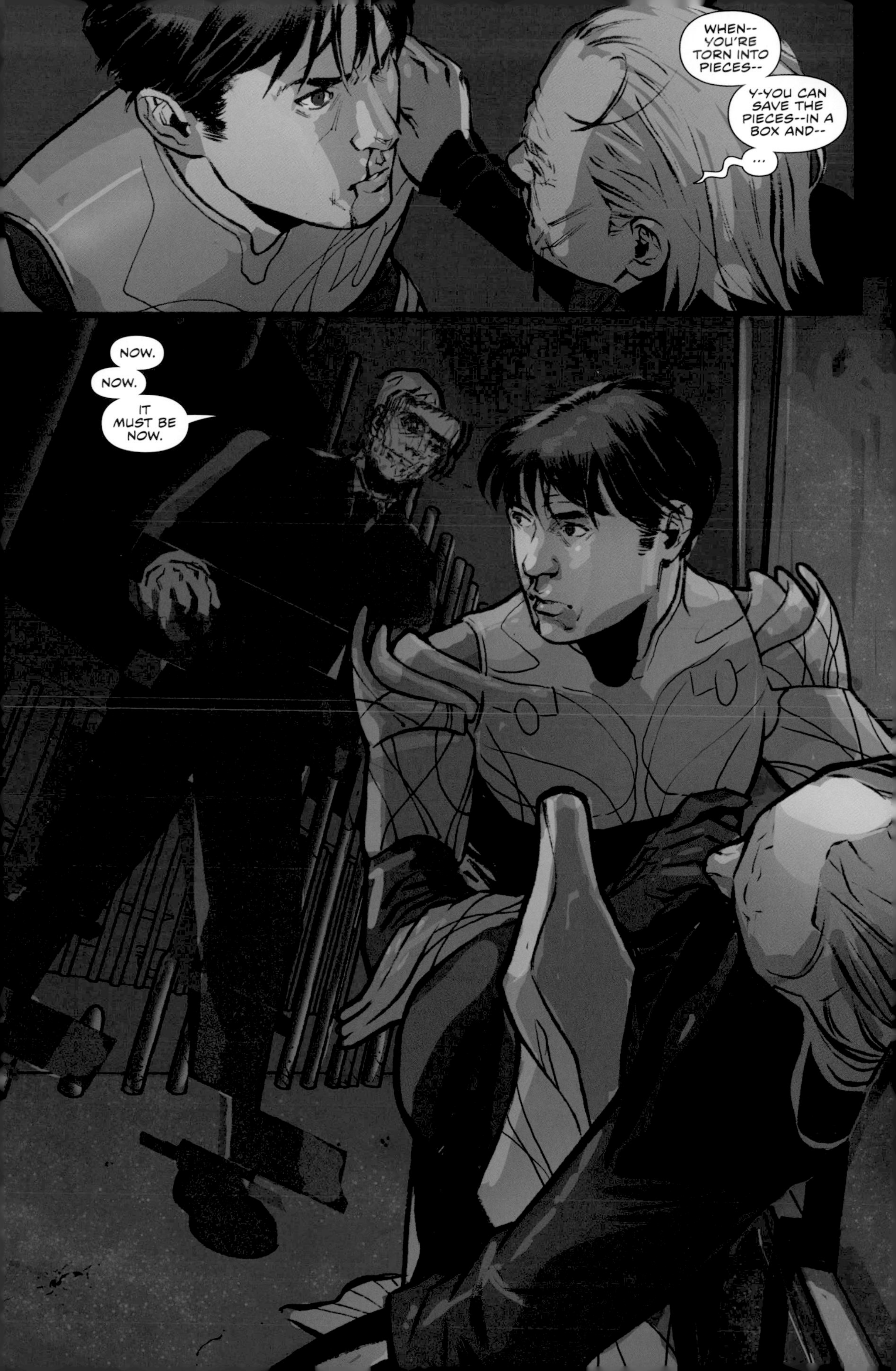
WHEN-- YOU'RE TORN INTO PIECES--
Y-YOU CAN SAVE THE PIECES--IN A BOX AND--
...
NOW.
NOW.
IT MUST BE NOW.

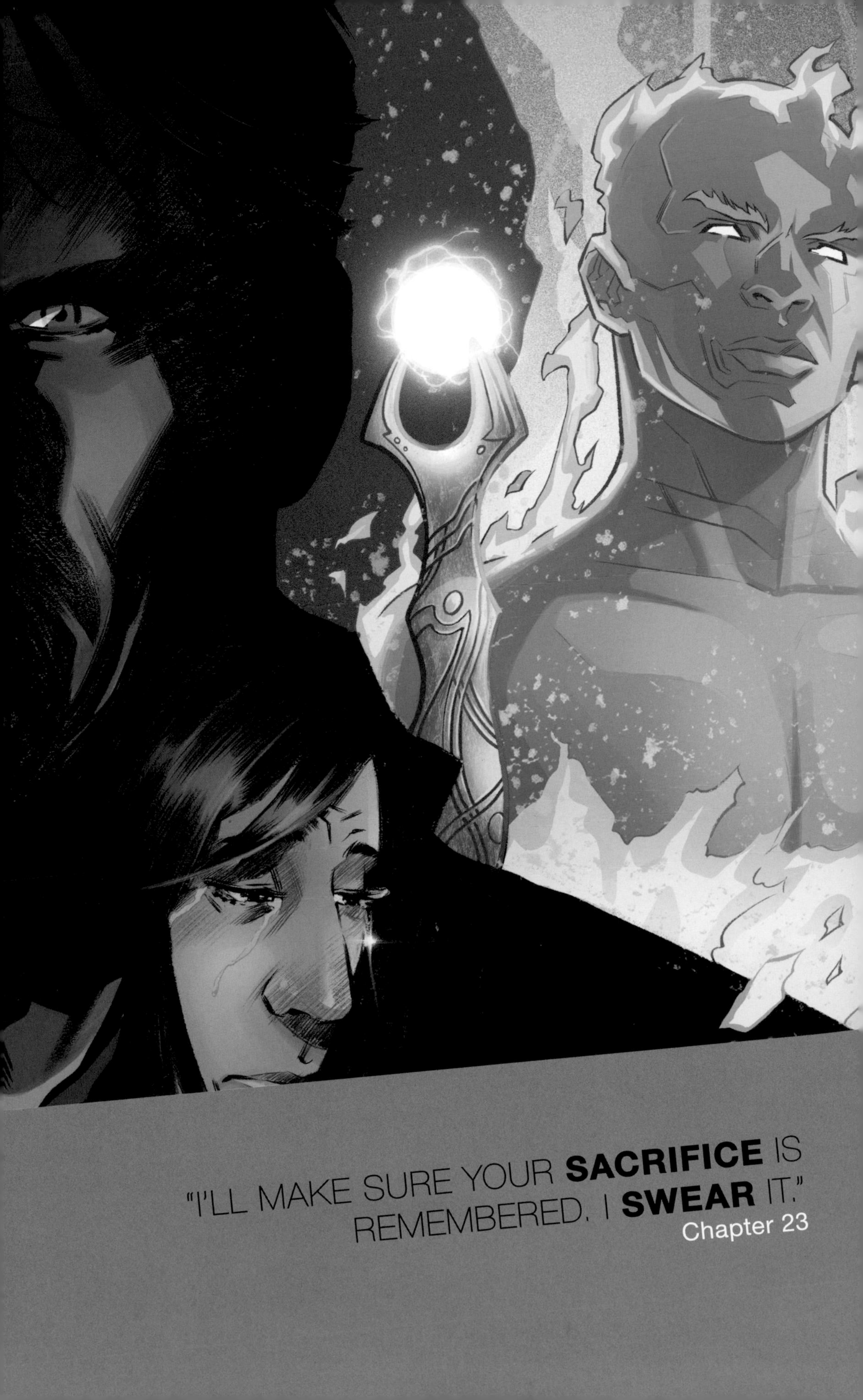

"I'LL MAKE SURE YOUR **SACRIFICE** IS REMEMBERED. I **SWEAR** IT."

Chapter 23

SHE'S STILL *ALIVE.* BUT HEMORRHAGING.

What?

AND HER BRAIN HAS ALREADY *FLAT-LINED.*

Oh spit! That does *not* sound good.

Doesn't *feel* good, either. Ceiling coming down.

Lights going out.

Got to do something *fast.*

Find

somewhere

won't

safe

soon

can't

if   I

fall

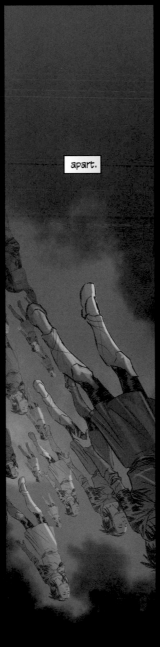

apart.

Okay.

That went well.

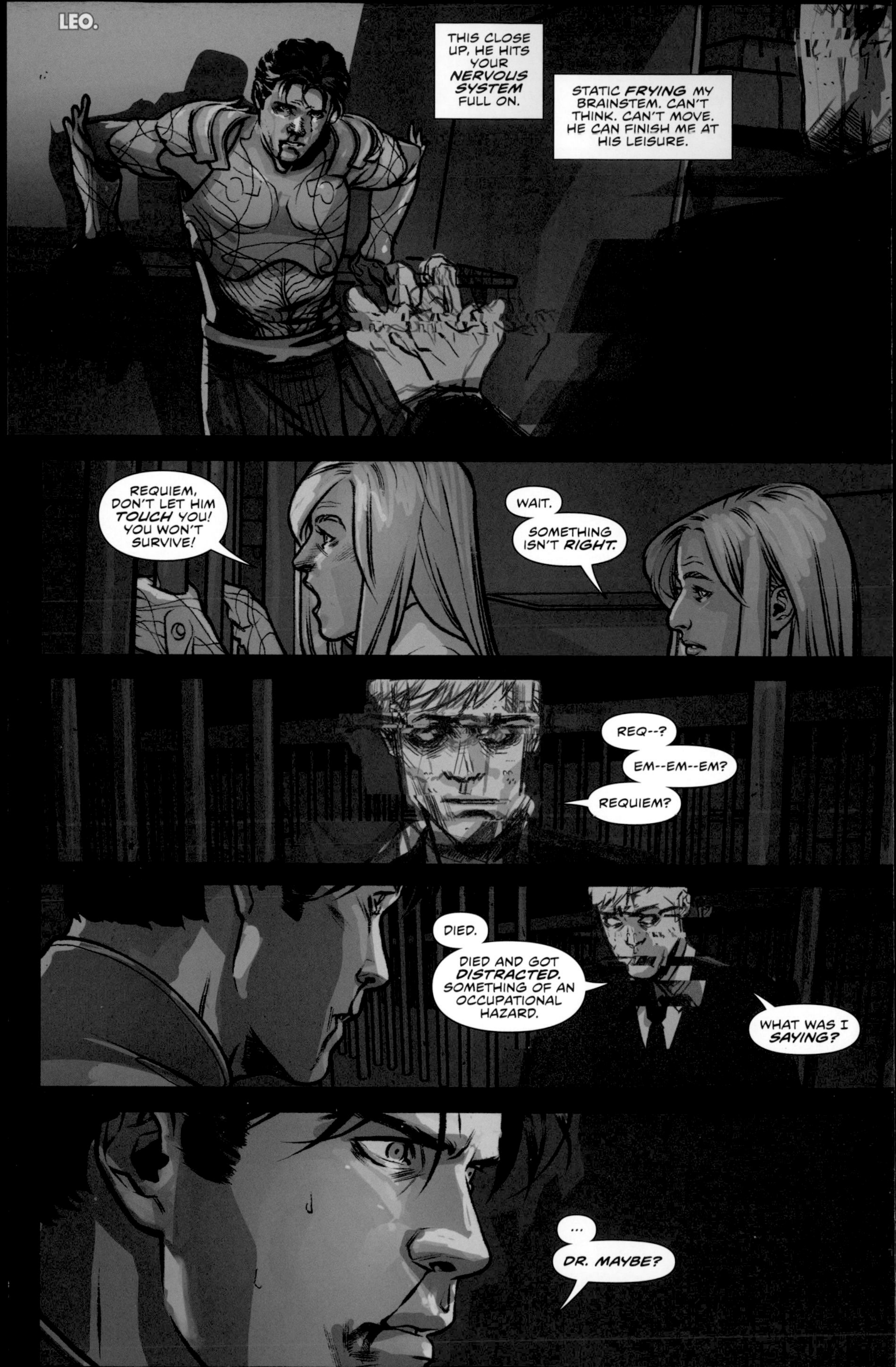
LEO.
THIS CLOSE UP, HE HITS YOUR NERVOUS SYSTEM FULL ON.
STATIC FRYING MY BRAINSTEM. CAN'T THINK. CAN'T MOVE. HE CAN FINISH ME AT HIS LEISURE.
REQUIEM, DON'T LET HIM TOUCH YOU! YOU WON'T SURVIVE!
WAIT.
SOMETHING ISN'T RIGHT.
REQ--?
EM--EM--EM?
REQUIEM?
DIED.
DIED AND GOT DISTRACTED. SOMETHING OF AN OCCUPATIONAL HAZARD.
WHAT WAS I SAYING?
...
DR. MAYBE?

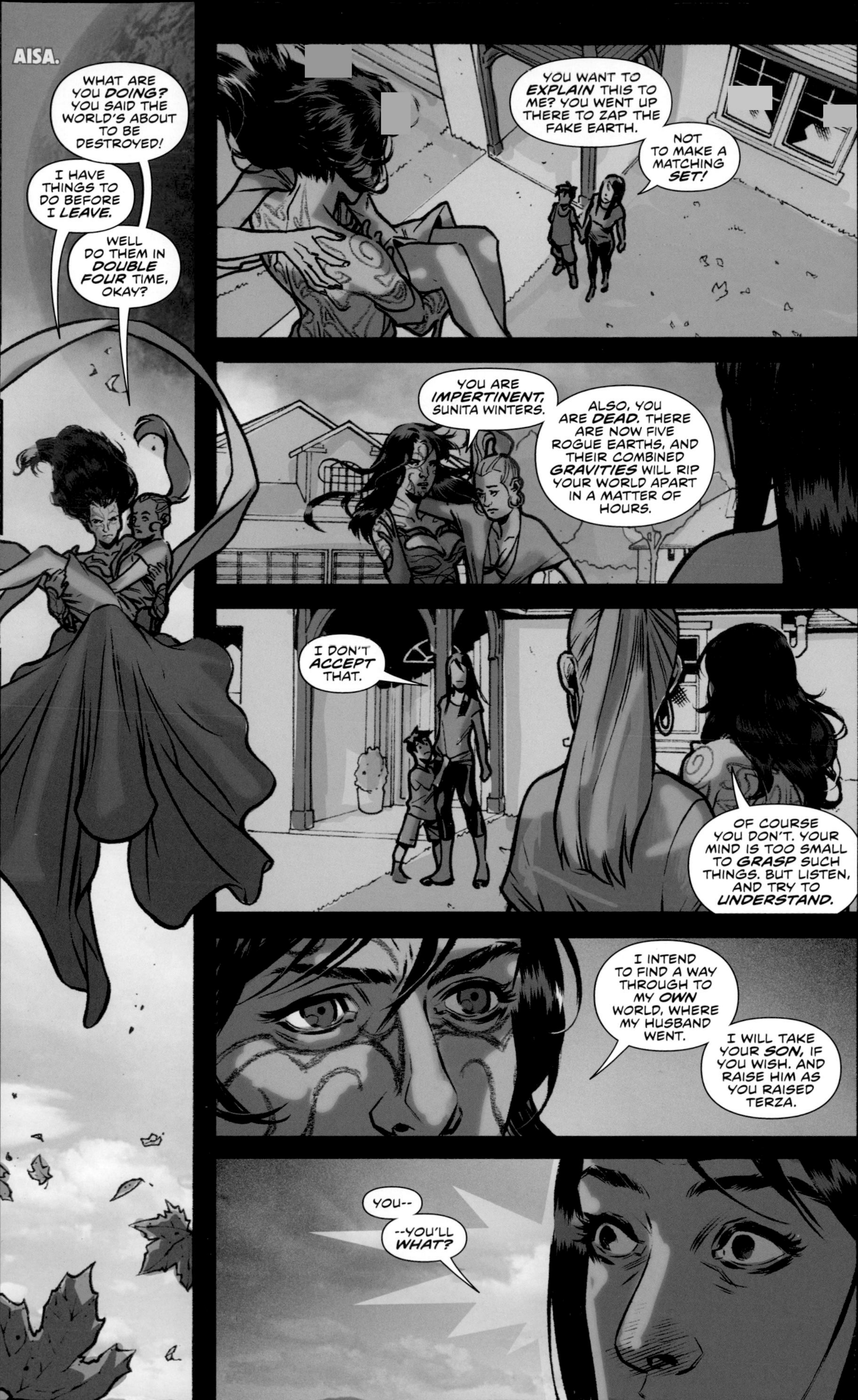
AISA.
WHAT ARE YOU DOING? YOU SAID THE WORLD'S ABOUT TO BE DESTROYED!
I HAVE THINGS TO DO BEFORE I LEAVE.
WELL DO THEM IN DOUBLE FOUR TIME, OKAY?
YOU WANT TO EXPLAIN THIS TO ME? YOU WENT UP THERE TO ZAP THE FAKE EARTH.
NOT TO MAKE A MATCHING SET!
YOU ARE IMPERTINENT, SUNITA WINTERS.
ALSO, YOU ARE DEAD. THERE ARE NOW FIVE ROGUE EARTHS, AND THEIR COMBINED GRAVITIES WILL RIP YOUR WORLD APART IN A MATTER OF HOURS.
I DON'T ACCEPT THAT.
OF COURSE YOU DON'T. YOUR MIND IS TOO SMALL TO GRASP SUCH THINGS. BUT LISTEN, AND TRY TO UNDERSTAND.
I INTEND TO FIND A WAY THROUGH TO MY OWN WORLD, WHERE MY HUSBAND WENT.
I WILL TAKE YOUR SON, IF YOU WISH. AND RAISE HIM AS YOU RAISED TERZA.
YOU--
--YOU'LL WHAT?

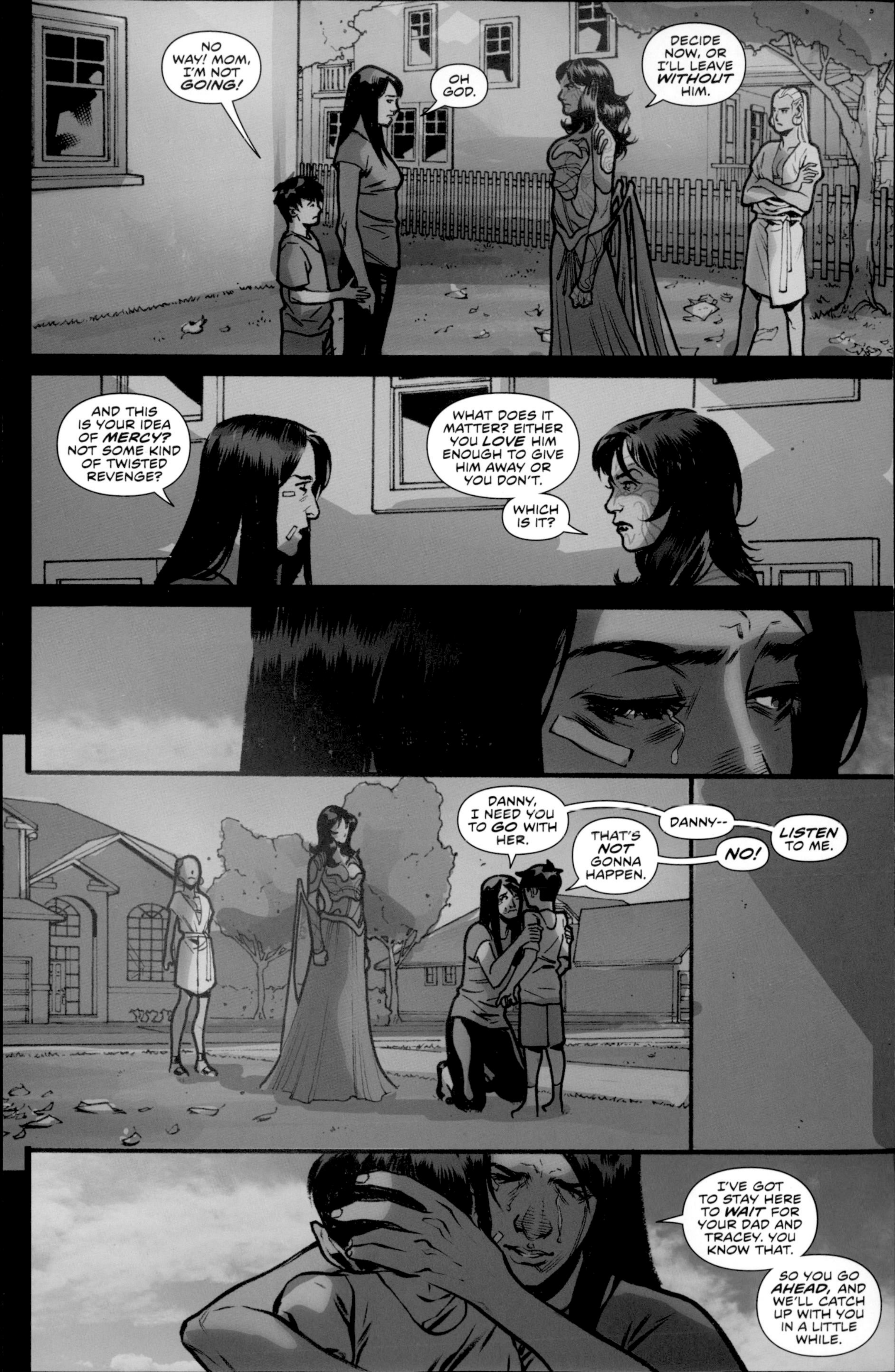
NO WAY! MOM, I'M NOT GOING!
OH GOD.
DECIDE NOW, OR I'LL LEAVE WITHOUT HIM.
AND THIS IS YOUR IDEA OF MERCY? NOT SOME KIND OF TWISTED REVENGE?
WHAT DOES IT MATTER? EITHER YOU LOVE HIM ENOUGH TO GIVE HIM AWAY OR YOU DON'T.
WHICH IS IT?
DANNY, I NEED YOU TO GO WITH HER.
THAT'S NOT GONNA HAPPEN.
DANNY--
NO!
LISTEN TO ME.
I'VE GOT TO STAY HERE TO WAIT FOR YOUR DAD AND TRACEY. YOU KNOW THAT.
SO YOU GO AHEAD, AND WE'LL CATCH UP WITH YOU IN A LITTLE WHILE.

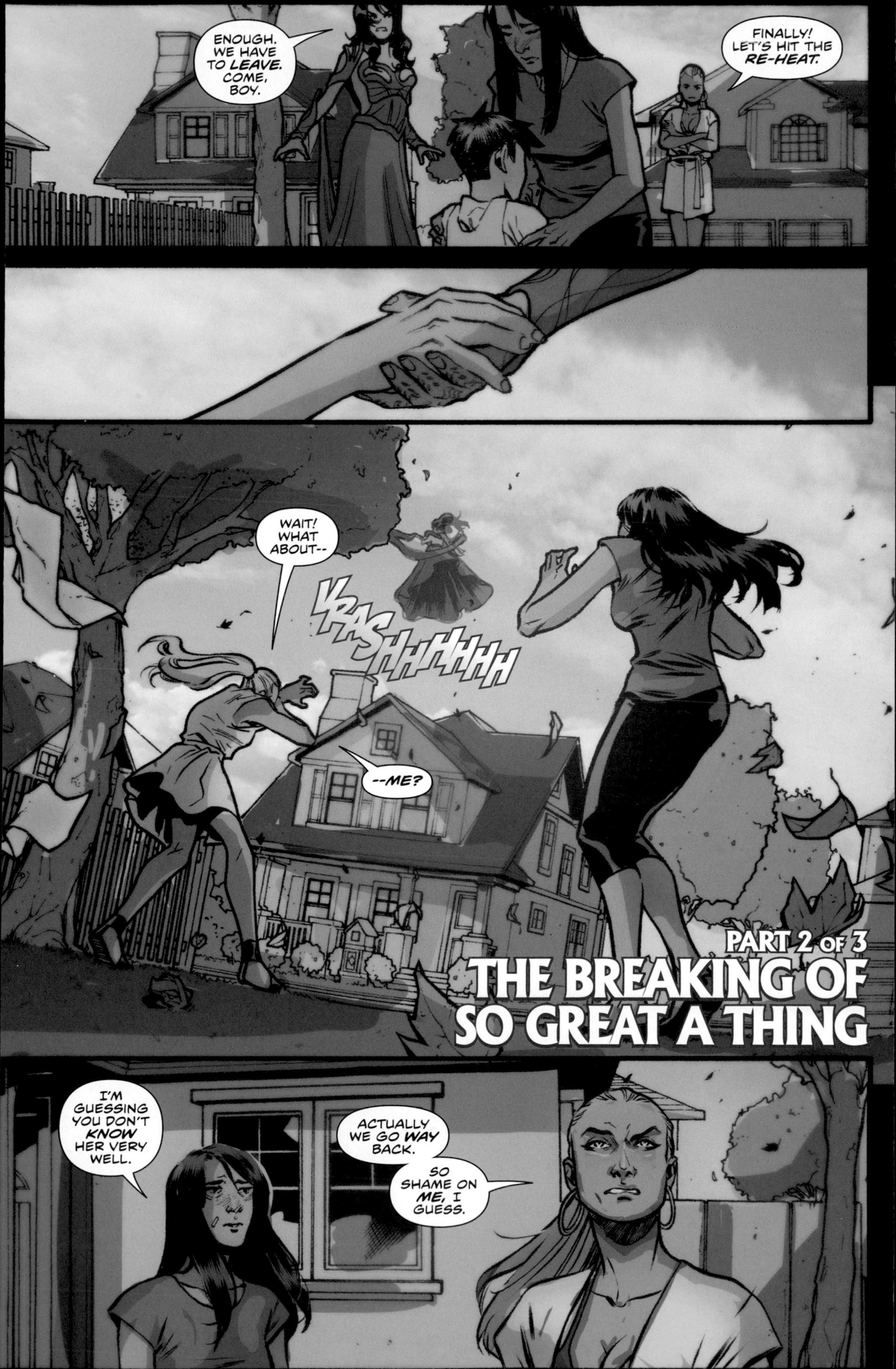
ENOUGH. WE HAVE TO LEAVE. COME, BOY.
FINALLY! LET'S HIT THE RE-HEAT.
WAIT! WHAT ABOUT--
VRASHHHHHH
--ME?
PART 2 OF 3
THE BREAKING OF SO GREAT A THING
I'M GUESSING YOU DON'T KNOW HER VERY WELL.
ACTUALLY WE GO WAY BACK.
SO SHAME ON ME, I GUESS.

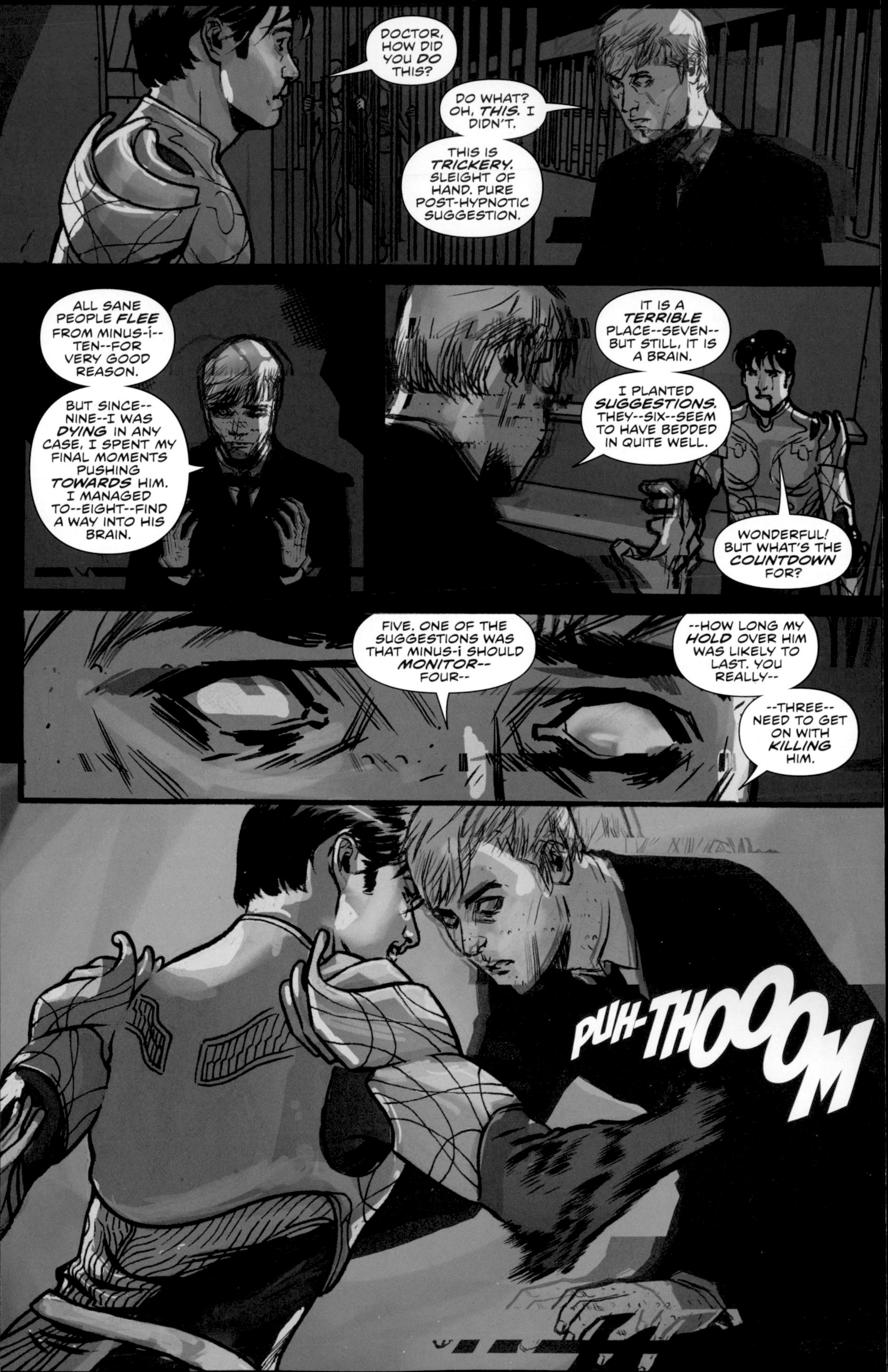
DOCTOR, HOW DID YOU DO THIS?
DO WHAT? OH, THIS. I DIDN'T.
THIS IS TRICKERY. SLEIGHT OF HAND. PURE POST-HYPNOTIC SUGGESTION.
ALL SANE PEOPLE FLEE FROM MINUS-i--TEN--FOR VERY GOOD REASON.
BUT SINCE--NINE--I WAS DYING IN ANY CASE, I SPENT MY FINAL MOMENTS PUSHING TOWARDS HIM. I MANAGED TO--EIGHT--FIND A WAY INTO HIS BRAIN.
IT IS A TERRIBLE PLACE--SEVEN--BUT STILL, IT IS A BRAIN.
I PLANTED SUGGESTIONS. THEY--SIX--SEEM TO HAVE BEDDED IN QUITE WELL.
WONDERFUL! BUT WHAT'S THE COUNTDOWN FOR?
FIVE. ONE OF THE SUGGESTIONS WAS THAT MINUS-i SHOULD MONITOR--FOUR--
--HOW LONG MY HOLD OVER HIM WAS LIKELY TO LAST. YOU REALLY--
--THREE--NEED TO GET ON WITH KILLING HIM.
PUH-THOOOOM

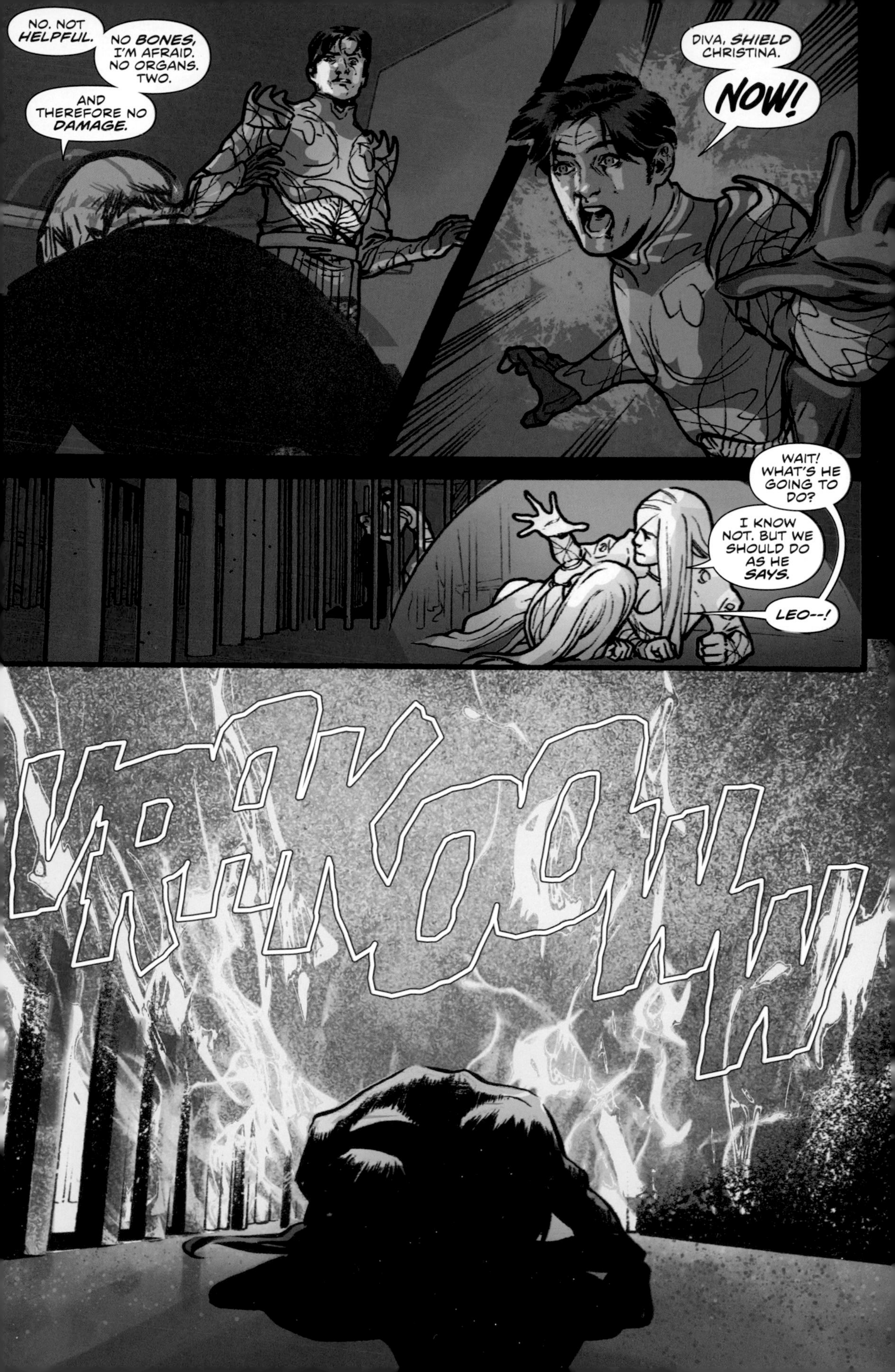
NO. NOT HELPFUL.
NO BONES, I'M AFRAID. NO ORGANS. TWO.
AND THEREFORE NO DAMAGE.
DIVA, SHIELD CHRISTINA.
NOW!
WAIT! WHAT'S HE GOING TO DO?
I KNOW NOT. BUT WE SHOULD DO AS HE SAYS.
LEO--!
VRRMOOOM

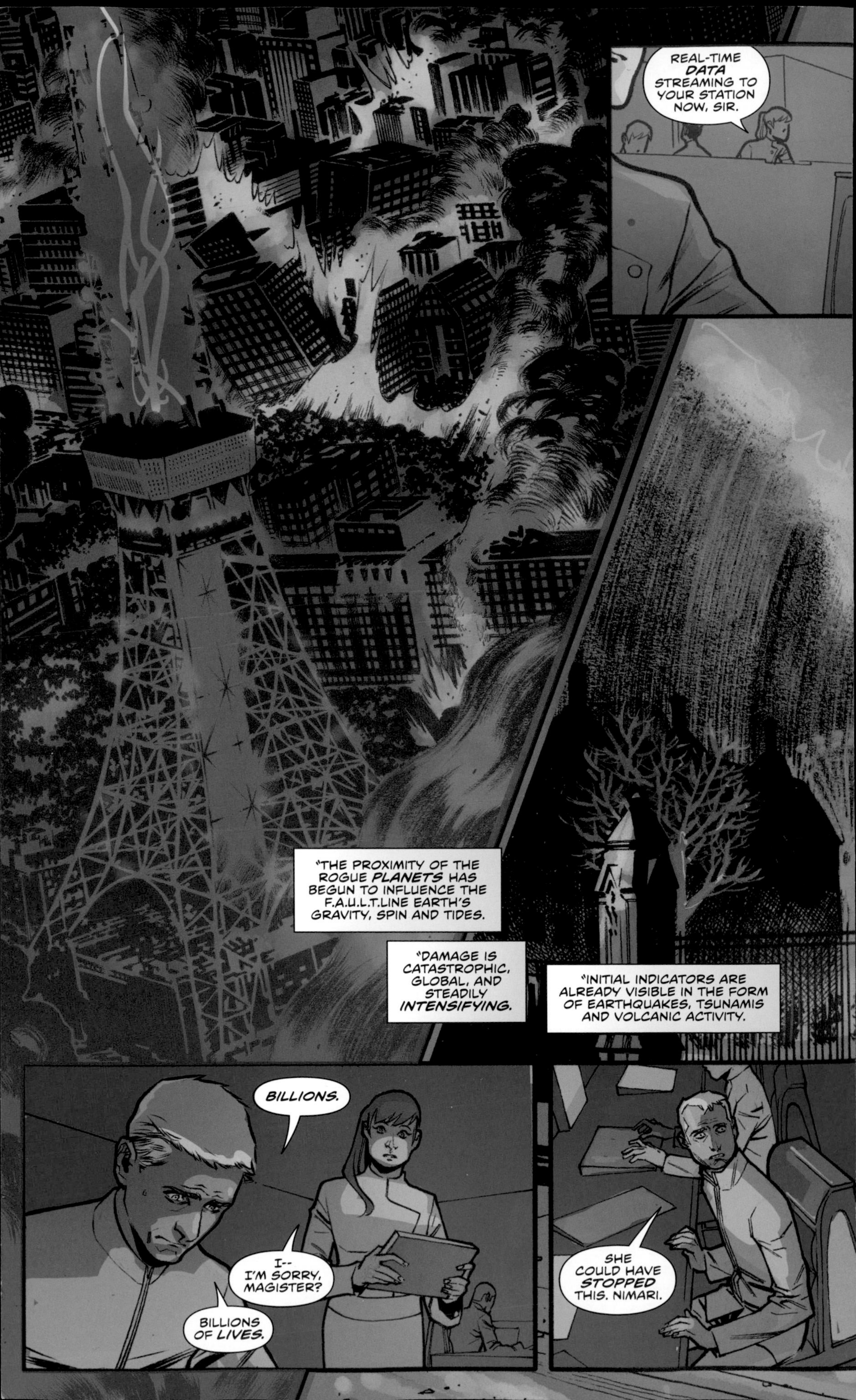
REAL-TIME DATA STREAMING TO YOUR STATION NOW, SIR.
"THE PROXIMITY OF THE ROGUE PLANETS HAS BEGUN TO INFLUENCE THE F.A.U.L.T.LINE EARTH'S GRAVITY, SPIN AND TIDES.
"DAMAGE IS CATASTROPHIC, GLOBAL, AND STEADILY INTENSIFYING.
"INITIAL INDICATORS ARE ALREADY VISIBLE IN THE FORM OF EARTHQUAKES, TSUNAMIS AND VOLCANIC ACTIVITY.
BILLIONS.
I-- I'M SORRY, MAGISTER?
BILLIONS OF LIVES.
SHE COULD HAVE STOPPED THIS. NIMARI.

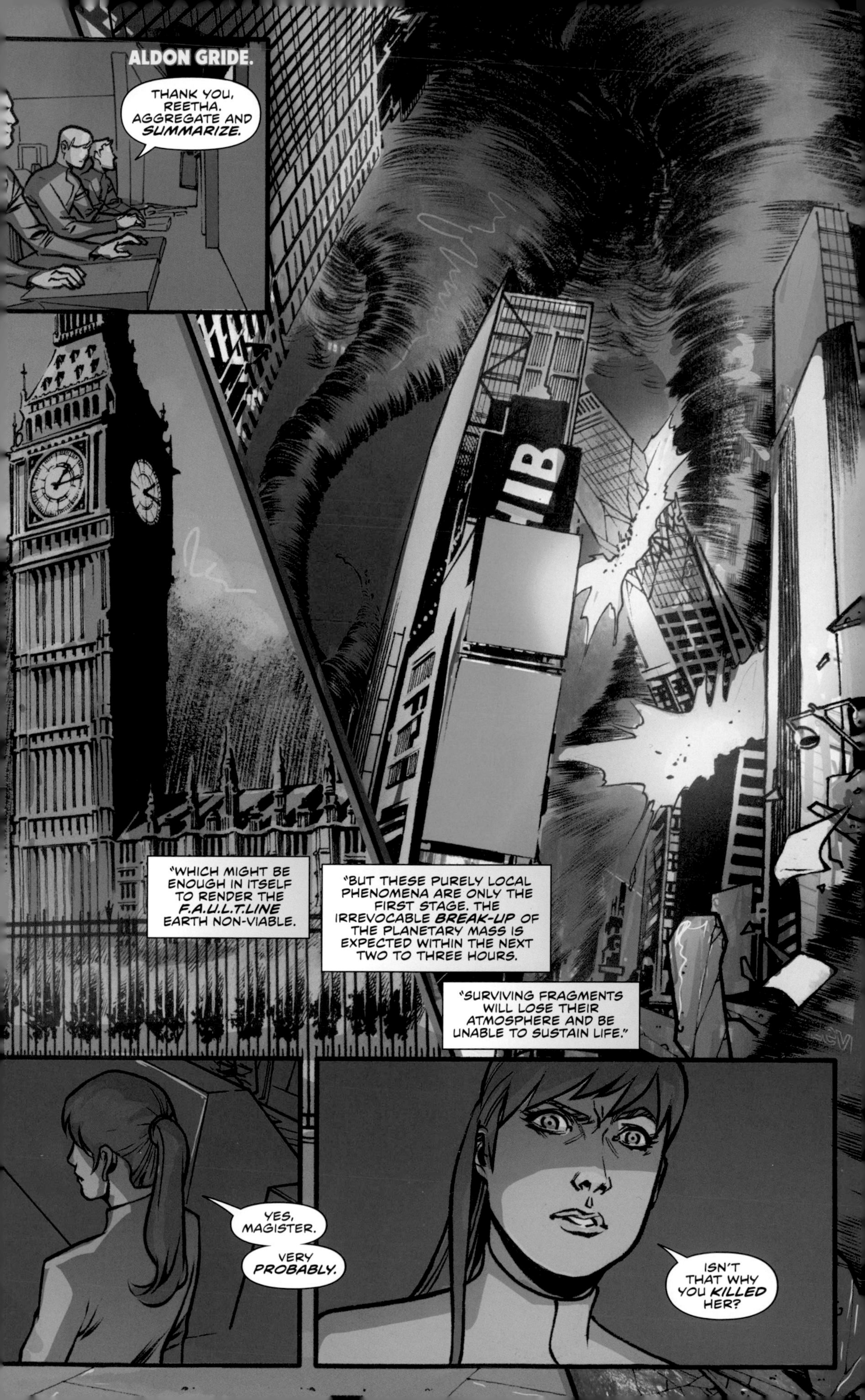
ALDON GRIDE.
THANK YOU, REETHA. AGGREGATE AND SUMMARIZE.
"WHICH MIGHT BE ENOUGH IN ITSELF TO RENDER THE F.A.U.L.T.LINE EARTH NON-VIABLE.
"BUT THESE PURELY LOCAL PHENOMENA ARE ONLY THE FIRST STAGE. THE IRREVOCABLE BREAK-UP OF THE PLANETARY MASS IS EXPECTED WITHIN THE NEXT TWO TO THREE HOURS.
"SURVIVING FRAGMENTS WILL LOSE THEIR ATMOSPHERE AND BE UNABLE TO SUSTAIN LIFE."
YES, MAGISTER.
VERY PROBABLY.
ISN'T THAT WHY YOU KILLED HER?

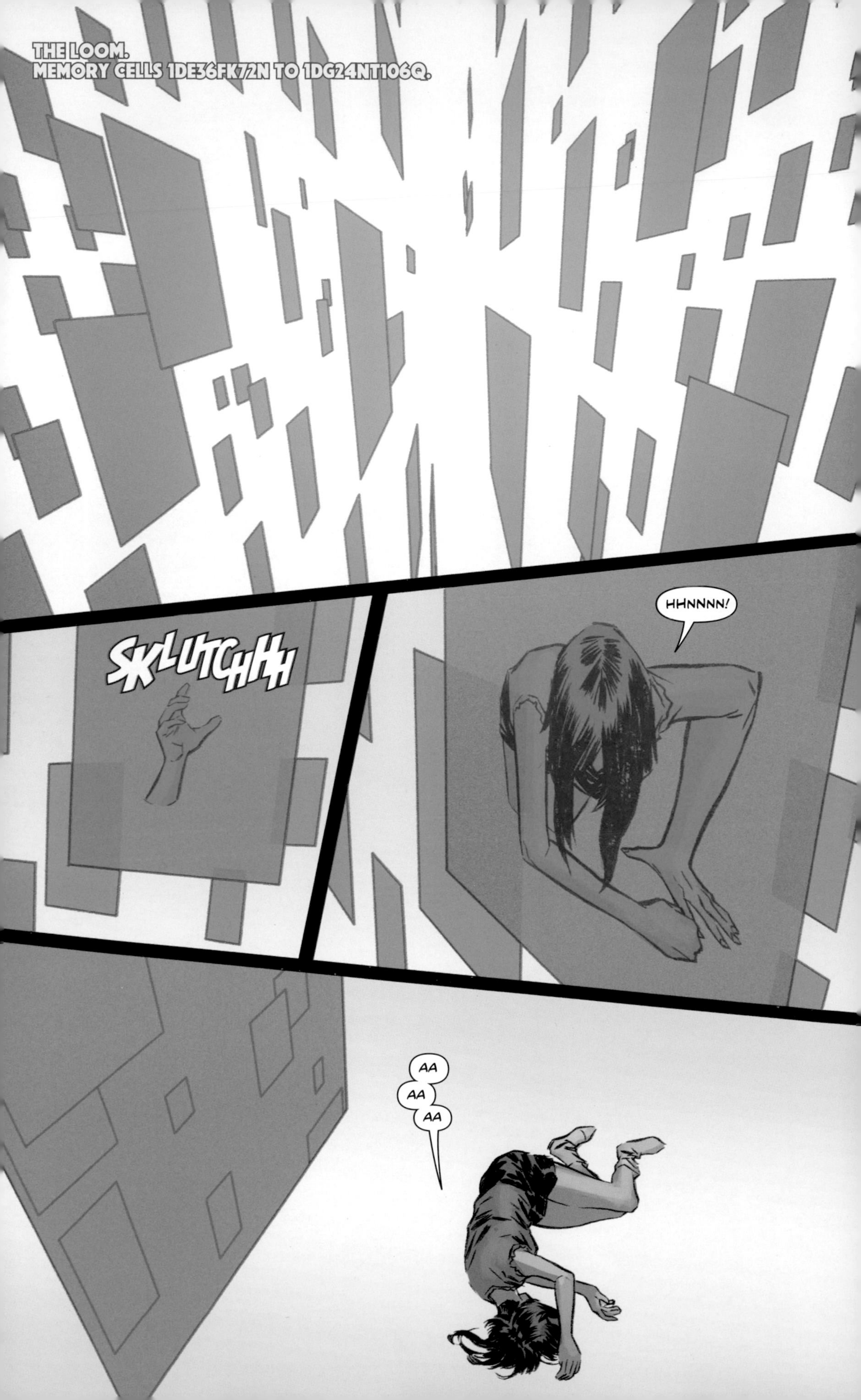

THE LOOM.
MEMORY CELLS 1DE36FK72N TO 1DG24NT106Q.
SKLUTCHHH
HHNNNN!
AA
AA
AA

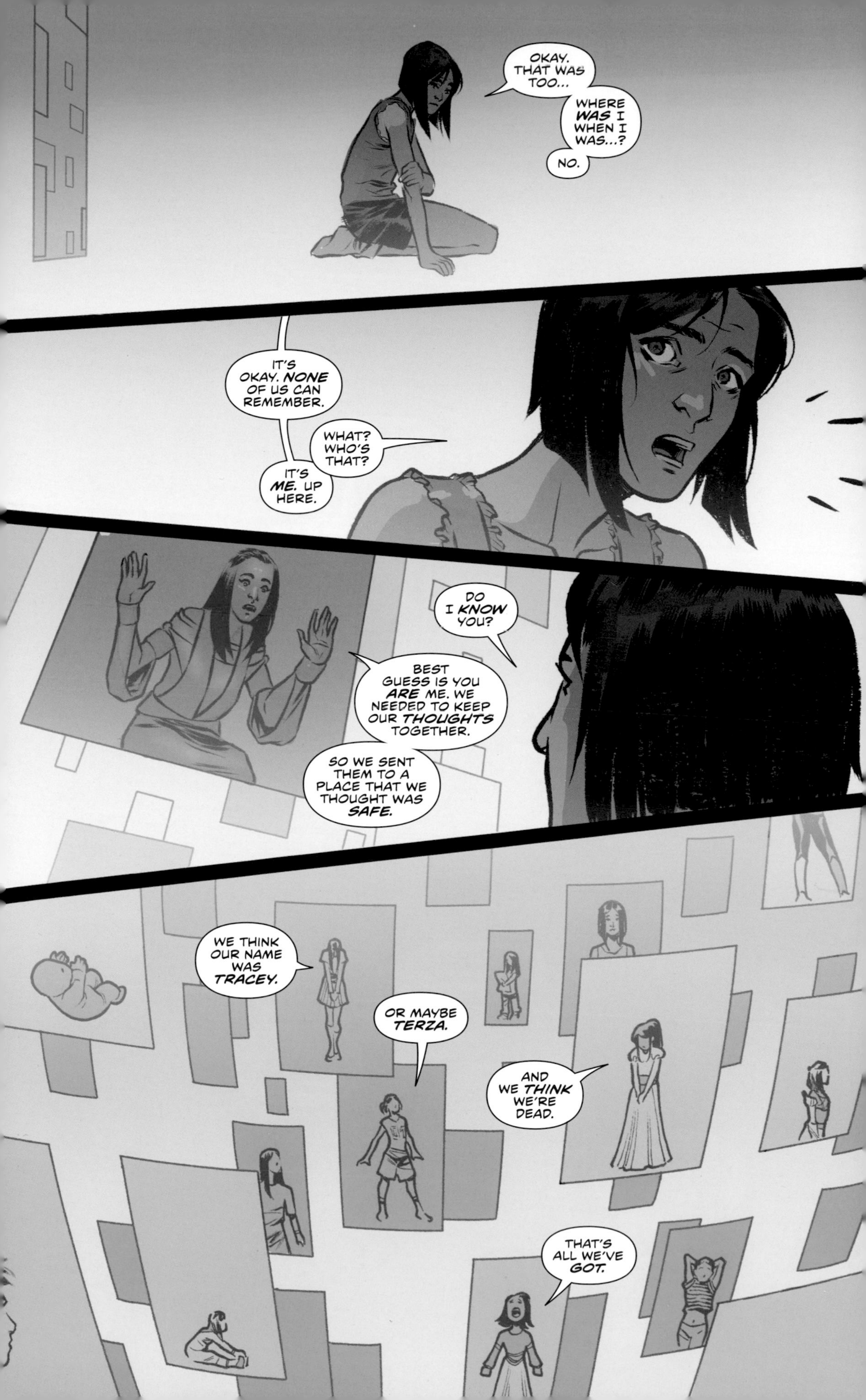
OKAY. THAT WAS TOO...
WHERE WAS I WHEN I WAS...?
NO.
IT'S OKAY. NONE OF US CAN REMEMBER.
WHAT? WHO'S THAT?
IT'S ME. UP HERE.
DO I KNOW YOU?
BEST GUESS IS YOU ARE ME. WE NEEDED TO KEEP OUR THOUGHTS TOGETHER.
SO WE SENT THEM TO A PLACE THAT WE THOUGHT WAS SAFE.
WE THINK OUR NAME WAS TRACEY.
OR MAYBE TERZA.
AND WE THINK WE'RE DEAD.
THAT'S ALL WE'VE GOT.

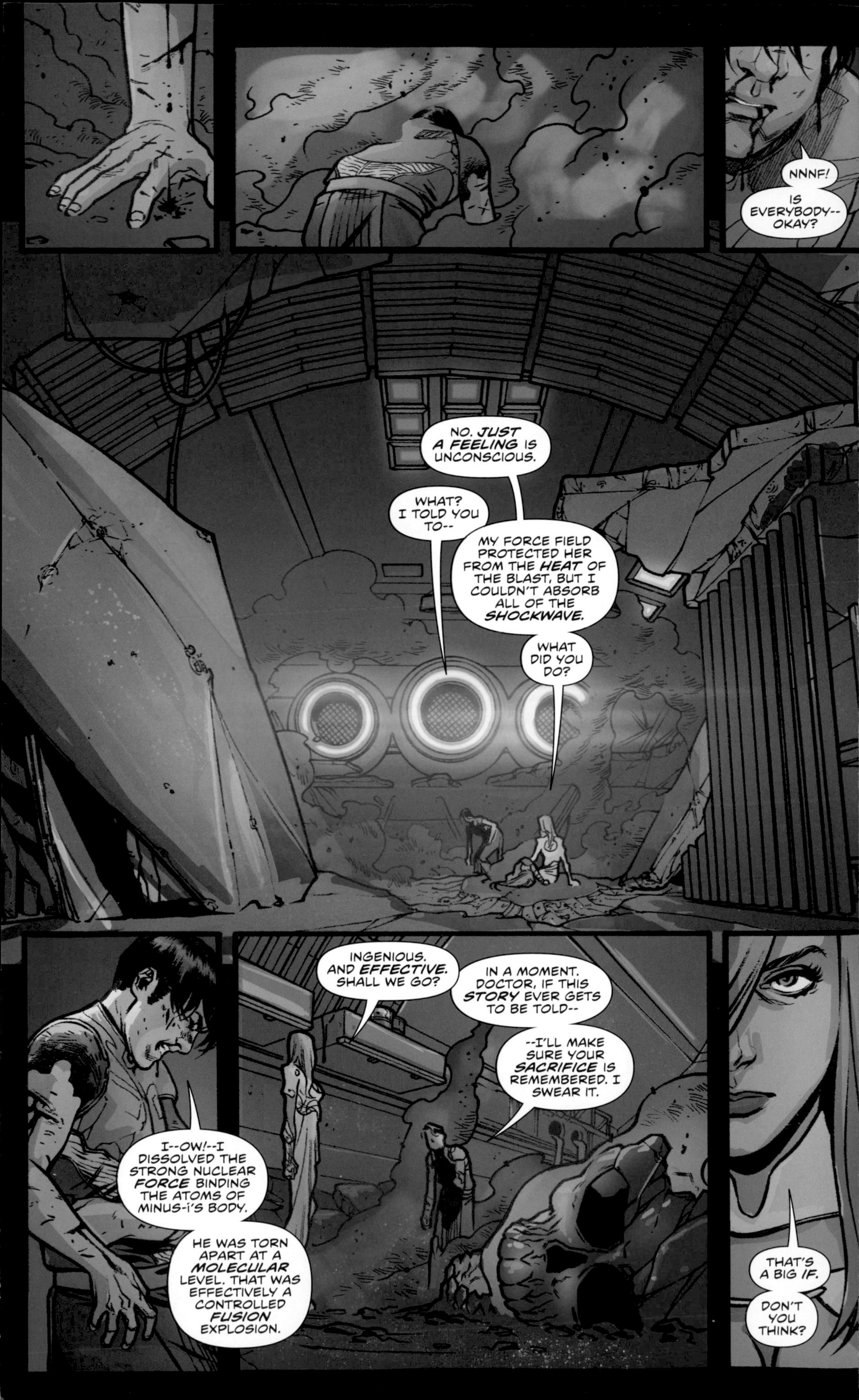
NNNF!
IS EVERYBODY-- OKAY?
NO. JUST A FEELING IS UNCONSCIOUS.
WHAT? I TOLD YOU TO--
MY FORCE FIELD PROTECTED HER FROM THE HEAT OF THE BLAST, BUT I COULDN'T ABSORB ALL OF THE SHOCKWAVE.
WHAT DID YOU DO?
I--OW!--I DISSOLVED THE STRONG NUCLEAR FORCE BINDING THE ATOMS OF MINUS-i'S BODY.
HE WAS TORN APART AT A MOLECULAR LEVEL. THAT WAS EFFECTIVELY A CONTROLLED FUSION EXPLOSION.
INGENIOUS. AND EFFECTIVE. SHALL WE GO?
IN A MOMENT. DOCTOR, IF THIS STORY EVER GETS TO BE TOLD--
--I'LL MAKE SURE YOUR SACRIFICE IS REMEMBERED. I SWEAR IT.
THAT'S A BIG IF.
DON'T YOU THINK?

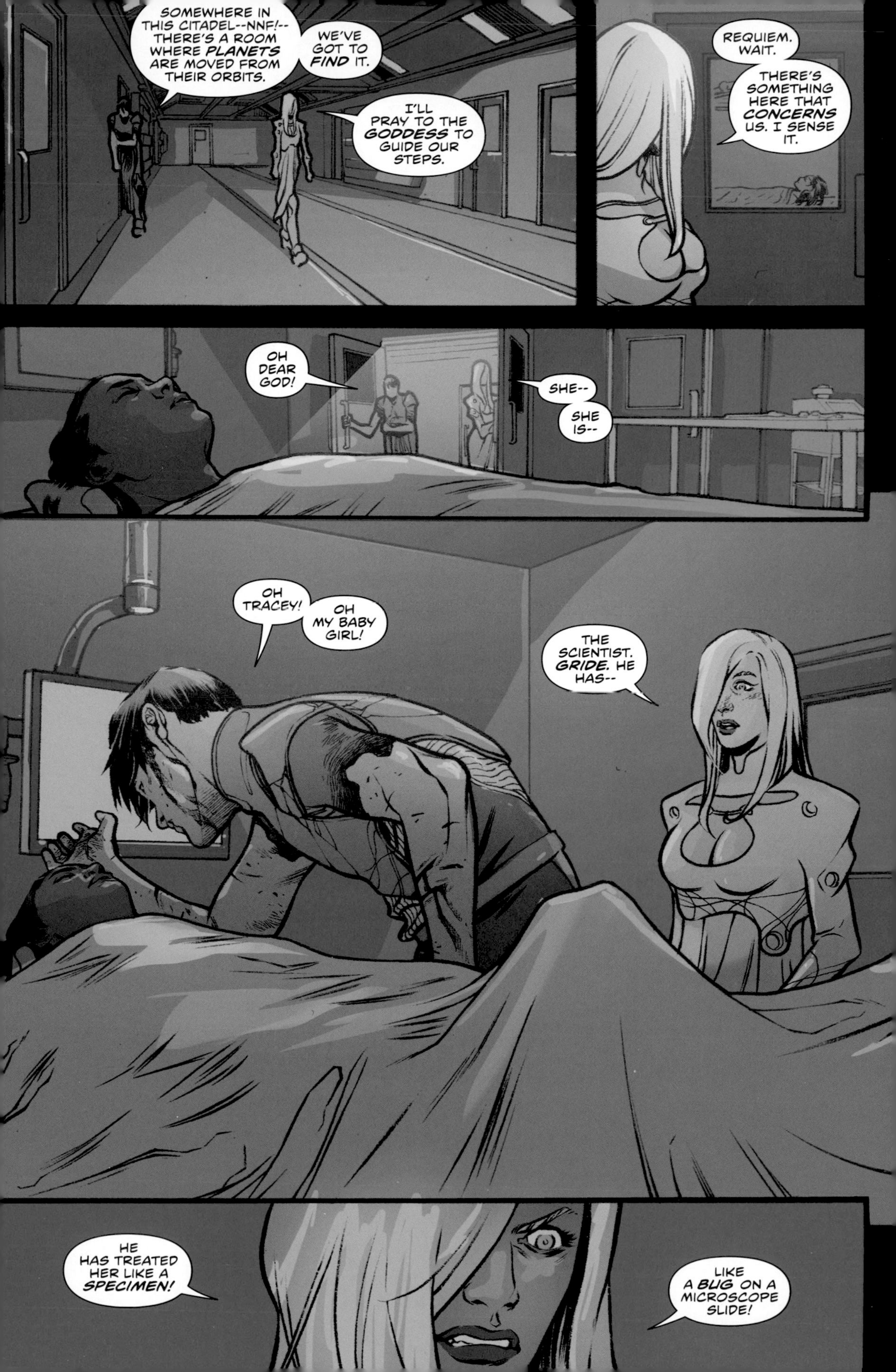
SOMEWHERE IN THIS CITADEL--NNF!-- THERE'S A ROOM WHERE PLANETS ARE MOVED FROM THEIR ORBITS.
WE'VE GOT TO FIND IT.
I'LL PRAY TO THE GODDESS TO GUIDE OUR STEPS.
REQUIEM. WAIT.
THERE'S SOMETHING HERE THAT CONCERNS US. I SENSE IT.
OH DEAR GOD!
SHE--
SHE IS--
OH TRACEY!
OH MY BABY GIRL!
THE SCIENTIST. GRIDE. HE HAS--
HE HAS TREATED HER LIKE A SPECIMEN!
LIKE A BUG ON A MICROSCOPE SLIDE!

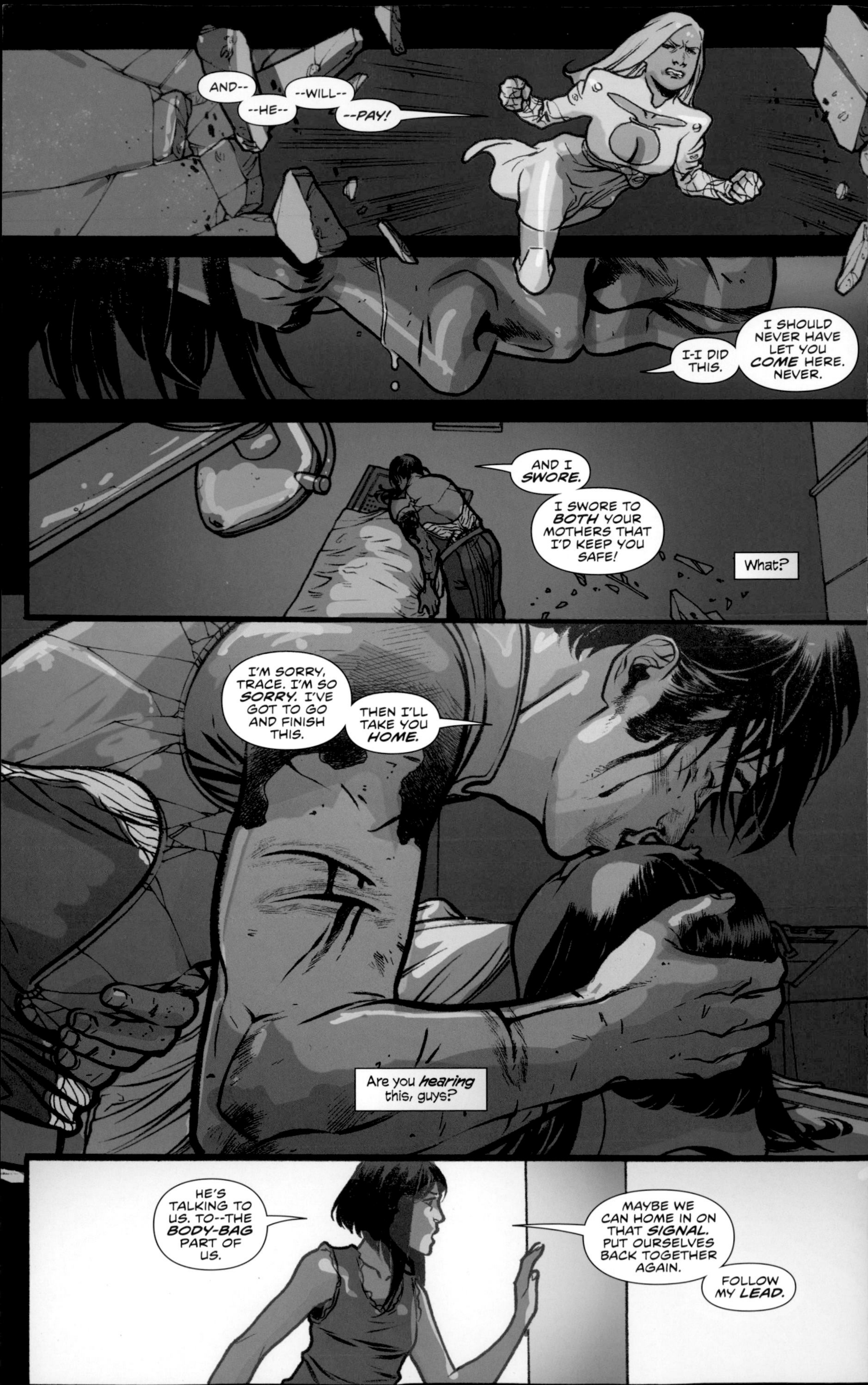
AND--
--HE--
--WILL--
--PAY!
I-I DID THIS.
I SHOULD NEVER HAVE LET YOU COME HERE. NEVER.
AND I SWORE.
I SWORE TO BOTH YOUR MOTHERS THAT I'D KEEP YOU SAFE!
What?
I'M SORRY, TRACE. I'M SO SORRY. I'VE GOT TO GO AND FINISH THIS.
THEN I'LL TAKE YOU HOME.
Are you hearing this, guys?
HE'S TALKING TO US. TO--THE BODY-BAG PART OF US.
MAYBE WE CAN HOME IN ON THAT SIGNAL. PUT OURSELVES BACK TOGETHER AGAIN.
FOLLOW MY LEAD.

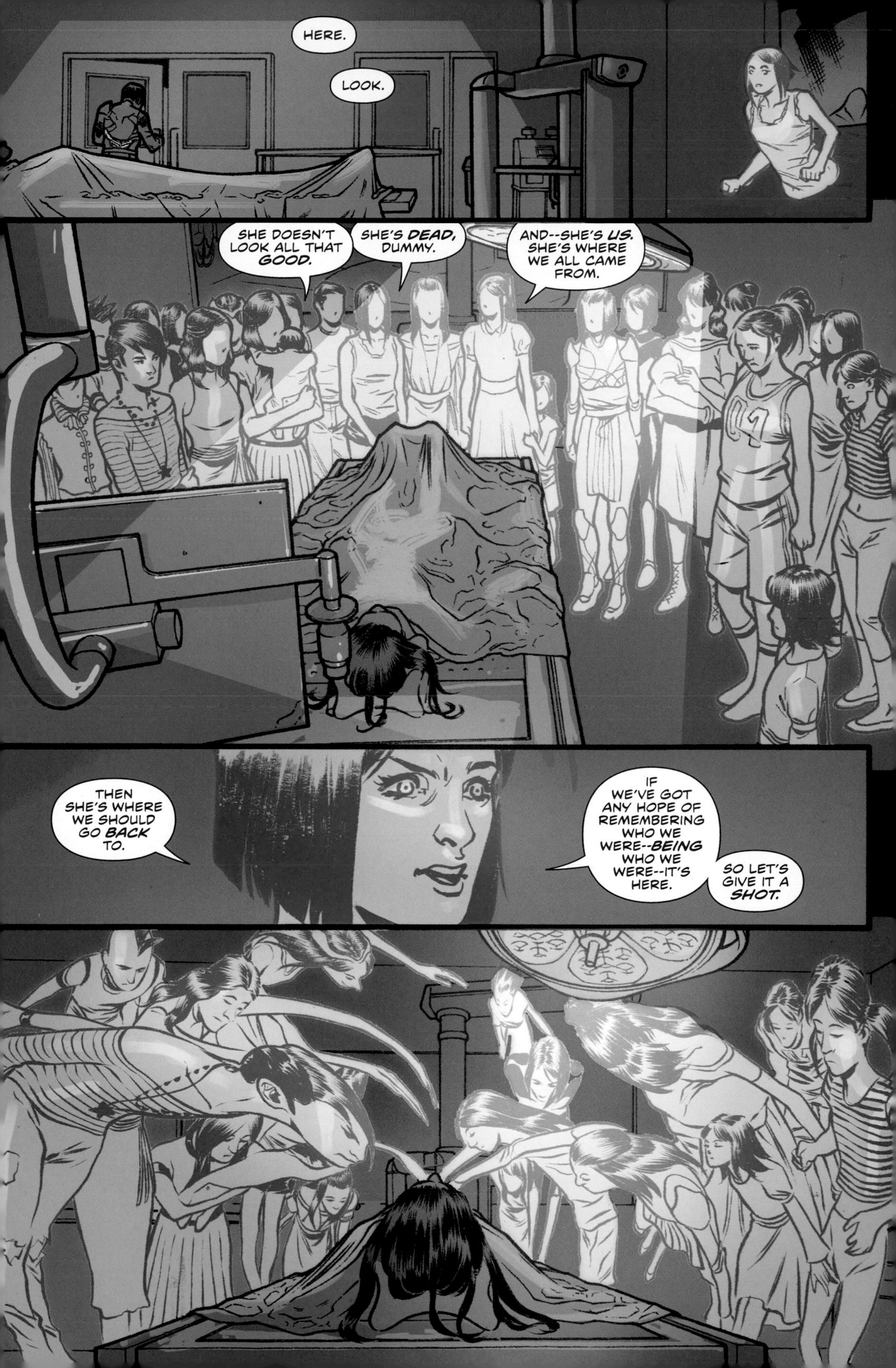
HERE.
LOOK.
SHE DOESN'T LOOK ALL THAT GOOD.
SHE'S DEAD, DUMMY.
AND--SHE'S US. SHE'S WHERE WE ALL CAME FROM.
THEN SHE'S WHERE WE SHOULD GO BACK TO.
IF WE'VE GOT ANY HOPE OF REMEMBERING WHO WE WERE--BEING WHO WE WERE--IT'S HERE.
SO LET'S GIVE IT A SHOT.

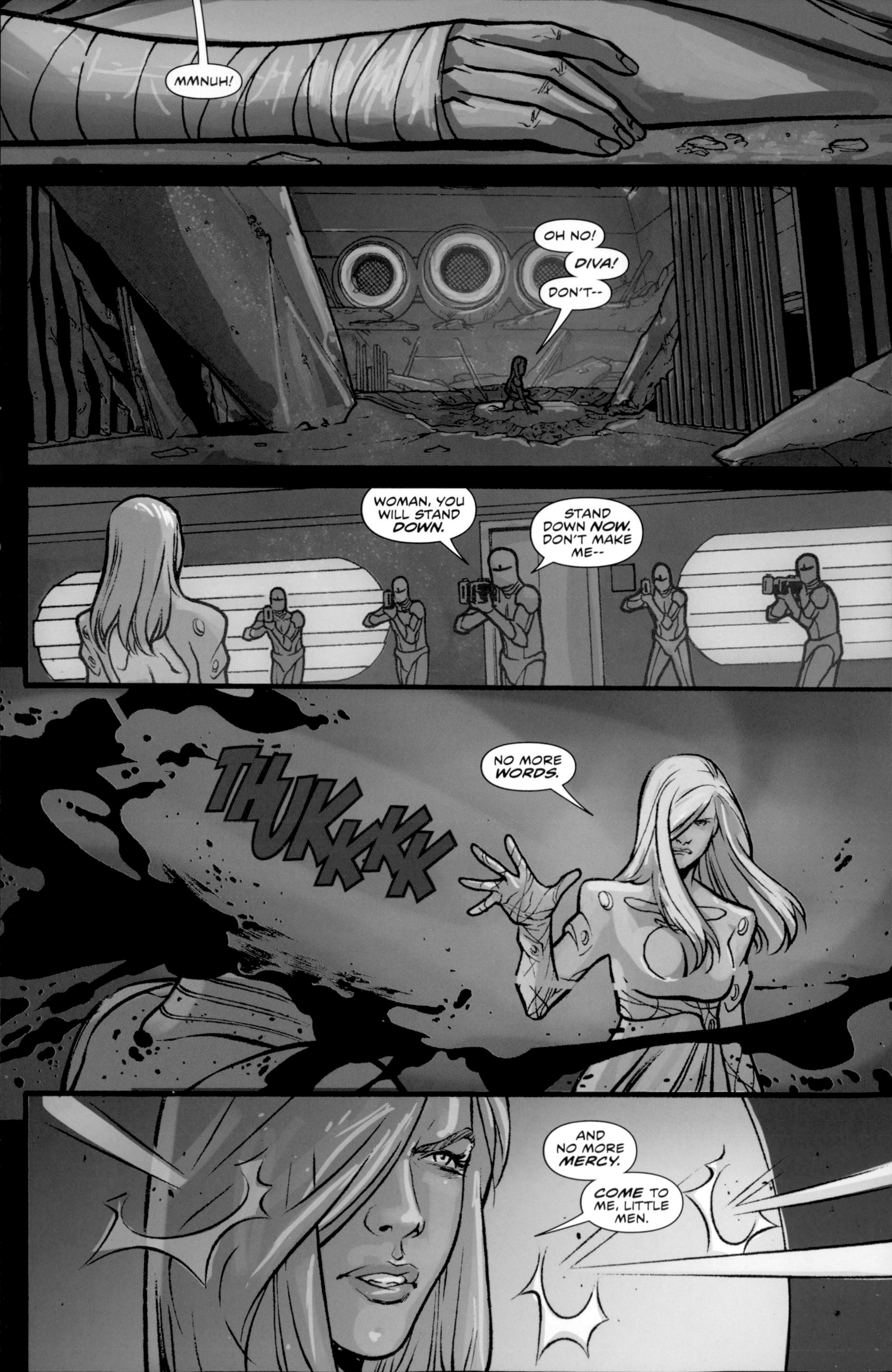
MMNUH!
OH NO!
DIVA!
DON'T--
WOMAN, YOU WILL STAND DOWN.
STAND DOWN NOW. DON'T MAKE ME--
THUKKKK
NO MORE WORDS.
AND NO MORE MERCY.
COME TO ME, LITTLE MEN.

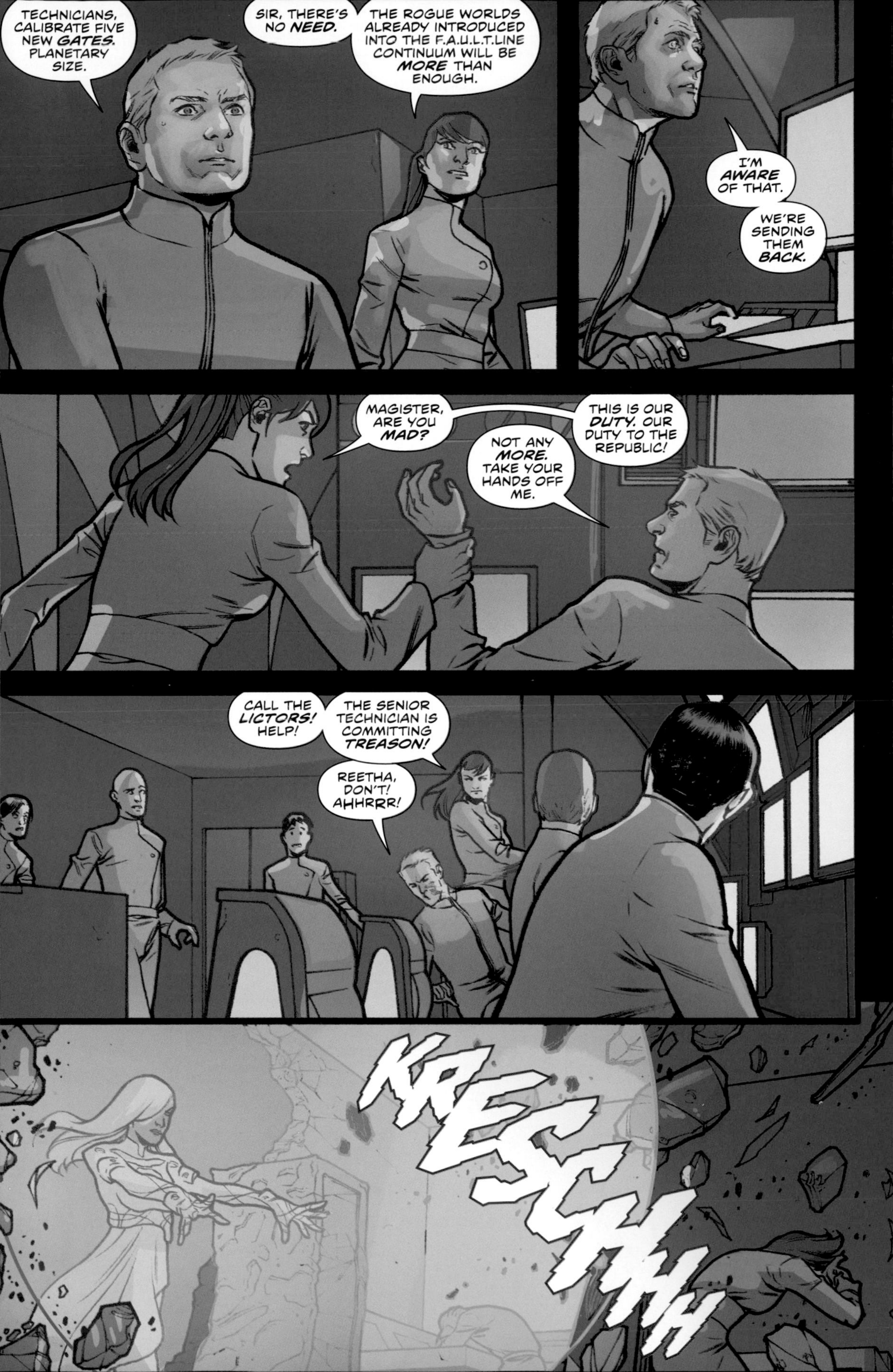
TECHNICIANS, CALIBRATE FIVE NEW GATES. PLANETARY SIZE.
SIR, THERE'S NO NEED.
THE ROGUE WORLDS ALREADY INTRODUCED INTO THE F.A.U.L.T.LINE CONTINUUM WILL BE MORE THAN ENOUGH.
I'M AWARE OF THAT.
WE'RE SENDING THEM BACK.
MAGISTER, ARE YOU MAD?
THIS IS OUR DUTY. OUR DUTY TO THE REPUBLIC!
NOT ANY MORE. TAKE YOUR HANDS OFF ME.
CALL THE LICTORS! HELP!
THE SENIOR TECHNICIAN IS COMMITTING TREASON!
REETHA, DON'T! AHHRRR!
KRESCHMM

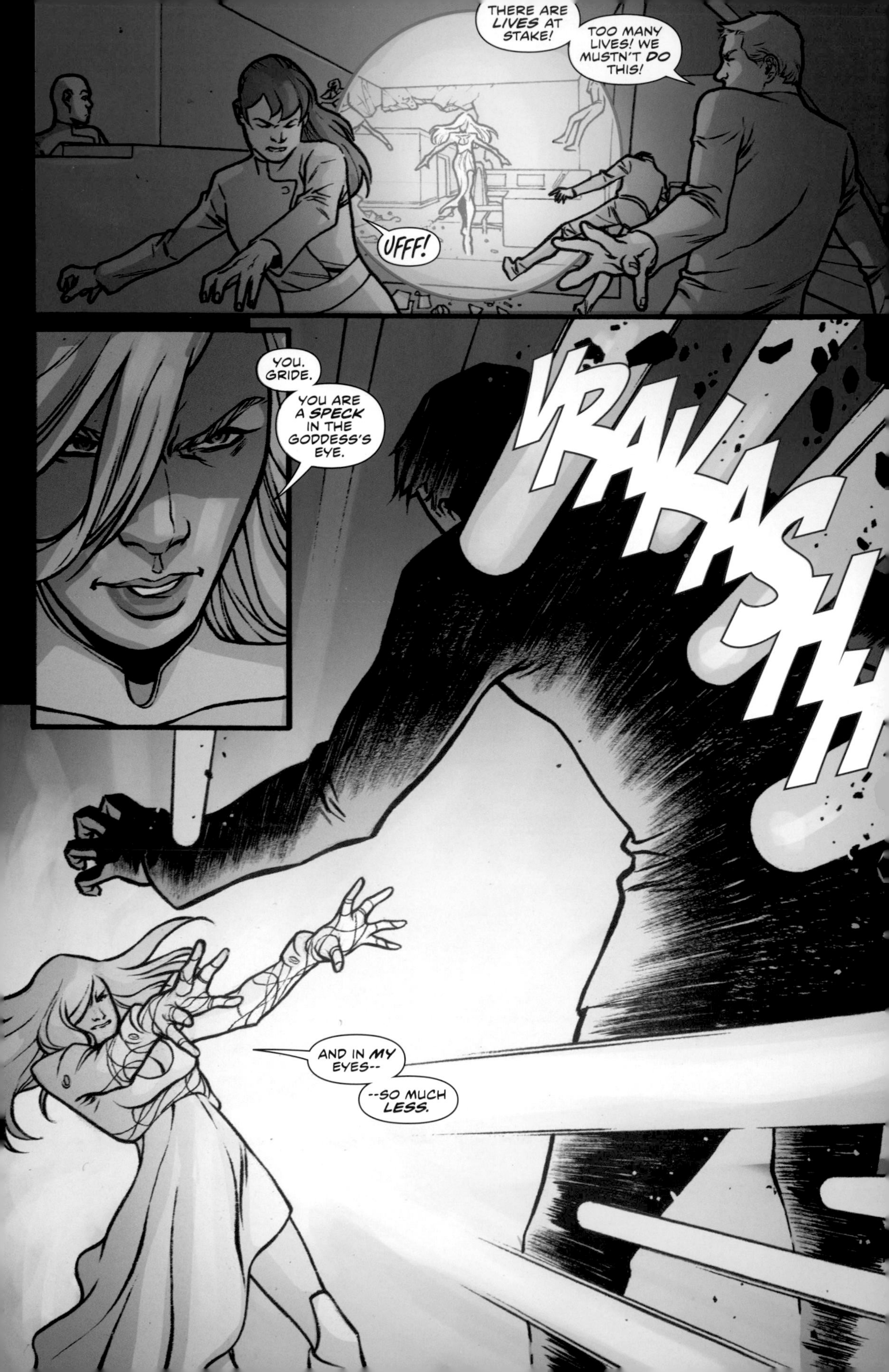
THERE ARE LIVES AT STAKE!
TOO MANY LIVES! WE MUSTN'T DO THIS!
UFFF!
YOU. GRIDE.
YOU ARE A SPECK IN THE GODDESS'S EYE.
VRAKASHH
AND IN MY EYES--
--SO MUCH LESS.

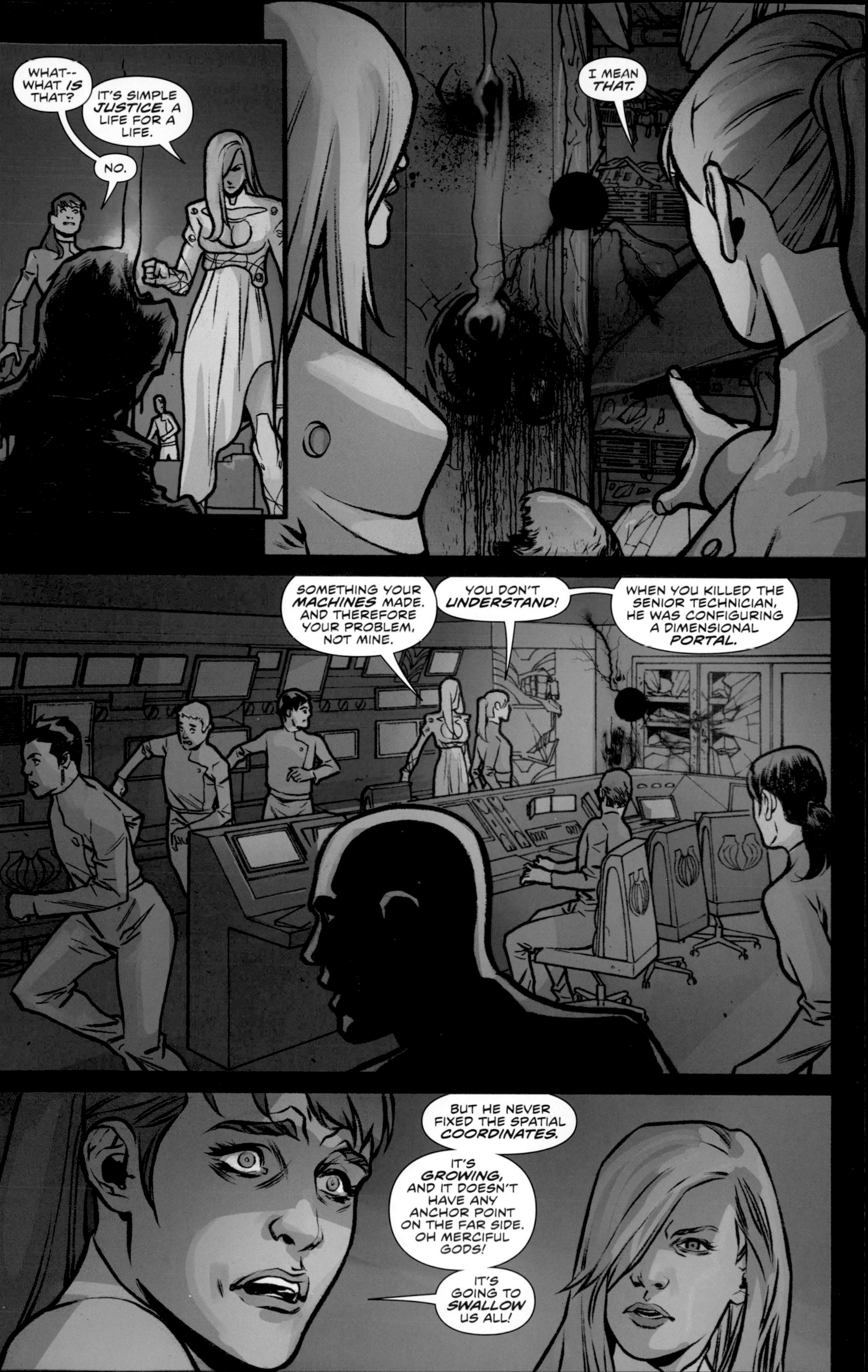
WHAT-- WHAT IS THAT?
IT'S SIMPLE JUSTICE. A LIFE FOR A LIFE.
NO.
I MEAN THAT.
SOMETHING YOUR MACHINES MADE. AND THEREFORE YOUR PROBLEM, NOT MINE.
YOU DON'T UNDERSTAND!
WHEN YOU KILLED THE SENIOR TECHNICIAN, HE WAS CONFIGURING A DIMENSIONAL PORTAL.
BUT HE NEVER FIXED THE SPATIAL COORDINATES.
IT'S GROWING, AND IT DOESN'T HAVE ANY ANCHOR POINT ON THE FAR SIDE. OH MERCIFUL GODS!
IT'S GOING TO SWALLOW US ALL!

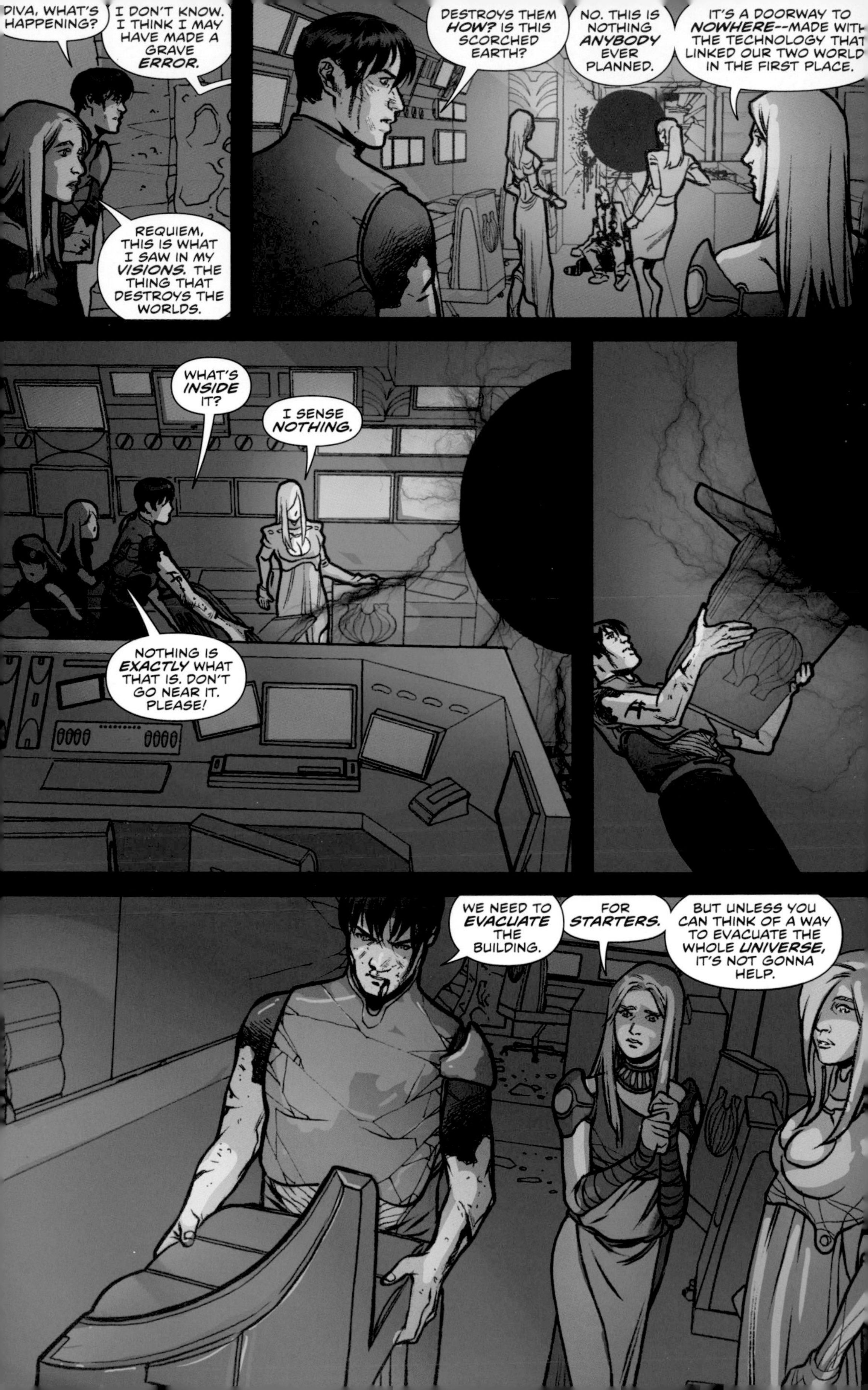
DIVA, WHAT'S HAPPENING?
I DON'T KNOW. I THINK I MAY HAVE MADE A GRAVE *ERROR.*
REQUIEM, THIS IS WHAT I SAW IN MY *VISIONS.* THE THING THAT DESTROYS THE WORLDS.
DESTROYS THEM *HOW?* IS THIS SCORCHED EARTH?
NO. THIS IS NOTHING *ANYBODY* EVER PLANNED.
IT'S A DOORWAY TO *NOWHERE*--MADE WITH THE TECHNOLOGY THAT LINKED OUR TWO WORLD IN THE FIRST PLACE.
WHAT'S *INSIDE* IT?
I SENSE *NOTHING.*
NOTHING IS *EXACTLY* WHAT THAT IS. DON'T GO NEAR IT. PLEASE!
WE NEED TO *EVACUATE* THE BUILDING.
FOR *STARTERS.*
BUT UNLESS YOU CAN THINK OF A WAY TO EVACUATE THE WHOLE *UNIVERSE,* IT'S NOT GONNA HELP.

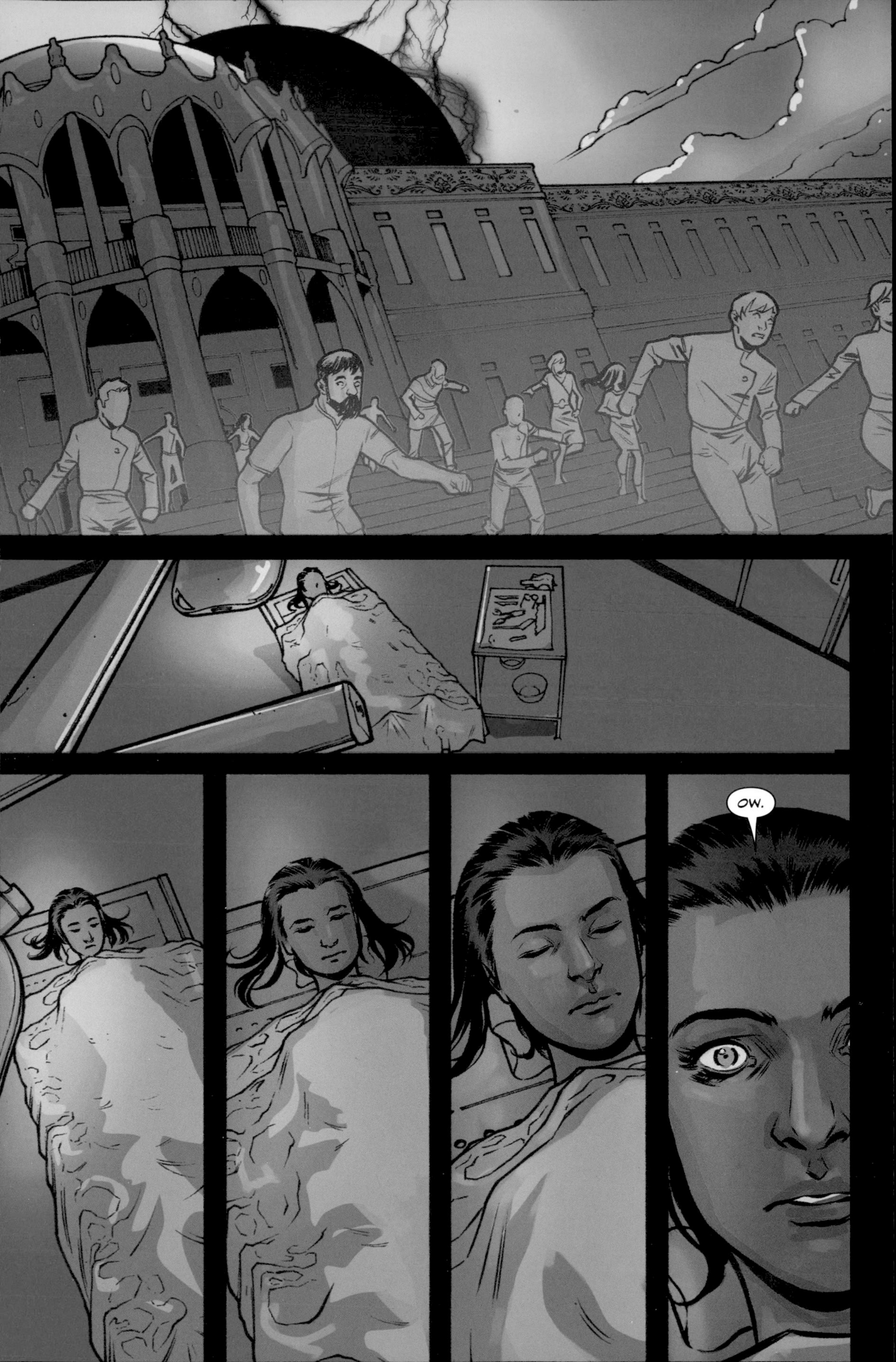
OW.

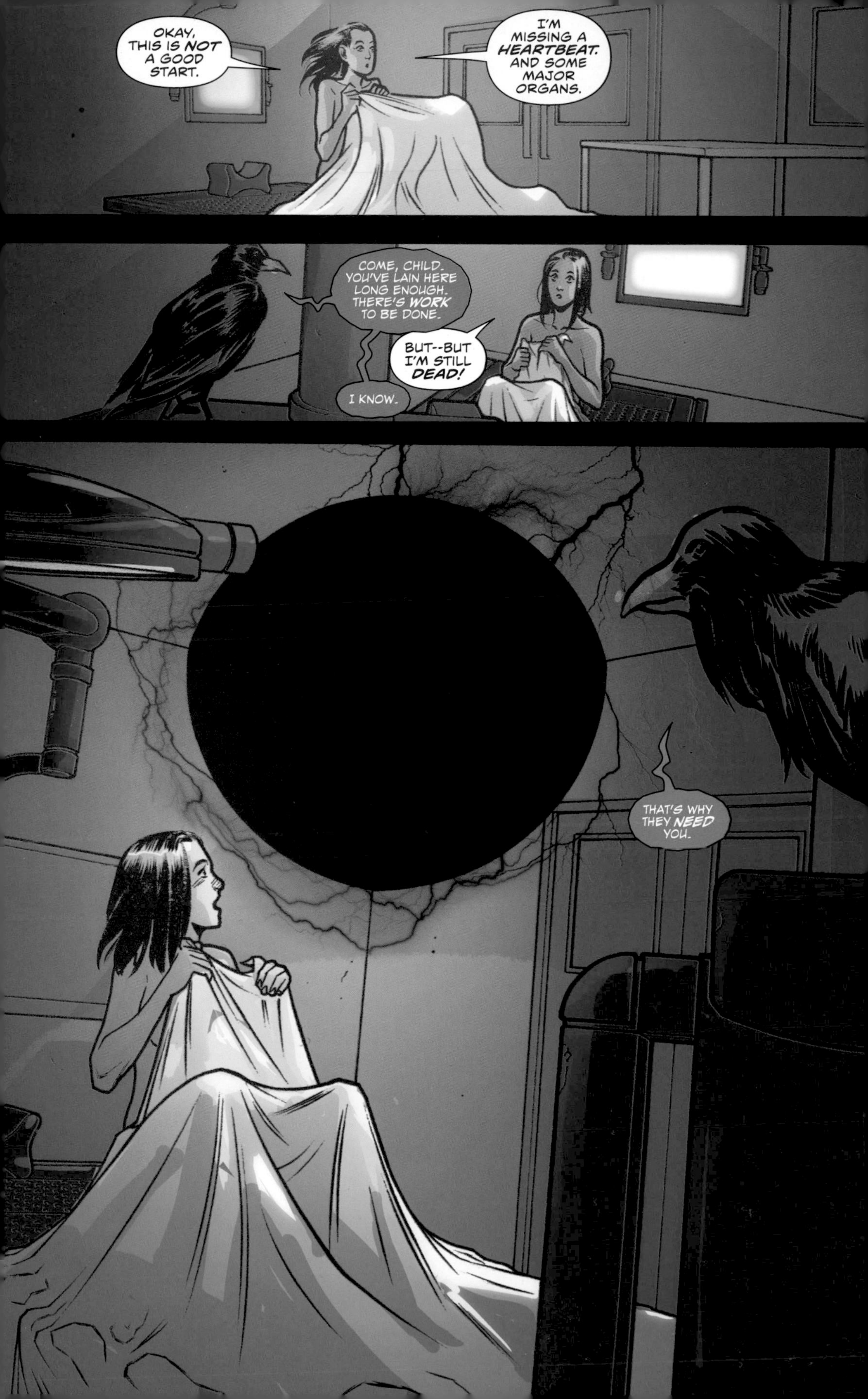
OKAY, THIS IS NOT A GOOD START.
I'M MISSING A HEARTBEAT. AND SOME MAJOR ORGANS.
COME, CHILD. YOU'VE LAIN HERE LONG ENOUGH. THERE'S WORK TO BE DONE.
BUT--BUT I'M STILL DEAD!
I KNOW.
THAT'S WHY THEY NEED YOU.

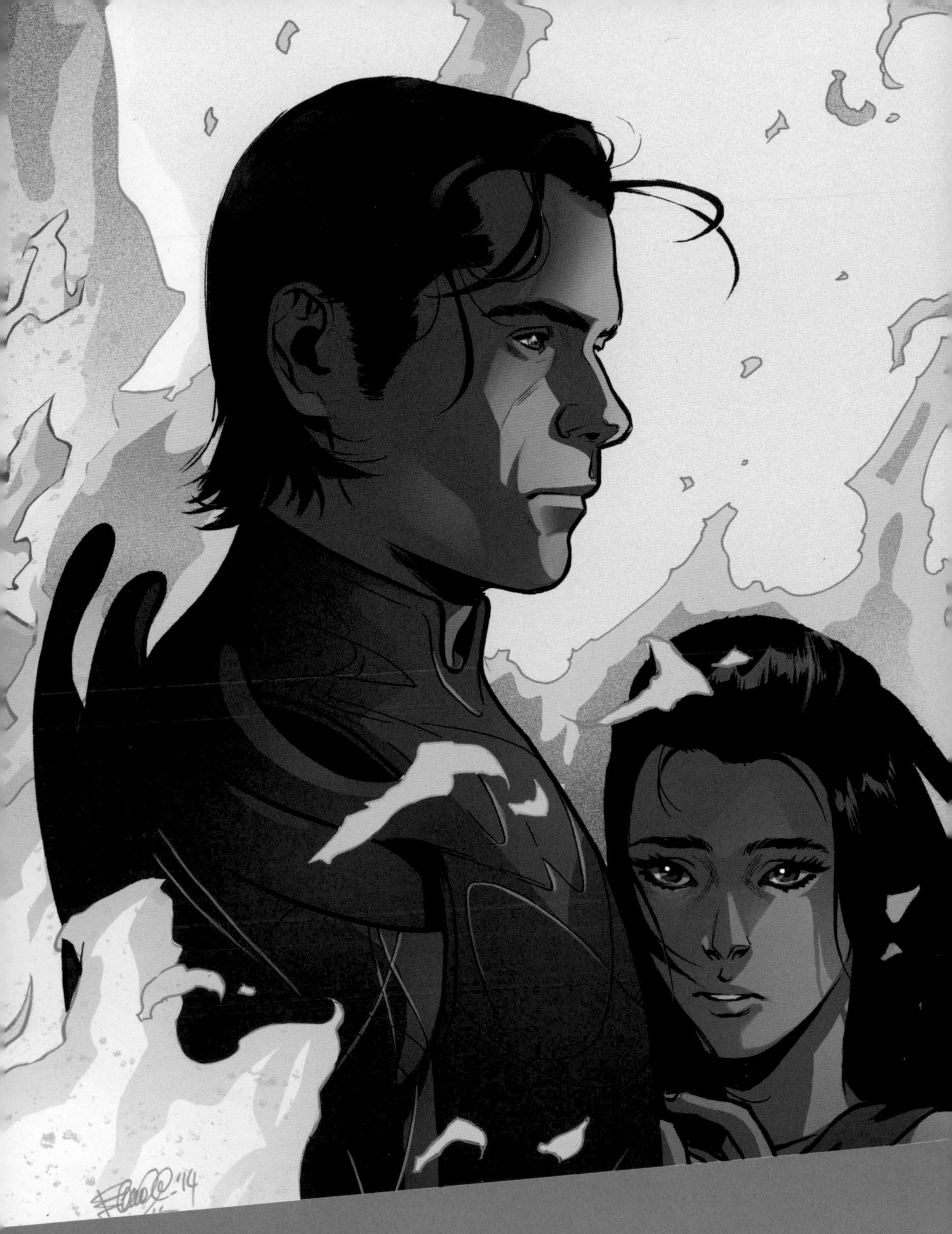

"I'VE HAD IT WITH BEING **COLLATERAL DAMAGE**.
I WANT TO GO WHERE **MY FAMILY** IS."

Chapter 24

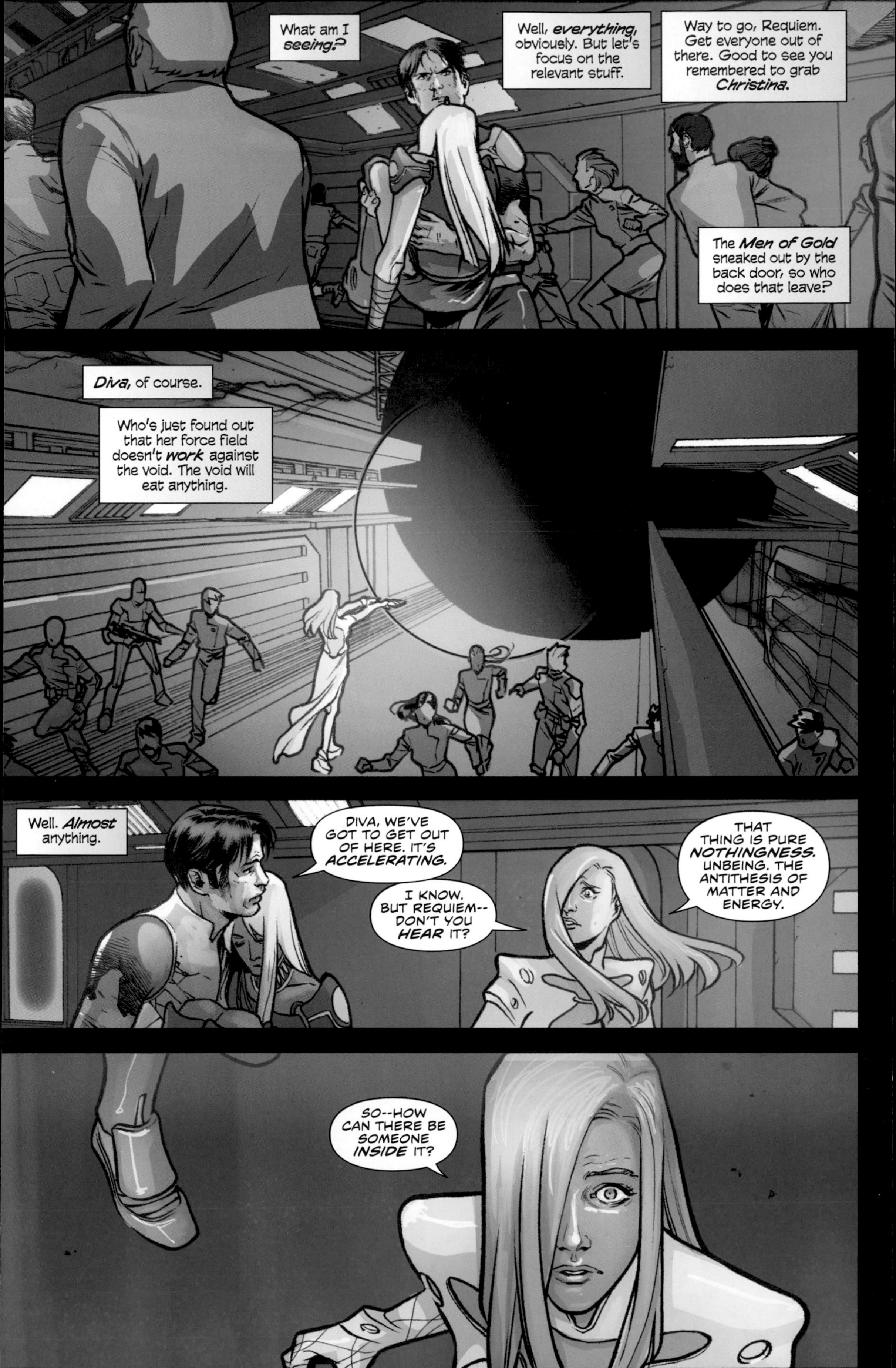

What am I seeing?
Well, everything, obviously. But let's focus on the relevant stuff.
Way to go, Requiem. Get everyone out of there. Good to see you remembered to grab Christina.
The Men of Gold sneaked out by the back door, so who does that leave?
Diva, of course.
Who's just found out that her force field doesn't work against the void. The void will eat anything.
Well. Almost anything.
DIVA, WE'VE GOT TO GET OUT OF HERE. IT'S ACCELERATING.
I KNOW. BUT REQUIEM-- DON'T YOU HEAR IT?
THAT THING IS PURE NOTHINGNESS. UNBEING. THE ANTITHESIS OF MATTER AND ENERGY.
SO--HOW CAN THERE BE SOMEONE INSIDE IT?

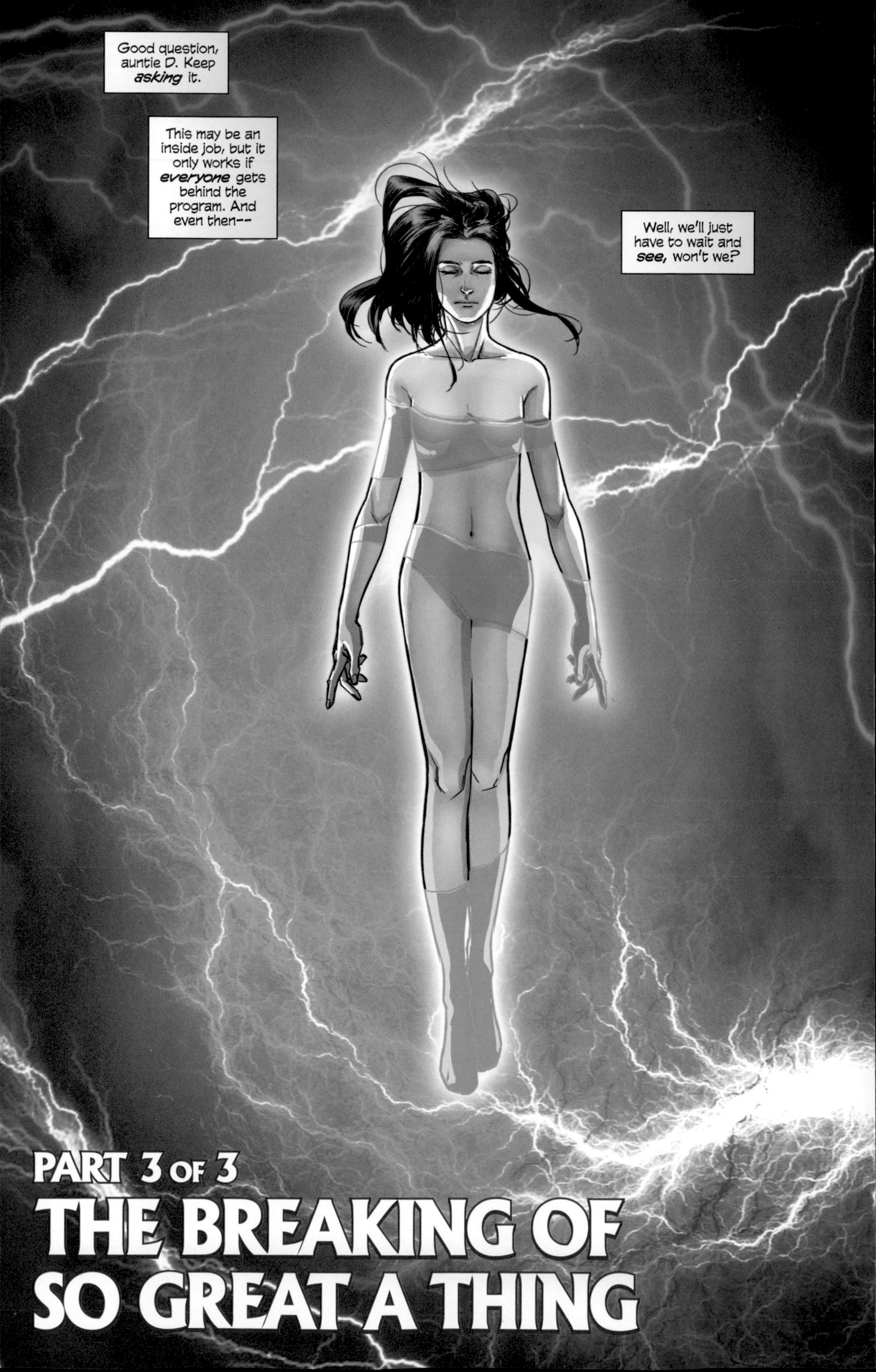

Good question, auntie D. Keep *asking* it.
This may be an inside job, but it only works if *everyone* gets behind the program. And even then--
Well, we'll just have to wait and *see,* won't we?
PART 3 OF 3
THE BREAKING OF SO GREAT A THING

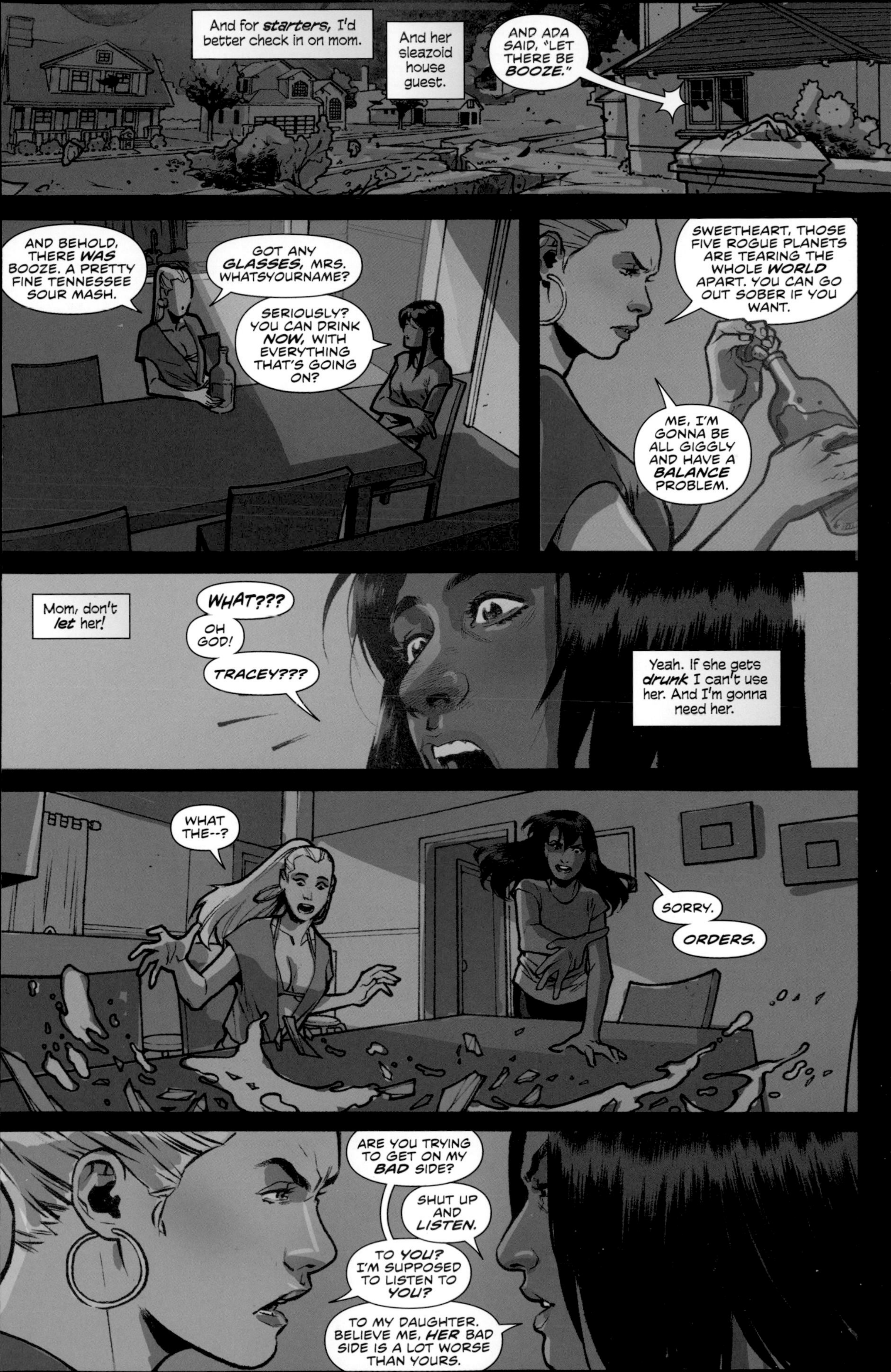
And for starters, I'd better check in on mom.
And her sleazoid house guest.
AND ADA SAID, "LET THERE BE BOOZE."
AND BEHOLD, THERE WAS BOOZE. A PRETTY FINE TENNESSEE SOUR MASH.
GOT ANY GLASSES, MRS. WHATSYOURNAME?
SERIOUSLY? YOU CAN DRINK NOW, WITH EVERYTHING THAT'S GOING ON?
SWEETHEART, THOSE FIVE ROGUE PLANETS ARE TEARING THE WHOLE WORLD APART. YOU CAN GO OUT SOBER IF YOU WANT.
ME, I'M GONNA BE ALL GIGGLY AND HAVE A BALANCE PROBLEM.
Mom, don't let her!
WHAT???
OH GOD!
TRACEY???
Yeah. If she gets drunk I can't use her. And I'm gonna need her.
WHAT THE--?
SORRY.
ORDERS.
ARE YOU TRYING TO GET ON MY BAD SIDE?
SHUT UP AND LISTEN.
TO YOU? I'M SUPPOSED TO LISTEN TO YOU?
TO MY DAUGHTER. BELIEVE ME, HER BAD SIDE IS A LOT WORSE THAN YOURS.

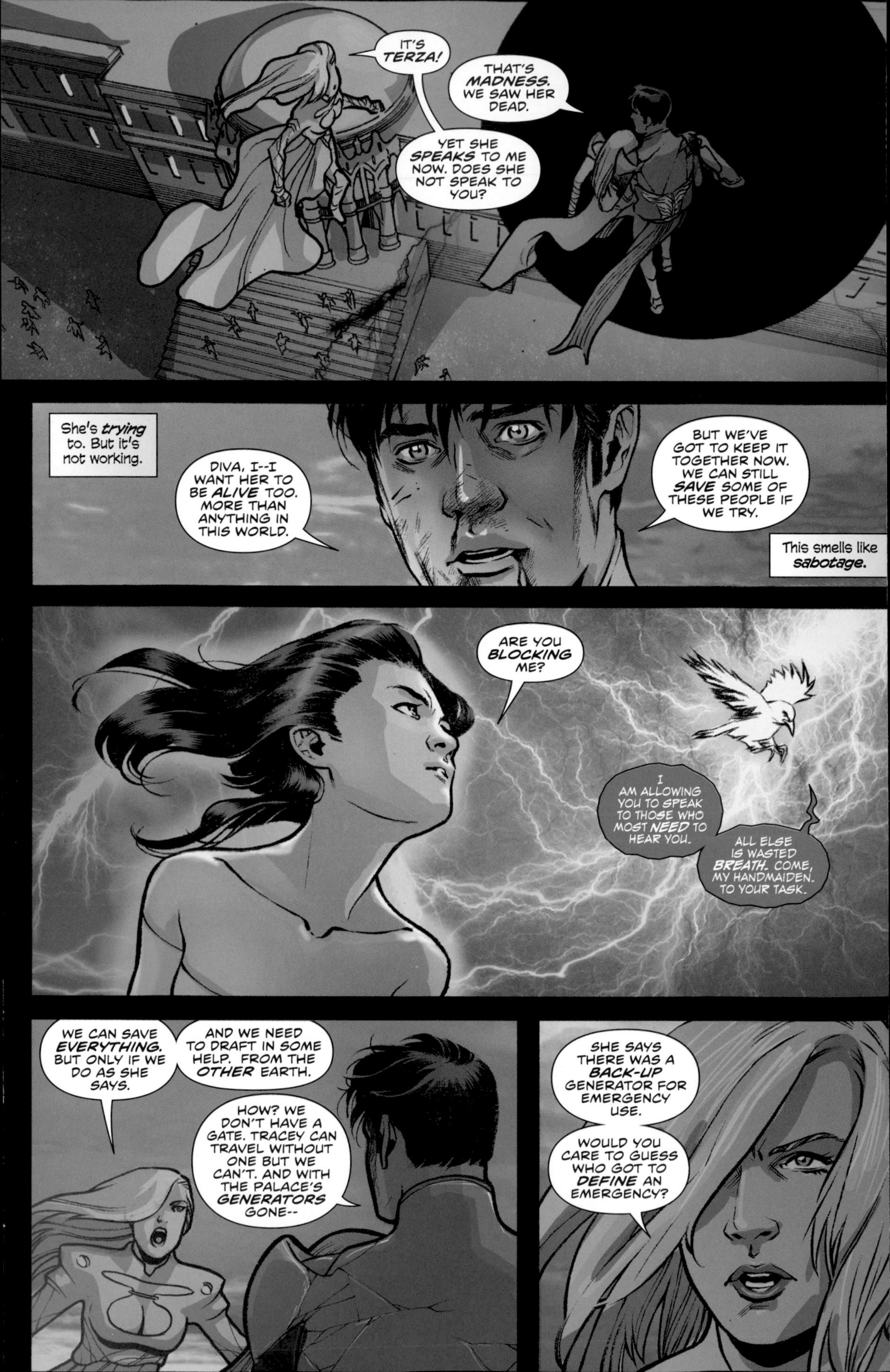
IT'S TERZA!
THAT'S MADNESS. WE SAW HER DEAD.
YET SHE SPEAKS TO ME NOW. DOES SHE NOT SPEAK TO YOU?
She's trying to. But it's not working.
DIVA, I--I WANT HER TO BE ALIVE TOO. MORE THAN ANYTHING IN THIS WORLD.
BUT WE'VE GOT TO KEEP IT TOGETHER NOW. WE CAN STILL SAVE SOME OF THESE PEOPLE IF WE TRY.
This smells like sabotage.
ARE YOU BLOCKING ME?
I AM ALLOWING YOU TO SPEAK TO THOSE WHO MOST NEED TO HEAR YOU.
ALL ELSE IS WASTED BREATH. COME, MY HANDMAIDEN. TO YOUR TASK.
WE CAN SAVE EVERYTHING. BUT ONLY IF WE DO AS SHE SAYS.
AND WE NEED TO DRAFT IN SOME HELP. FROM THE OTHER EARTH.
HOW? WE DON'T HAVE A GATE. TRACEY CAN TRAVEL WITHOUT ONE BUT WE CAN'T. AND WITH THE PALACE'S GENERATORS GONE--
SHE SAYS THERE WAS A BACK-UP GENERATOR FOR EMERGENCY USE.
WOULD YOU CARE TO GUESS WHO GOT TO DEFINE AN EMERGENCY?

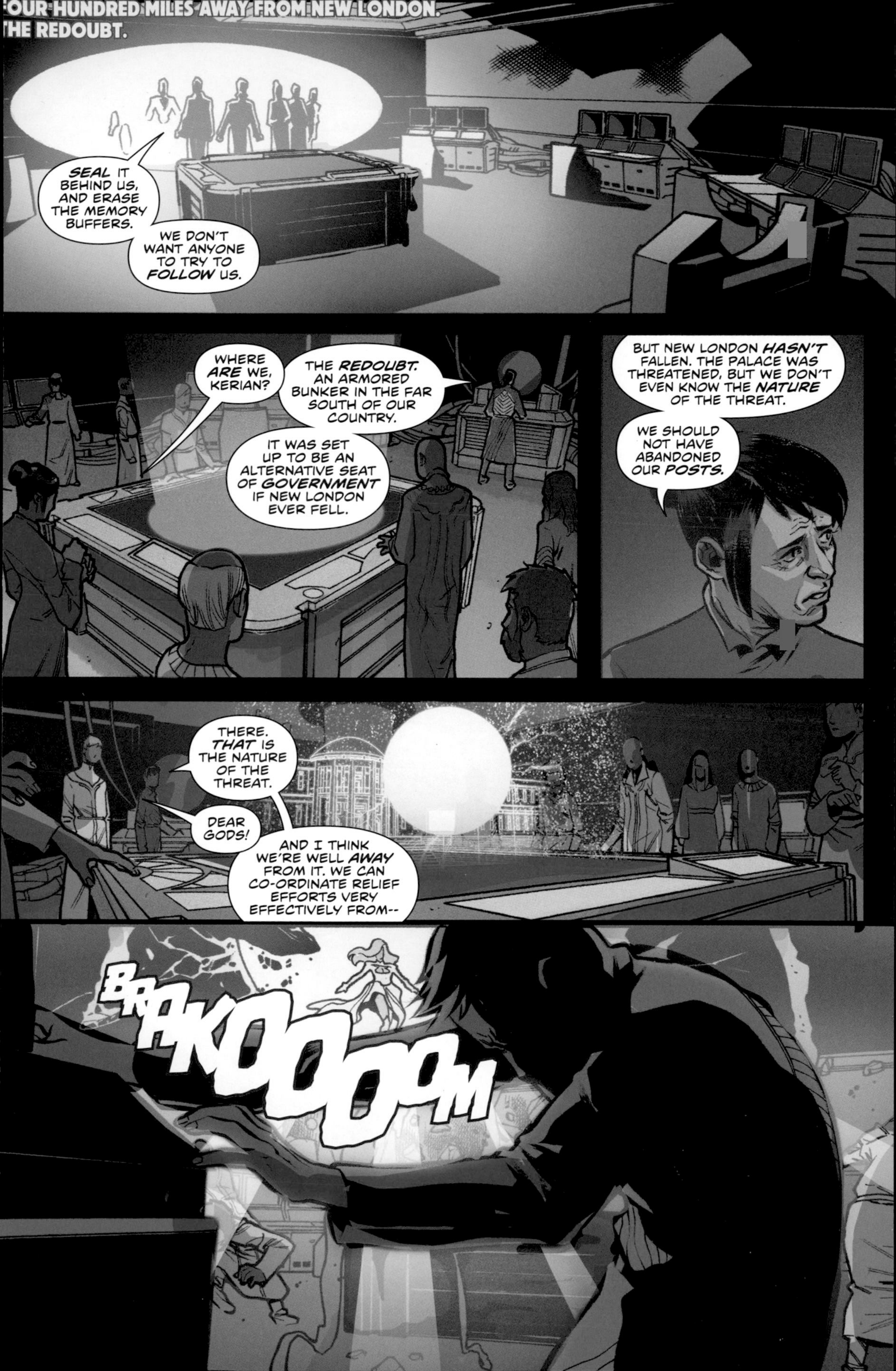
FOUR HUNDRED MILES AWAY FROM NEW LONDON.
THE REDOUBT.
SEAL IT BEHIND US, AND ERASE THE MEMORY BUFFERS.
WE DON'T WANT ANYONE TO TRY TO FOLLOW US.
WHERE ARE WE, KERIAN?
THE REDOUBT. AN ARMORED BUNKER IN THE FAR SOUTH OF OUR COUNTRY.
IT WAS SET UP TO BE AN ALTERNATIVE SEAT OF GOVERNMENT IF NEW LONDON EVER FELL.
BUT NEW LONDON HASN'T FALLEN. THE PALACE WAS THREATENED, BUT WE DON'T EVEN KNOW THE NATURE OF THE THREAT.
WE SHOULD NOT HAVE ABANDONED OUR POSTS.
THERE. THAT IS THE NATURE OF THE THREAT.
DEAR GODS!
AND I THINK WE'RE WELL AWAY FROM IT. WE CAN CO-ORDINATE RELIEF EFFORTS VERY EFFECTIVELY FROM--
BRAKOOOOOM

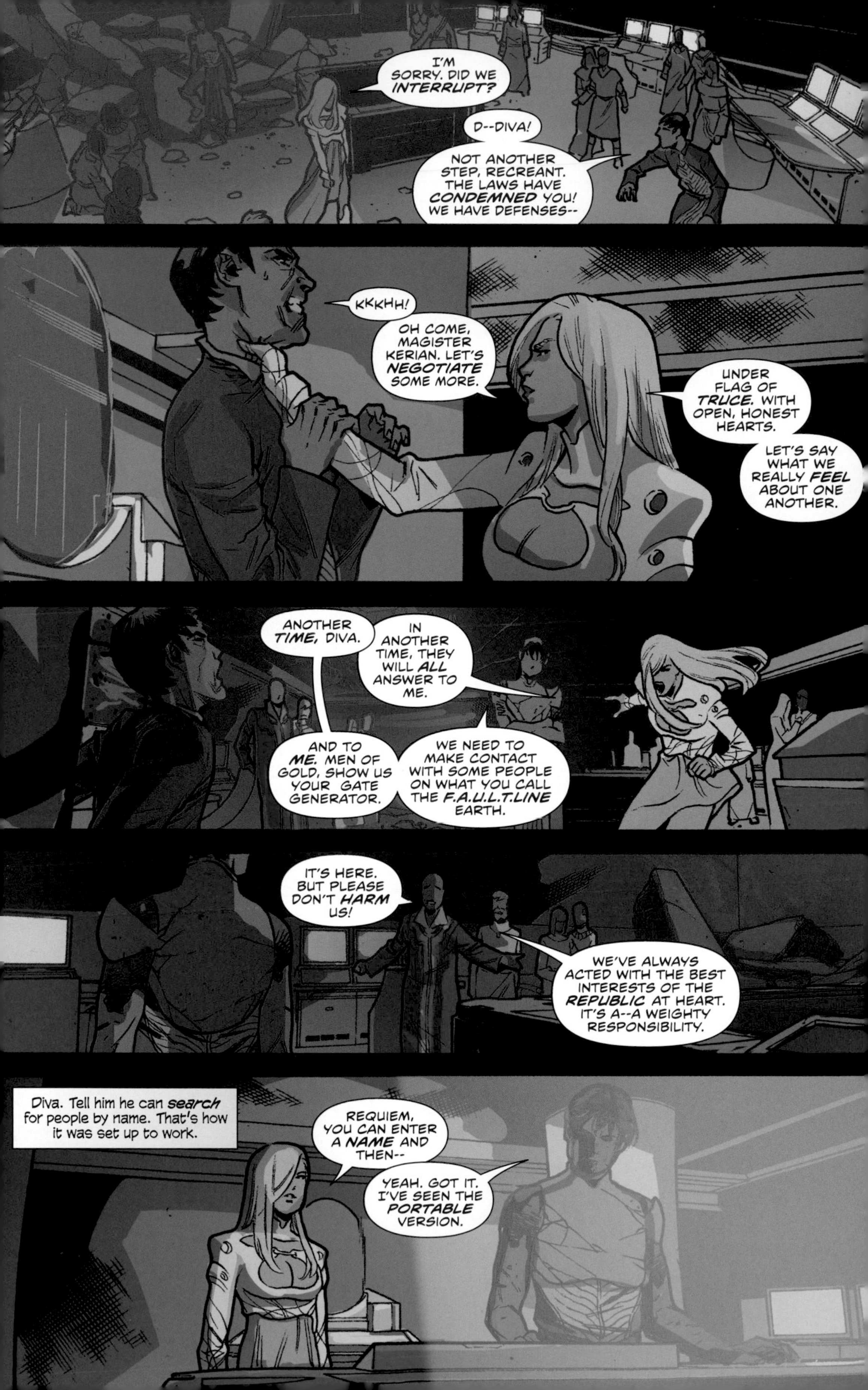
I'M SORRY. DID WE *INTERRUPT?*
D--DIVA!
NOT ANOTHER STEP, RECREANT. THE LAWS HAVE *CONDEMNED* YOU! WE HAVE DEFENSES--
KKKHH!
OH COME, MAGISTER KERIAN. LET'S *NEGOTIATE* SOME MORE.
UNDER FLAG OF *TRUCE.* WITH OPEN, HONEST HEARTS.
LET'S SAY WHAT WE REALLY *FEEL* ABOUT ONE ANOTHER.
ANOTHER *TIME,* DIVA.
IN ANOTHER TIME, THEY WILL *ALL* ANSWER TO ME.
AND TO *ME.* MEN OF GOLD, SHOW US YOUR GATE GENERATOR.
WE NEED TO MAKE CONTACT WITH SOME PEOPLE ON WHAT YOU CALL THE *F.A.U.L.T.LINE* EARTH.
IT'S HERE. BUT PLEASE DON'T *HARM* US!
WE'VE ALWAYS ACTED WITH THE BEST INTERESTS OF THE *REPUBLIC* AT HEART. IT'S A--A WEIGHTY RESPONSIBILITY.
Diva. Tell him he can *search* for people by name. That's how it was set up to work.
REQUIEM, YOU CAN ENTER A *NAME* AND THEN--
YEAH. GOT IT. I'VE SEEN THE *PORTABLE* VERSION.

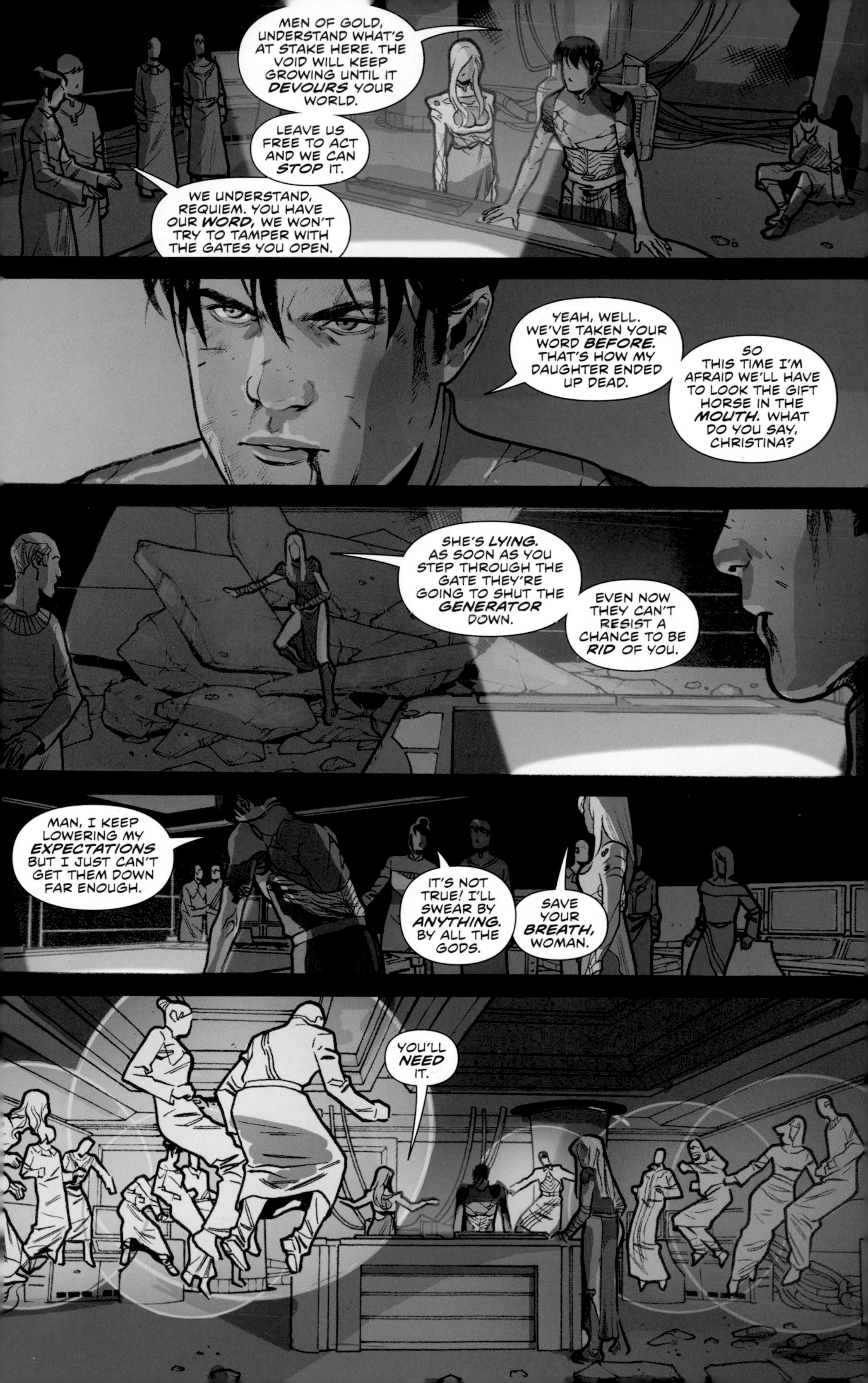
MEN OF GOLD, UNDERSTAND WHAT'S AT STAKE HERE. THE VOID WILL KEEP GROWING UNTIL IT DEVOURS YOUR WORLD.
LEAVE US FREE TO ACT AND WE CAN STOP IT.
WE UNDERSTAND, REQUIEM. YOU HAVE OUR WORD, WE WON'T TRY TO TAMPER WITH THE GATES YOU OPEN.
YEAH, WELL. WE'VE TAKEN YOUR WORD BEFORE. THAT'S HOW MY DAUGHTER ENDED UP DEAD.
SO THIS TIME I'M AFRAID WE'LL HAVE TO LOOK THE GIFT HORSE IN THE MOUTH. WHAT DO YOU SAY, CHRISTINA?
SHE'S LYING. AS SOON AS YOU STEP THROUGH THE GATE THEY'RE GOING TO SHUT THE GENERATOR DOWN.
EVEN NOW THEY CAN'T RESIST A CHANCE TO BE RID OF YOU.
MAN, I KEEP LOWERING MY EXPECTATIONS BUT I JUST CAN'T GET THEM DOWN FAR ENOUGH.
IT'S NOT TRUE! I'LL SWEAR BY ANYTHING. BY ALL THE GODS.
SAVE YOUR BREATH, WOMAN.
YOU'LL NEED IT.

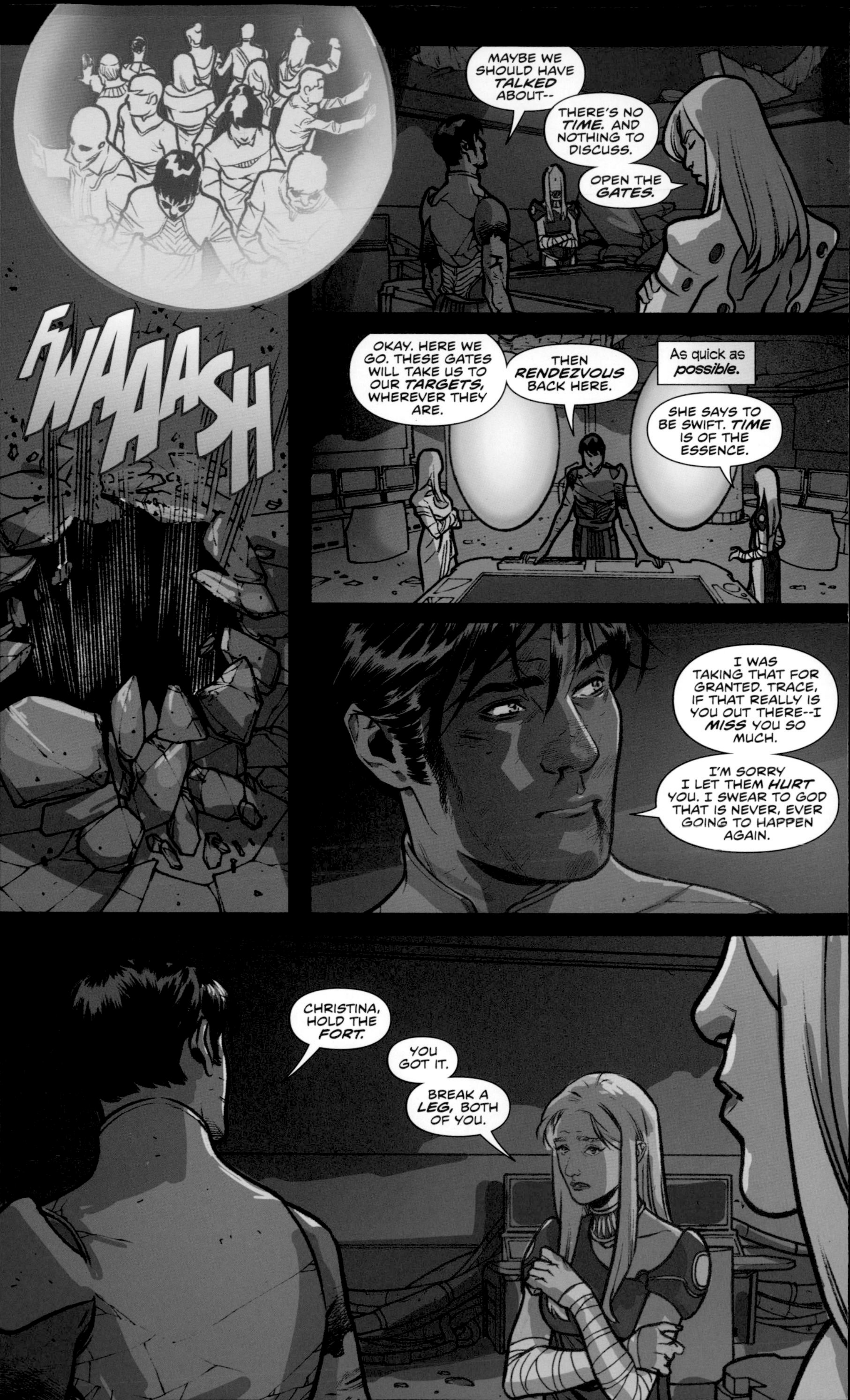
MAYBE WE SHOULD HAVE TALKED ABOUT--
THERE'S NO TIME. AND NOTHING TO DISCUSS.
OPEN THE GATES.
FWAAASH
OKAY. HERE WE GO. THESE GATES WILL TAKE US TO OUR TARGETS, WHEREVER THEY ARE.
THEN RENDEZVOUS BACK HERE.
As quick as possible.
SHE SAYS TO BE SWIFT. TIME IS OF THE ESSENCE.
I WAS TAKING THAT FOR GRANTED. TRACE, IF THAT REALLY IS YOU OUT THERE--I MISS YOU SO MUCH.
I'M SORRY I LET THEM HURT YOU. I SWEAR TO GOD THAT IS NEVER, EVER GOING TO HAPPEN AGAIN.
CHRISTINA, HOLD THE FORT.
YOU GOT IT.
BREAK A LEG, BOTH OF YOU.

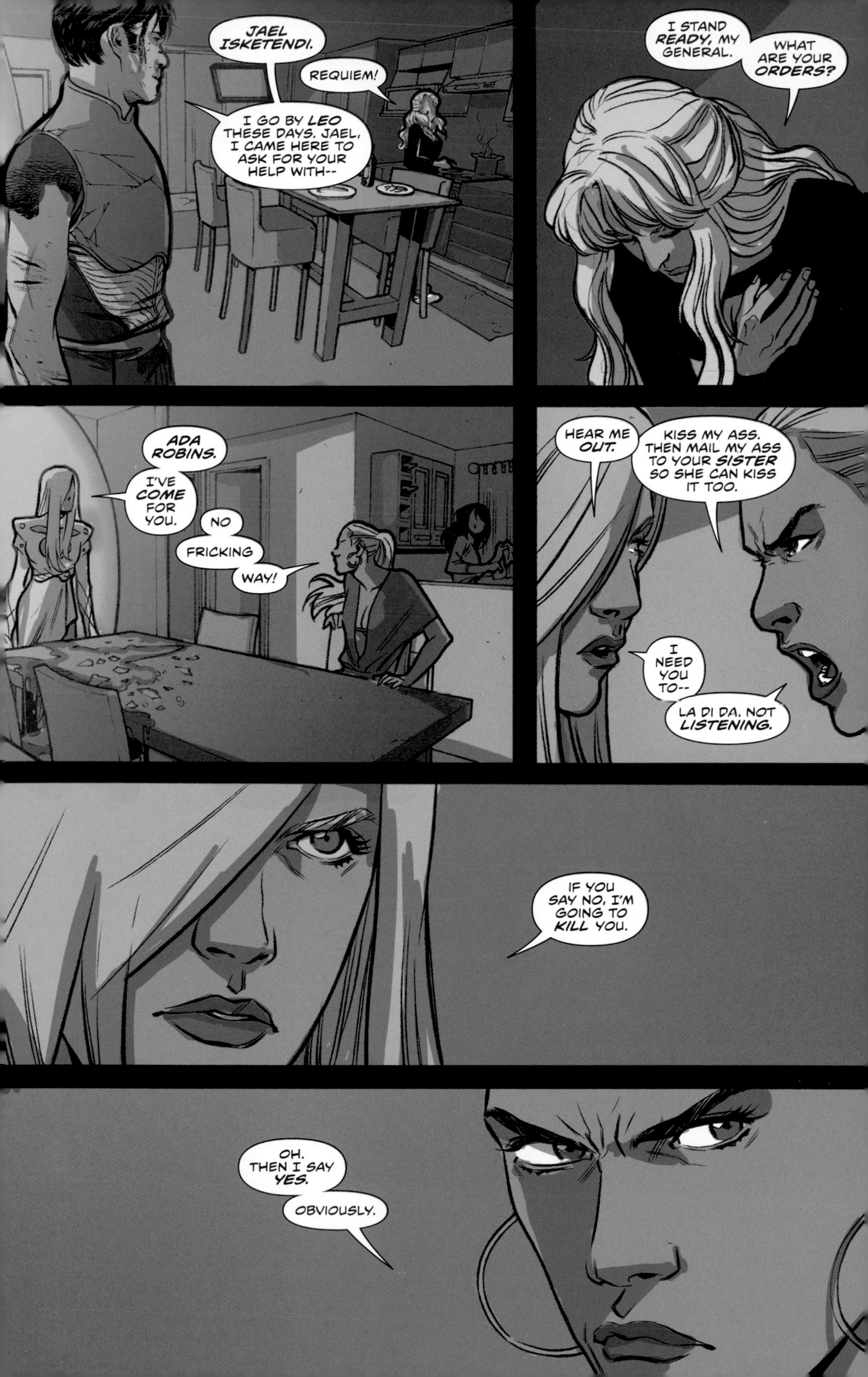
JAEL ISKETENDI.
REQUIEM!
I GO BY LEO THESE DAYS. JAEL, I CAME HERE TO ASK FOR YOUR HELP WITH--
I STAND READY, MY GENERAL.
WHAT ARE YOUR ORDERS?
ADA ROBINS.
I'VE COME FOR YOU.
NO
FRICKING
WAY!
HEAR ME OUT.
KISS MY ASS. THEN MAIL MY ASS TO YOUR SISTER SO SHE CAN KISS IT TOO.
I NEED YOU TO--
LA DI DA. NOT LISTENING.
IF YOU SAY NO, I'M GOING TO KILL YOU.
OH. THEN I SAY YES.
OBVIOUSLY.

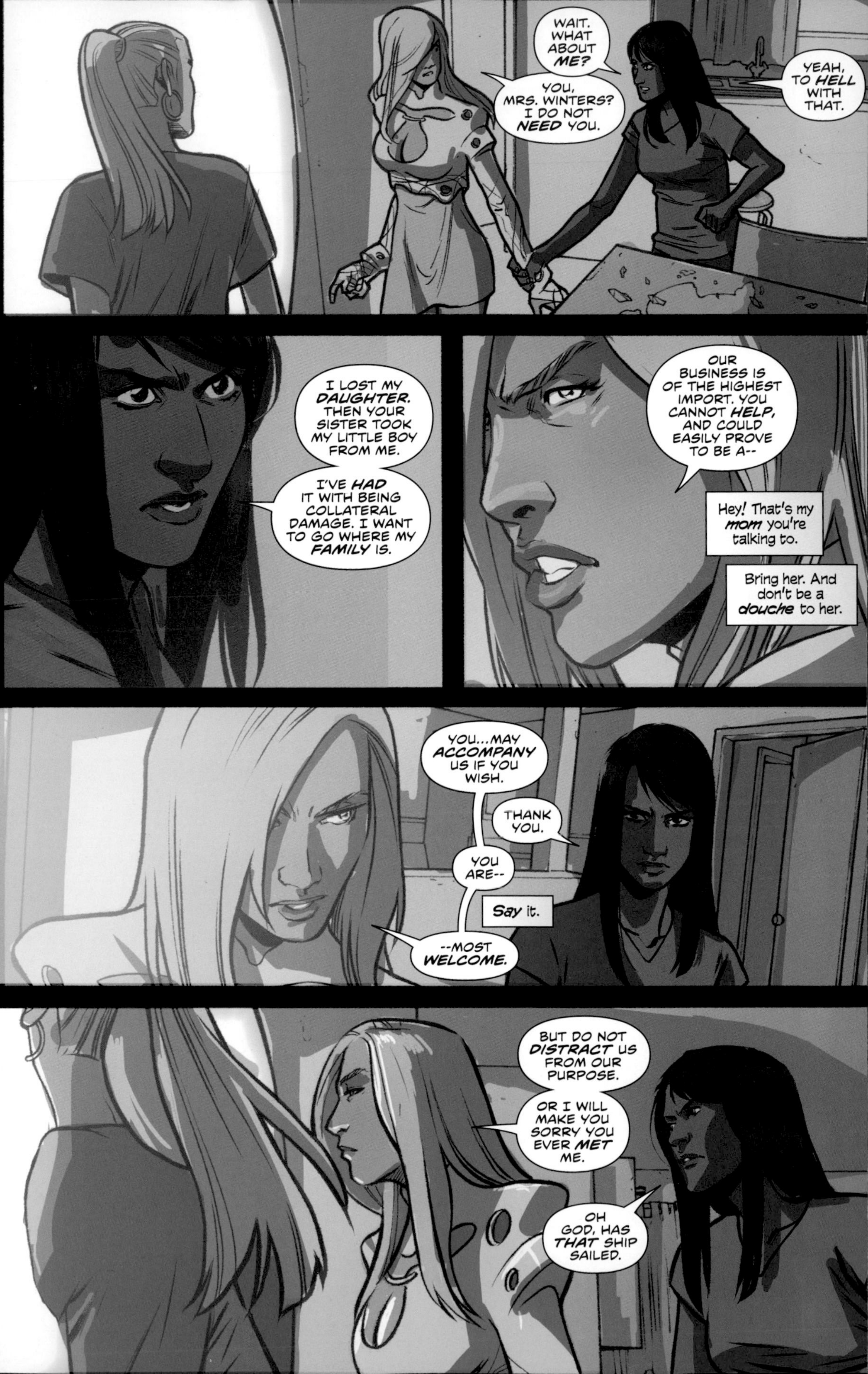
WAIT. WHAT ABOUT *ME?*
YOU, MRS. WINTERS? I DO NOT *NEED* YOU.
YEAH, TO *HELL* WITH THAT.
I LOST MY *DAUGHTER.* THEN YOUR SISTER TOOK MY LITTLE BOY FROM ME.
I'VE *HAD* IT WITH BEING COLLATERAL DAMAGE. I WANT TO GO WHERE MY *FAMILY* IS.
OUR BUSINESS IS OF THE HIGHEST IMPORT. YOU CANNOT *HELP,* AND COULD EASILY PROVE TO BE A--
Hey! That's my *mom* you're talking to.
Bring her. And don't be a *douche* to her.
YOU...MAY *ACCOMPANY* US IF YOU WISH.
THANK YOU.
YOU ARE--
Say it.
--MOST *WELCOME.*
BUT DO NOT *DISTRACT* US FROM OUR PURPOSE.
OR I WILL MAKE YOU SORRY YOU EVER *MET* ME.
OH GOD, HAS *THAT* SHIP SAILED.

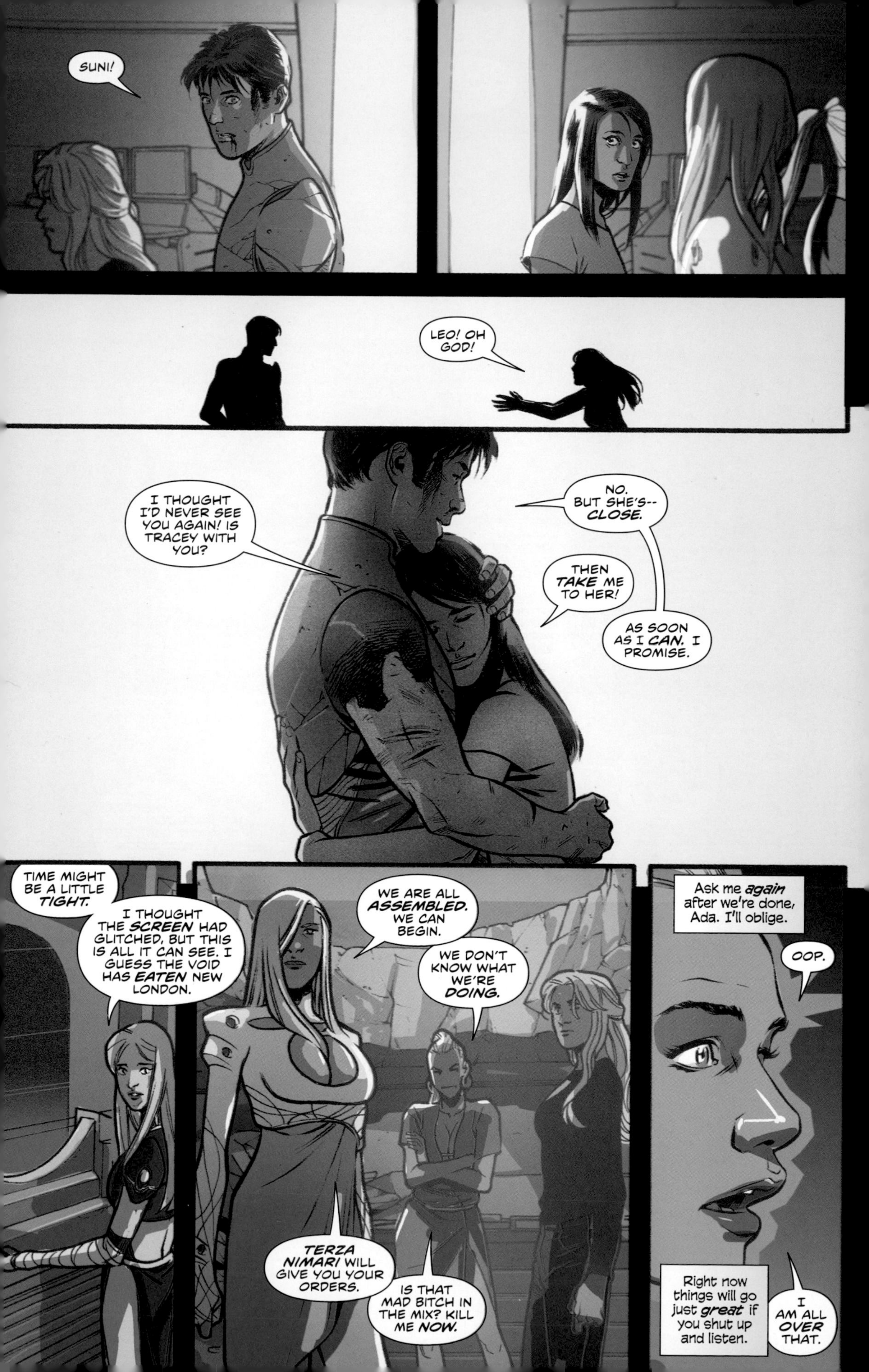
SUNI!
LEO! OH GOD!
I THOUGHT I'D NEVER SEE YOU AGAIN! IS TRACEY WITH YOU?
NO. BUT SHE'S-- CLOSE.
THEN TAKE ME TO HER!
AS SOON AS I CAN. I PROMISE.
TIME MIGHT BE A LITTLE TIGHT.
I THOUGHT THE SCREEN HAD GLITCHED, BUT THIS IS ALL IT CAN SEE. I GUESS THE VOID HAS EATEN NEW LONDON.
WE ARE ALL ASSEMBLED. WE CAN BEGIN.
WE DON'T KNOW WHAT WE'RE DOING.
TERZA NIMARI WILL GIVE YOU YOUR ORDERS.
IS THAT MAD BITCH IN THE MIX? KILL ME NOW.
Ask me again after we're done, Ada. I'll oblige.
OOP.
Right now things will go just great if you shut up and listen.
I AM ALL OVER THAT.

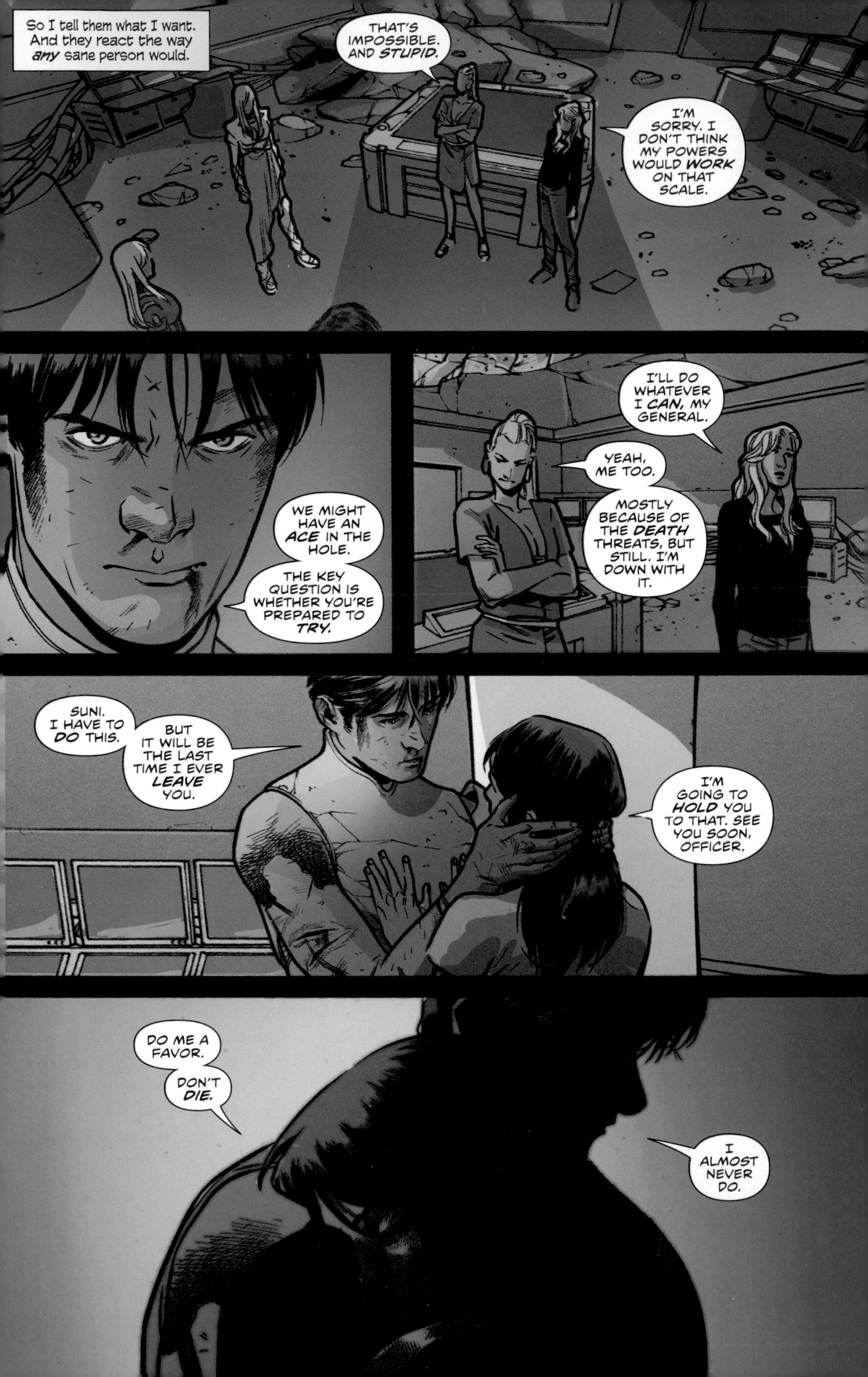

So I tell them what I want. And they react the way *any* sane person would.
THAT'S IMPOSSIBLE. AND ***STUPID.***
I'M SORRY. I DON'T THINK MY POWERS WOULD ***WORK*** ON THAT SCALE.
WE MIGHT HAVE AN ***ACE*** IN THE HOLE.
THE KEY QUESTION IS WHETHER YOU'RE PREPARED TO ***TRY.***
I'LL DO WHATEVER I ***CAN,*** MY GENERAL.
YEAH, ME TOO.
MOSTLY BECAUSE OF THE ***DEATH*** THREATS, BUT STILL. I'M DOWN WITH IT.
SUNI. I HAVE TO ***DO*** THIS.
BUT IT WILL BE THE LAST TIME I EVER ***LEAVE*** YOU.
I'M GOING TO ***HOLD*** YOU TO THAT. SEE YOU SOON, OFFICER.
DO ME A FAVOR.
DON'T ***DIE.***
I ALMOST NEVER DO.

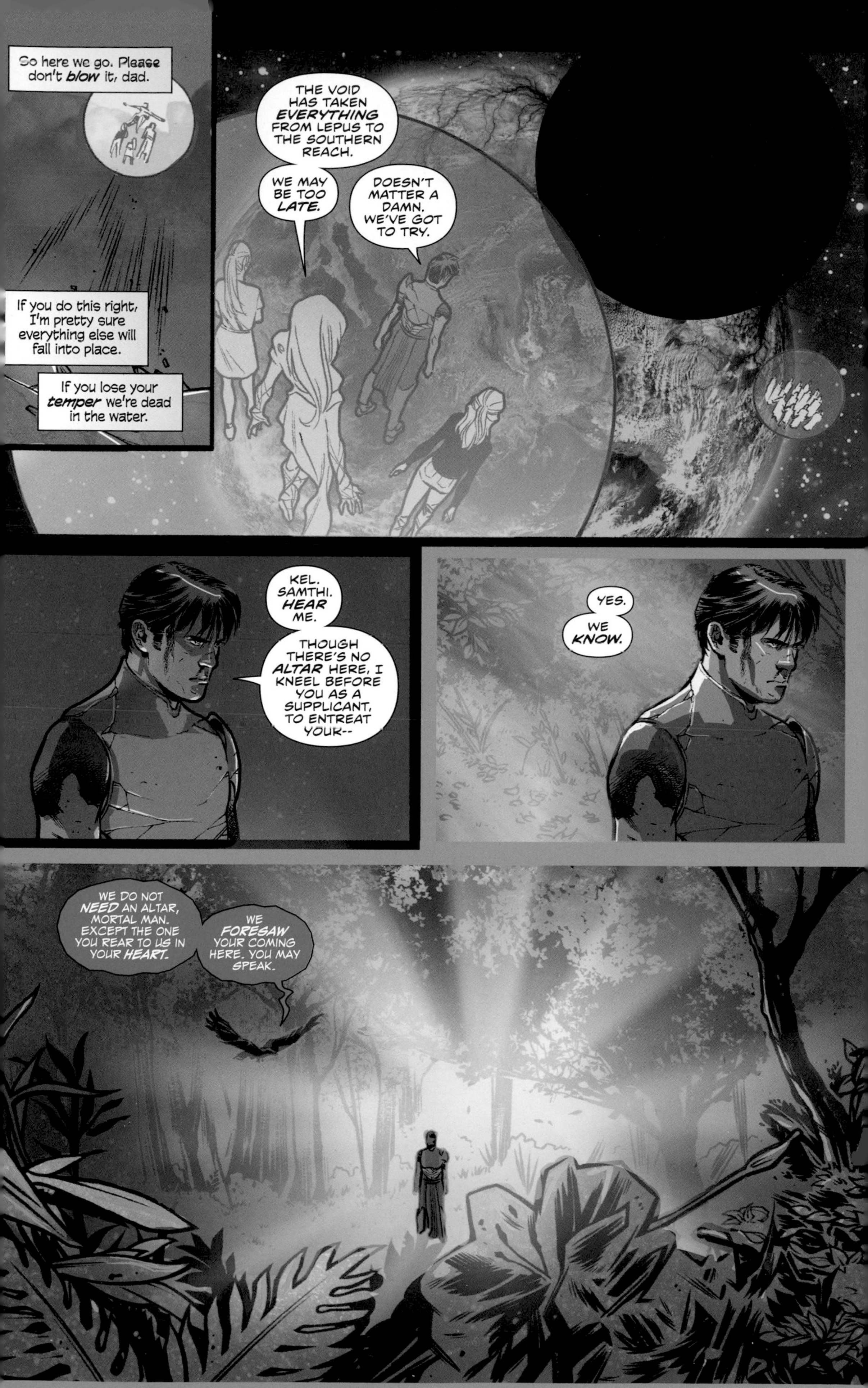
So here we go. Please don't *blow* it, dad.
THE VOID HAS TAKEN *EVERYTHING* FROM LEPUS TO THE SOUTHERN REACH.
WE MAY BE TOO *LATE.*
DOESN'T MATTER A DAMN. WE'VE GOT TO TRY.
If you do this right, I'm pretty sure everything else will fall into place.
If you lose your *temper* we're dead in the water.
KEL. SAMTHI. *HEAR* ME.
THOUGH THERE'S NO *ALTAR* HERE, I KNEEL BEFORE YOU AS A SUPPLICANT, TO ENTREAT YOUR--
YES.
WE *KNOW.*
WE DO NOT *NEED* AN ALTAR, MORTAL MAN. EXCEPT THE ONE YOU REAR TO US IN YOUR *HEART.*
WE *FORESAW* YOUR COMING HERE. YOU MAY SPEAK.

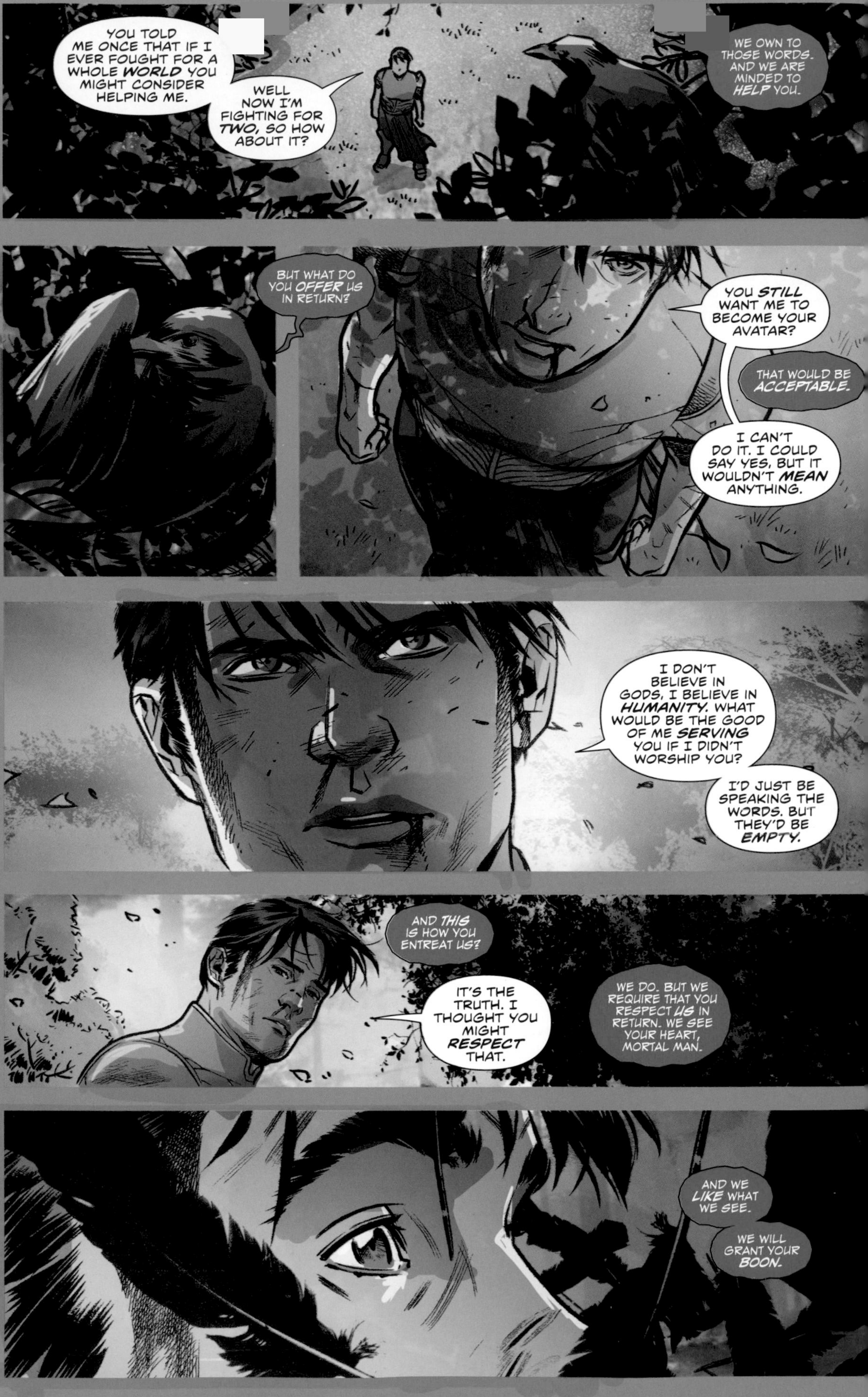
YOU TOLD ME ONCE THAT IF I EVER FOUGHT FOR A WHOLE WORLD YOU MIGHT CONSIDER HELPING ME.
WELL NOW I'M FIGHTING FOR TWO, SO HOW ABOUT IT?
WE OWN TO THOSE WORDS. AND WE ARE MINDED TO HELP YOU.
BUT WHAT DO YOU OFFER US IN RETURN?
YOU STILL WANT ME TO BECOME YOUR AVATAR?
THAT WOULD BE ACCEPTABLE.
I CAN'T DO IT. I COULD SAY YES, BUT IT WOULDN'T MEAN ANYTHING.
I DON'T BELIEVE IN GODS, I BELIEVE IN HUMANITY. WHAT WOULD BE THE GOOD OF ME SERVING YOU IF I DIDN'T WORSHIP YOU?
I'D JUST BE SPEAKING THE WORDS. BUT THEY'D BE EMPTY.
AND THIS IS HOW YOU ENTREAT US?
IT'S THE TRUTH. I THOUGHT YOU MIGHT RESPECT THAT.
WE DO. BUT WE REQUIRE THAT YOU RESPECT US IN RETURN. WE SEE YOUR HEART, MORTAL MAN.
AND WE LIKE WHAT WE SEE.
WE WILL GRANT YOUR BOON.

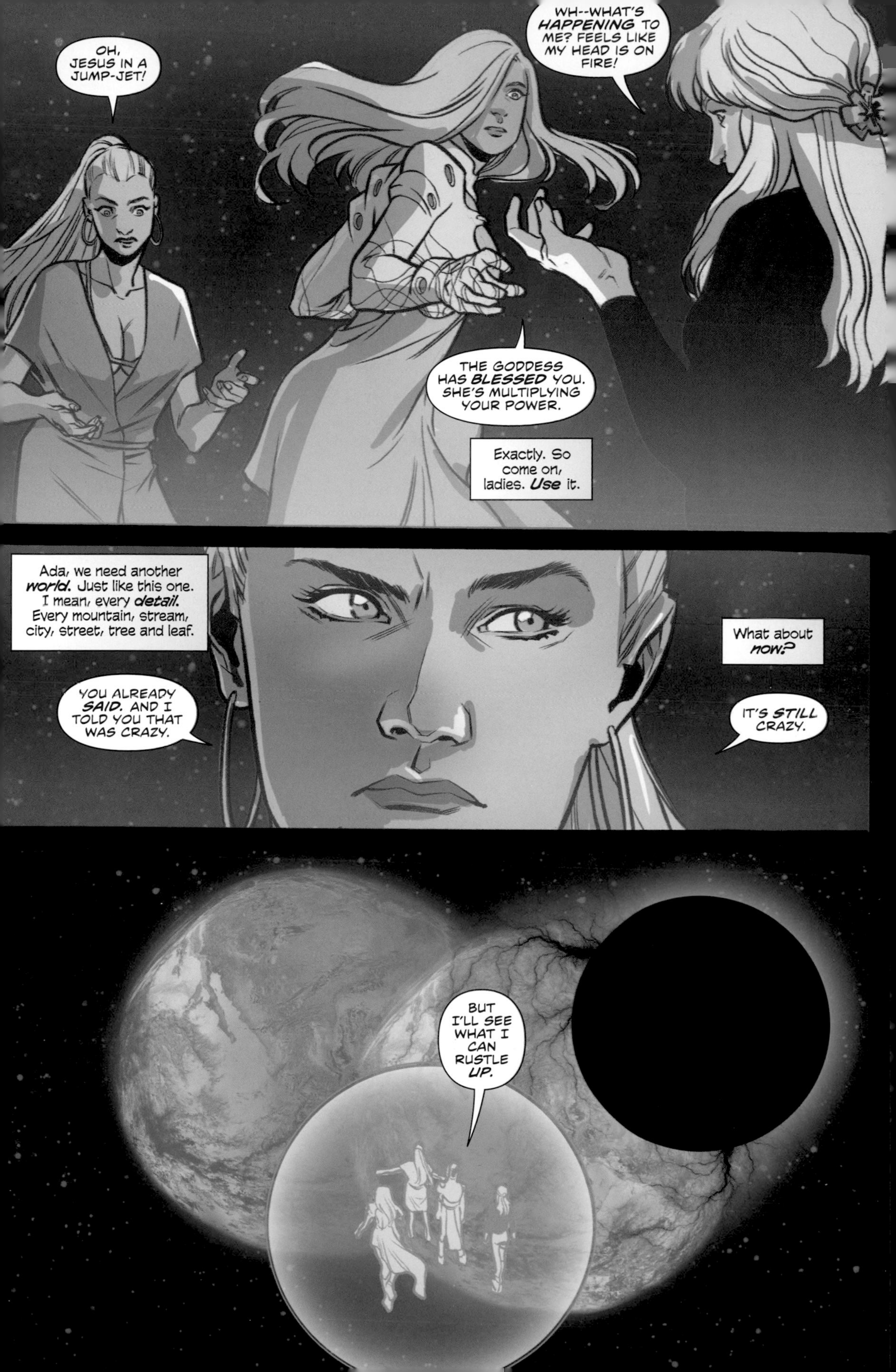
OH, JESUS IN A JUMP-JET!
WH--WHAT'S HAPPENING TO ME? FEELS LIKE MY HEAD IS ON FIRE!
THE GODDESS HAS BLESSED YOU. SHE'S MULTIPLYING YOUR POWER.
Exactly. So come on, ladies. Use it.
Ada, we need another world. Just like this one. I mean, every detail. Every mountain, stream, city, street, tree and leaf.
YOU ALREADY SAID. AND I TOLD YOU THAT WAS CRAZY.
What about now?
IT'S STILL CRAZY.
BUT I'LL SEE WHAT I CAN RUSTLE UP.

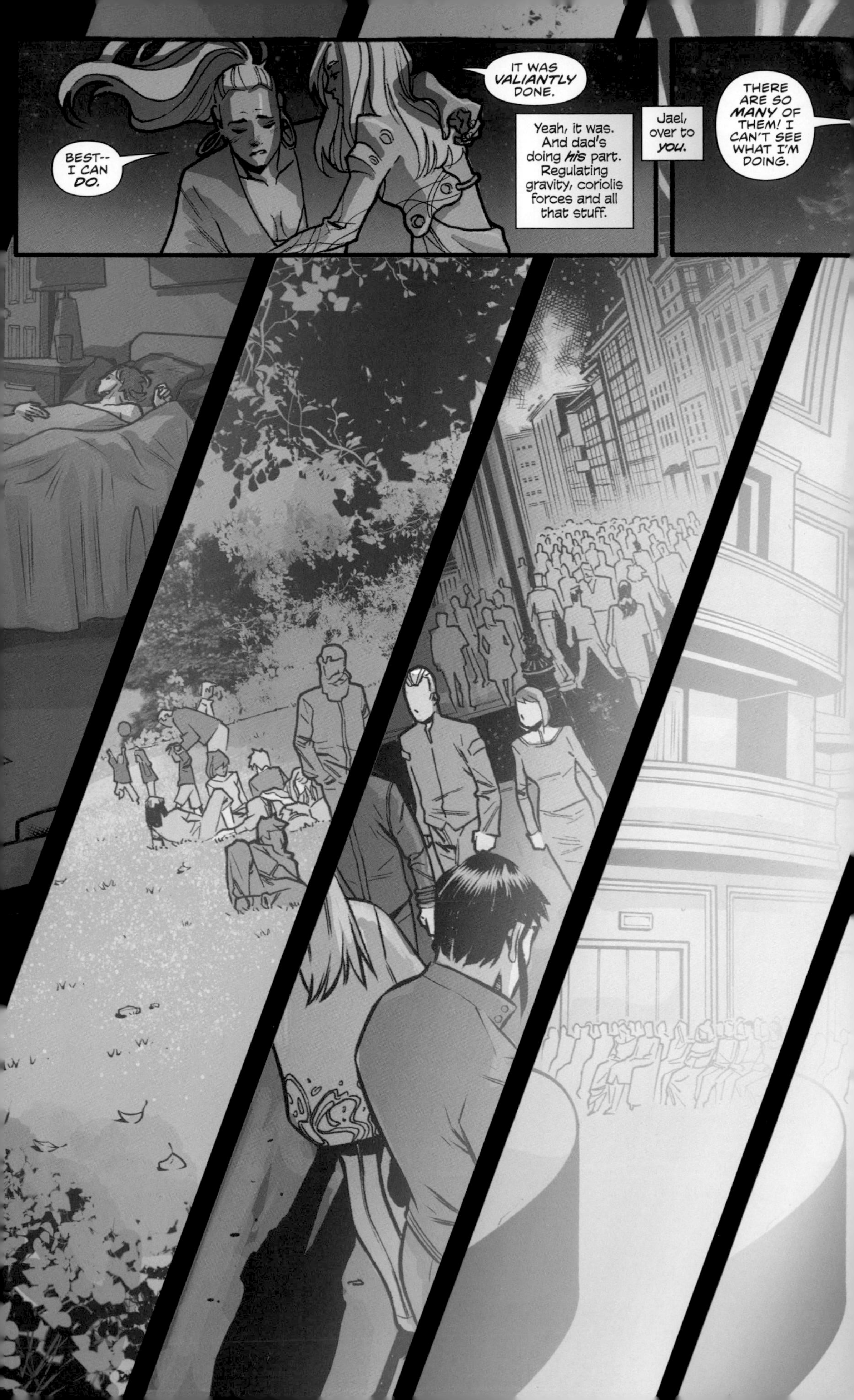
BEST--
I CAN
DO.
IT WAS
VALIANTLY
DONE.
Yeah, it was. And dad's doing his part. Regulating gravity, coriolis forces and all that stuff.
Jael, over to you.
THERE ARE SO MANY OF THEM! I CAN'T SEE WHAT I'M DOING.

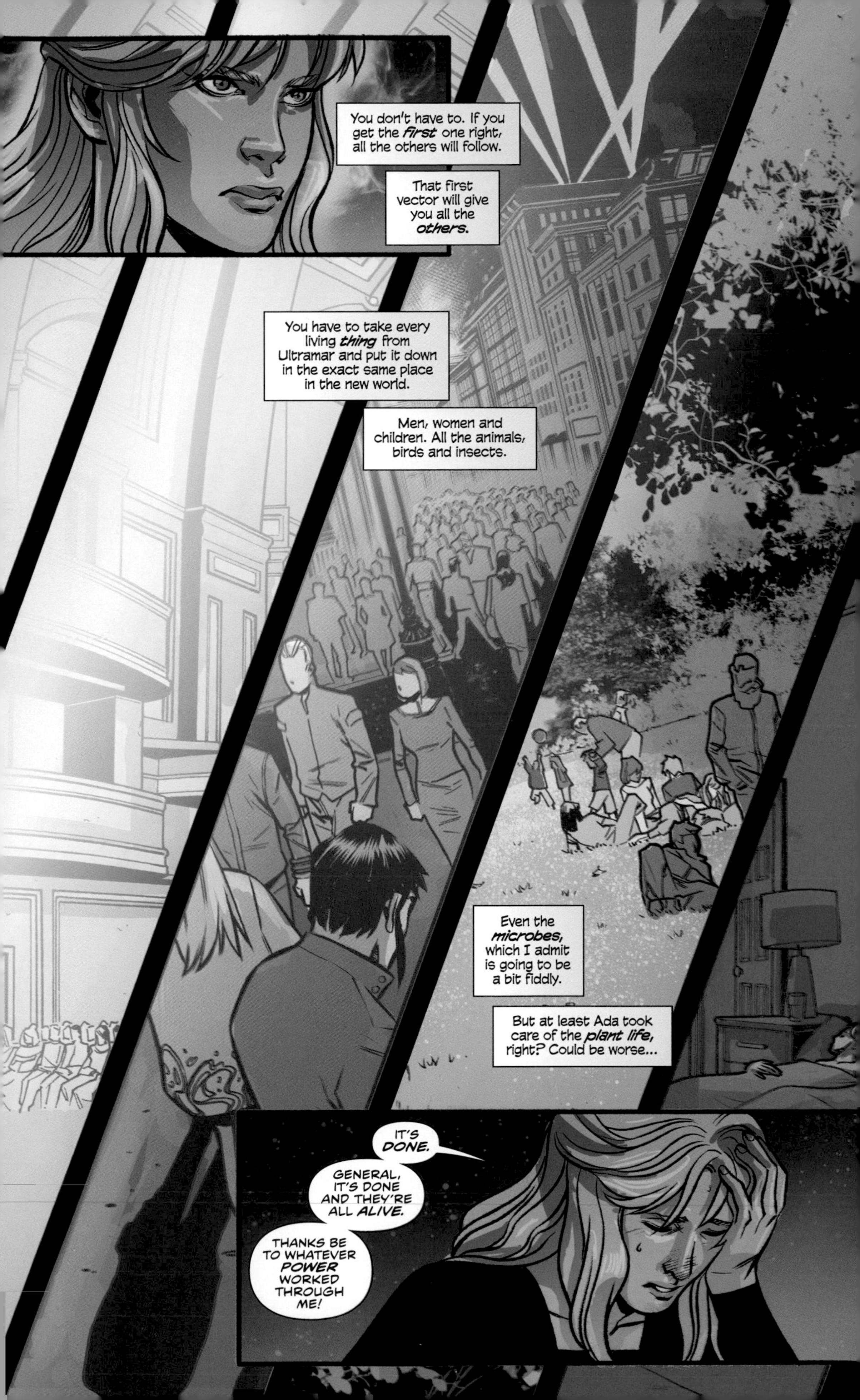
You don't have to. If you get the *first* one right, all the others will follow.
That first vector will give you all the *others.*
You have to take every living *thing* from Ultramar and put it down in the exact same place in the new world.
Men, women and children. All the animals, birds and insects.
Even the *microbes,* which I admit is going to be a bit fiddly.
But at least Ada took care of the *plant life,* right? Could be worse...
IT'S *DONE.*
GENERAL, IT'S DONE AND THEY'RE ALL *ALIVE.*
THANKS BE TO WHATEVER *POWER* WORKED THROUGH ME!

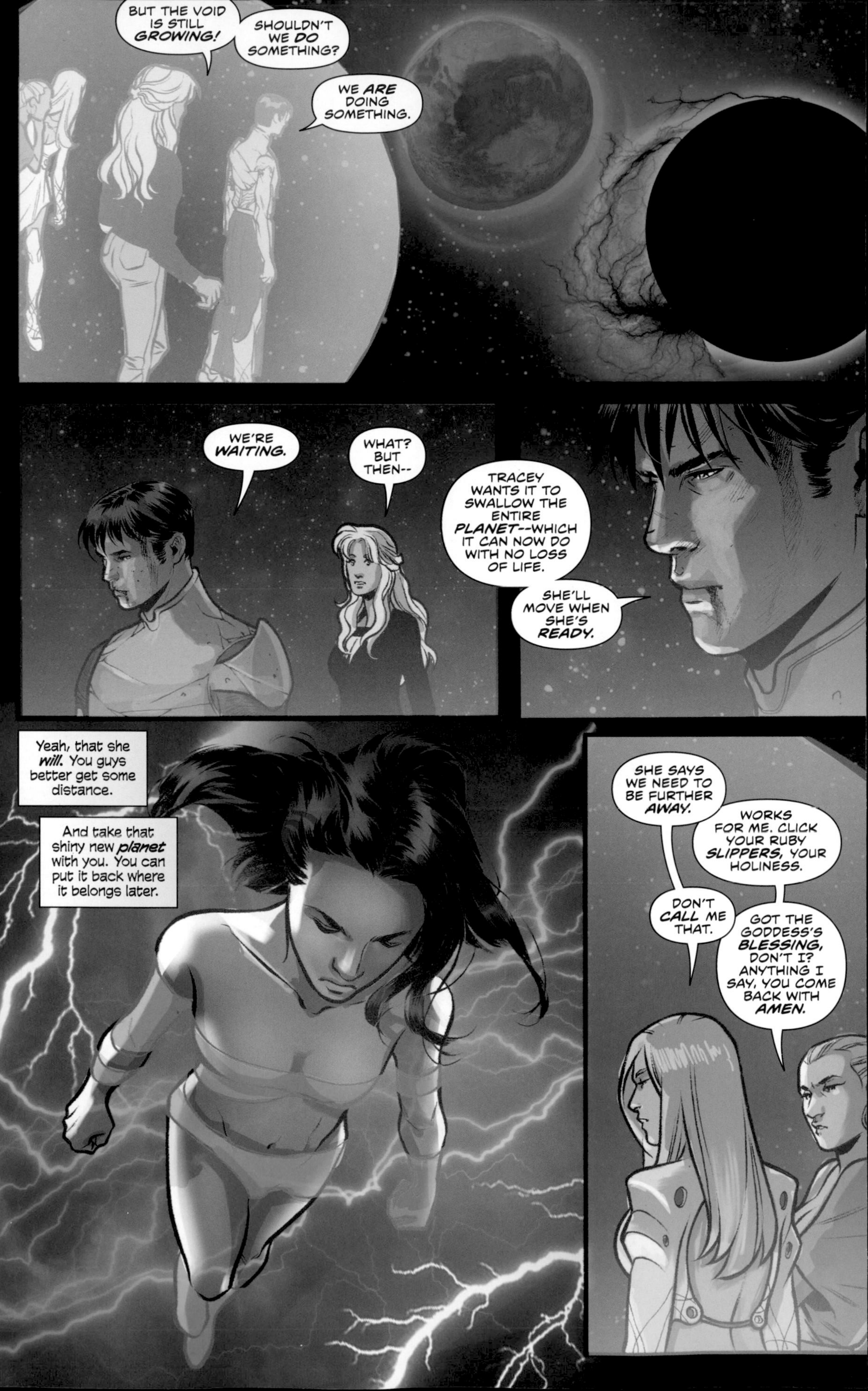

BUT THE VOID IS STILL GROWING!
SHOULDN'T WE DO SOMETHING?
WE ARE DOING SOMETHING.
WE'RE WAITING.
WHAT? BUT THEN--
TRACEY WANTS IT TO SWALLOW THE ENTIRE PLANET--WHICH IT CAN NOW DO WITH NO LOSS OF LIFE.
SHE'LL MOVE WHEN SHE'S READY.
Yeah, that she will. You guys better get some distance.
And take that shiny new planet with you. You can put it back where it belongs later.
SHE SAYS WE NEED TO BE FURTHER AWAY.
WORKS FOR ME. CLICK YOUR RUBY SLIPPERS, YOUR HOLINESS.
DON'T CALL ME THAT.
GOT THE GODDESS'S BLESSING, DON'T I? ANYTHING I SAY, YOU COME BACK WITH AMEN.

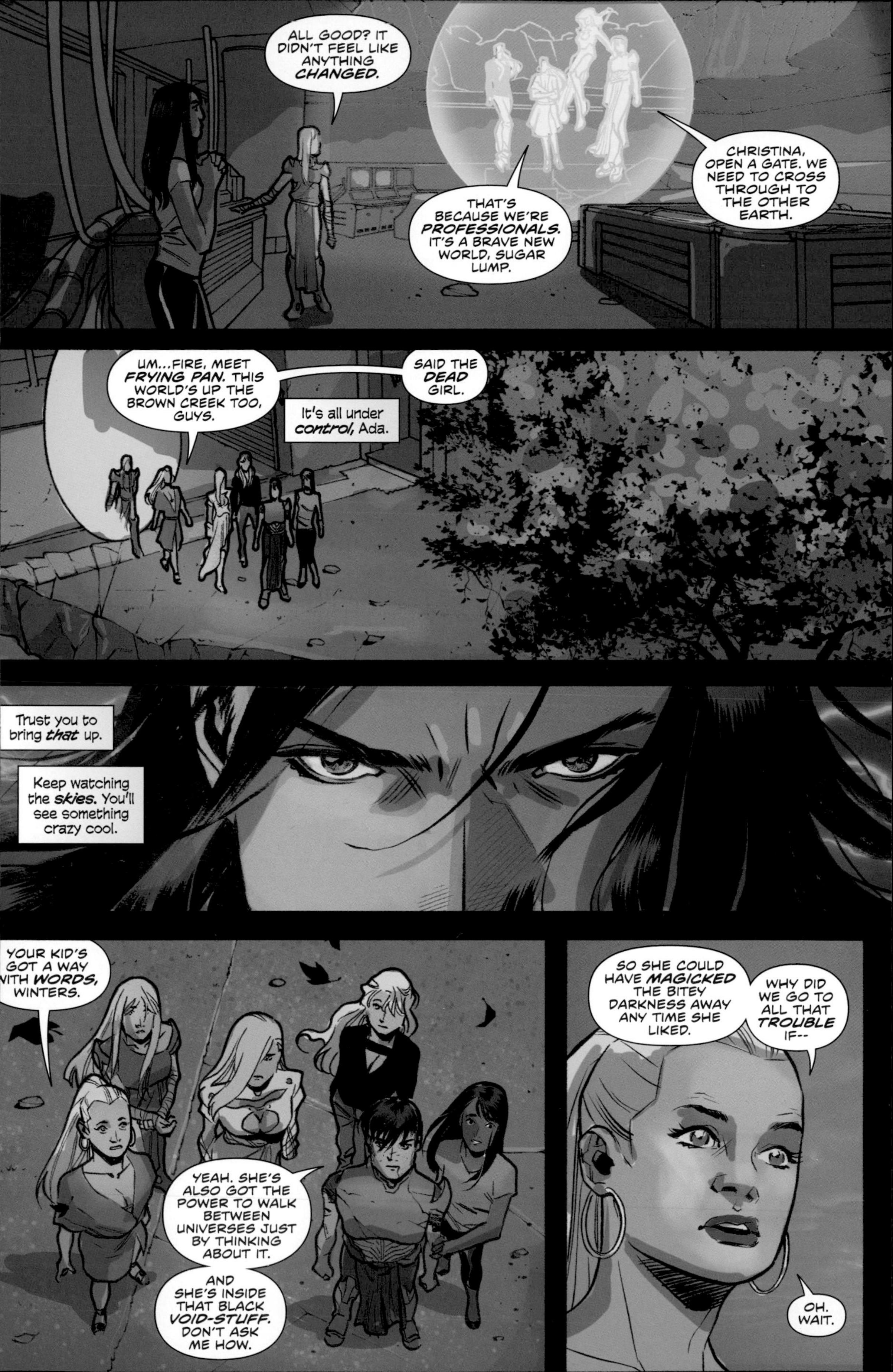
ALL GOOD? IT DIDN'T FEEL LIKE ANYTHING CHANGED.
THAT'S BECAUSE WE'RE PROFESSIONALS. IT'S A BRAVE NEW WORLD, SUGAR LUMP.
CHRISTINA, OPEN A GATE. WE NEED TO CROSS THROUGH TO THE OTHER EARTH.
UM...FIRE, MEET FRYING PAN. THIS WORLD'S UP THE BROWN CREEK TOO, GUYS.
SAID THE DEAD GIRL.
It's all under control, Ada.
Trust you to bring that up.
Keep watching the skies. You'll see something crazy cool.
YOUR KID'S GOT A WAY WITH WORDS, WINTERS.
YEAH. SHE'S ALSO GOT THE POWER TO WALK BETWEEN UNIVERSES JUST BY THINKING ABOUT IT.
AND SHE'S INSIDE THAT BLACK VOID-STUFF. DON'T ASK ME HOW.
WHY DID WE GO TO ALL THAT TROUBLE IF--
SO SHE COULD HAVE MAGICKED THE BITEY DARKNESS AWAY ANY TIME SHE LIKED.
OH. WAIT.

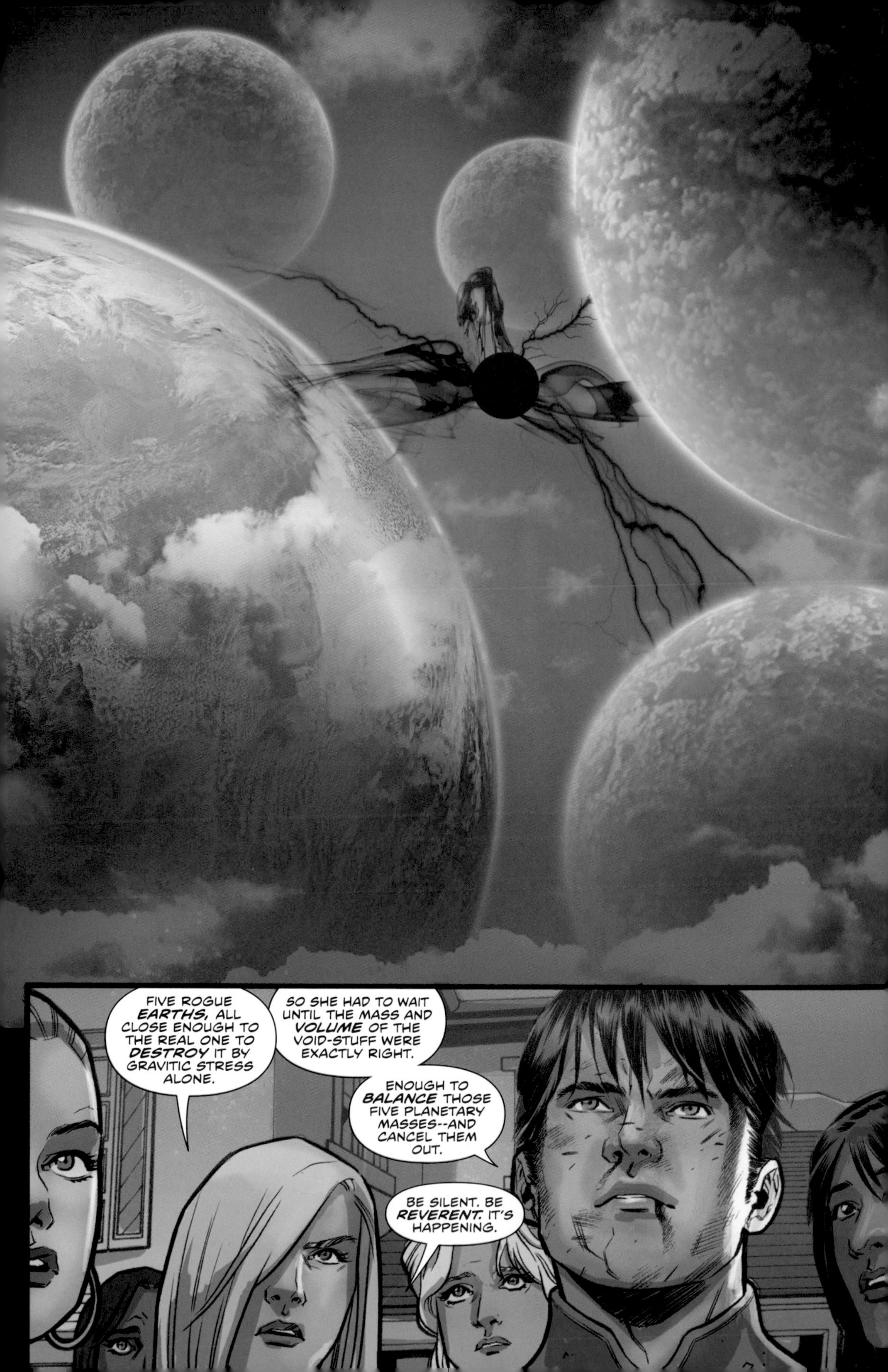
FIVE ROGUE EARTHS, ALL CLOSE ENOUGH TO THE REAL ONE TO DESTROY IT BY GRAVITIC STRESS ALONE.
SO SHE HAD TO WAIT UNTIL THE MASS AND VOLUME OF THE VOID-STUFF WERE EXACTLY RIGHT.
ENOUGH TO BALANCE THOSE FIVE PLANETARY MASSES--AND CANCEL THEM OUT.
BE SILENT. BE REVERENT. IT'S HAPPENING.

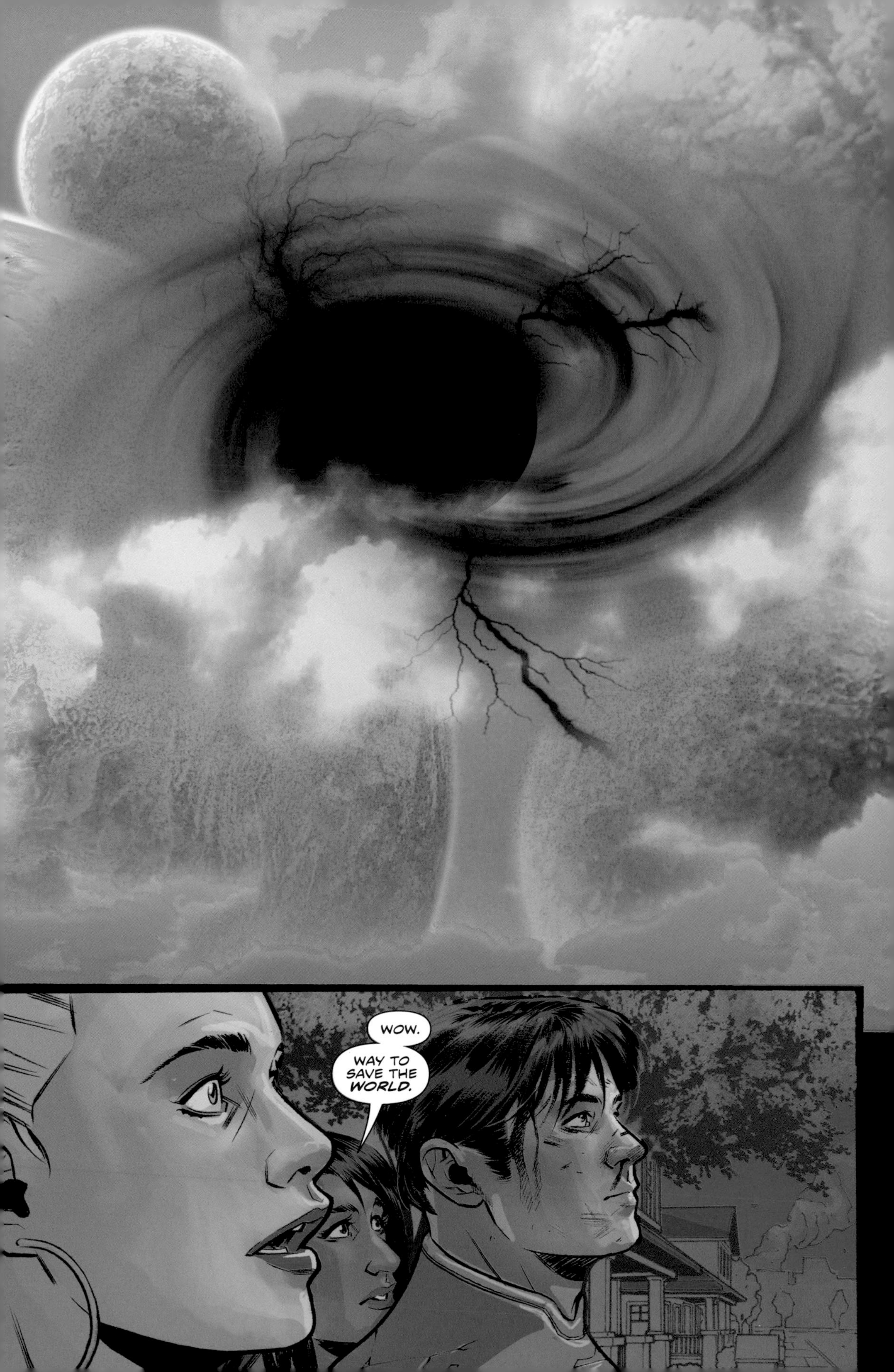
WOW.
WAY TO SAVE THE WORLD.

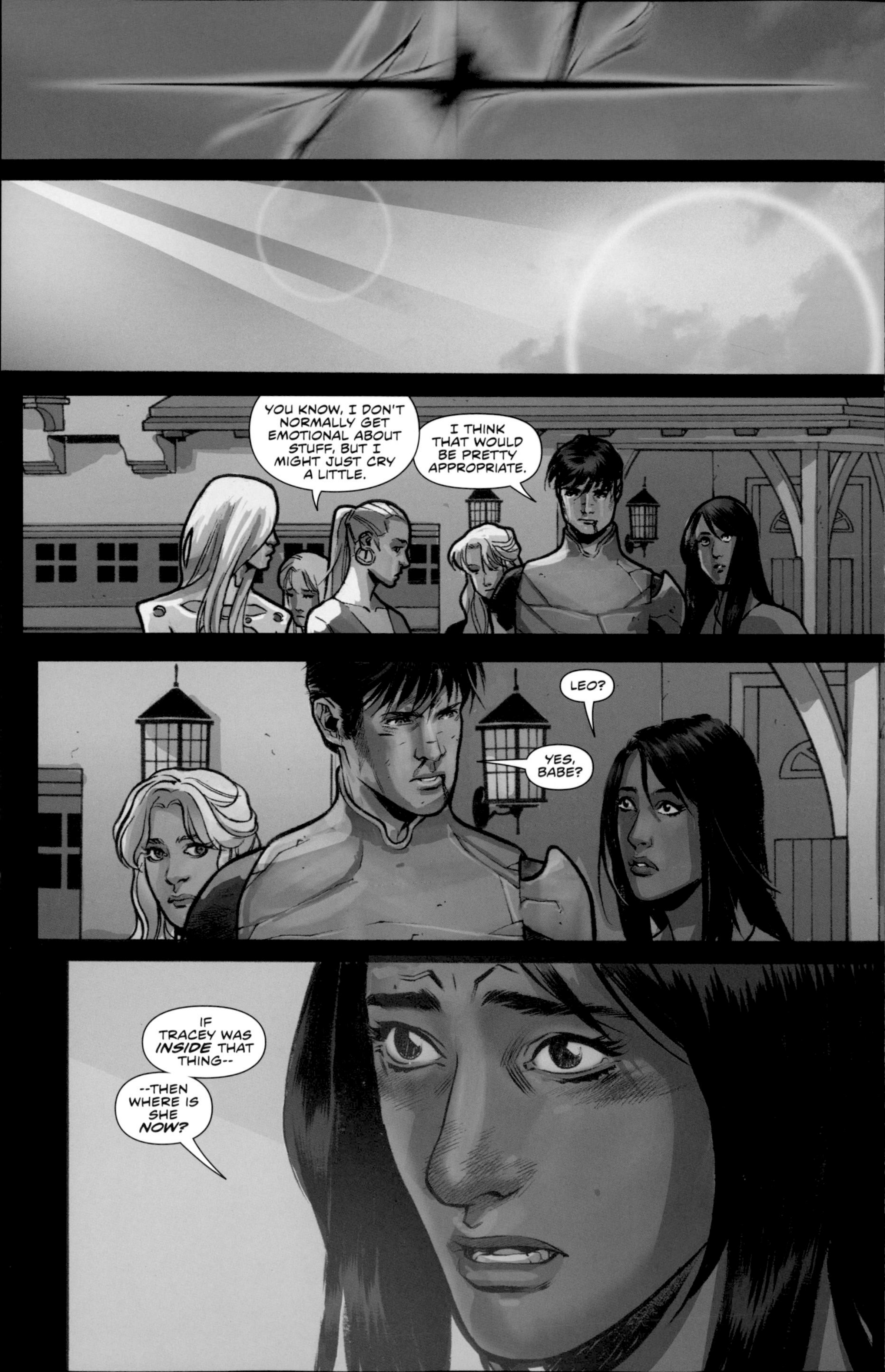
YOU KNOW, I DON'T NORMALLY GET EMOTIONAL ABOUT STUFF, BUT I MIGHT JUST CRY A LITTLE.
I THINK THAT WOULD BE PRETTY APPROPRIATE.
LEO?
YES, BABE?
IF TRACEY WAS *INSIDE* THAT THING--
--THEN WHERE IS SHE *NOW?*

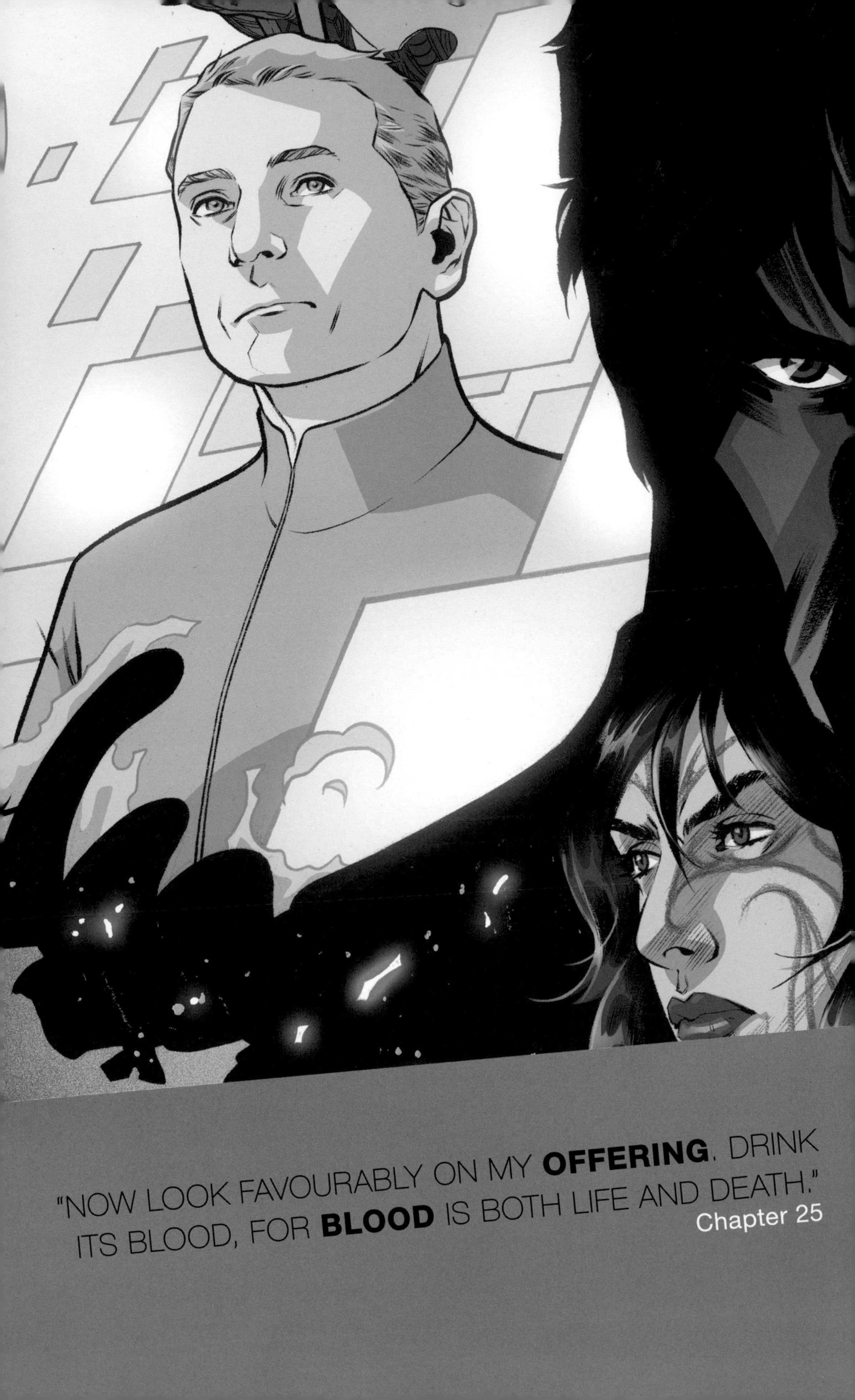

"NOW LOOK FAVOURABLY ON MY **OFFERING**. DRINK ITS BLOOD, FOR **BLOOD** IS BOTH LIFE AND DEATH."

Chapter 25

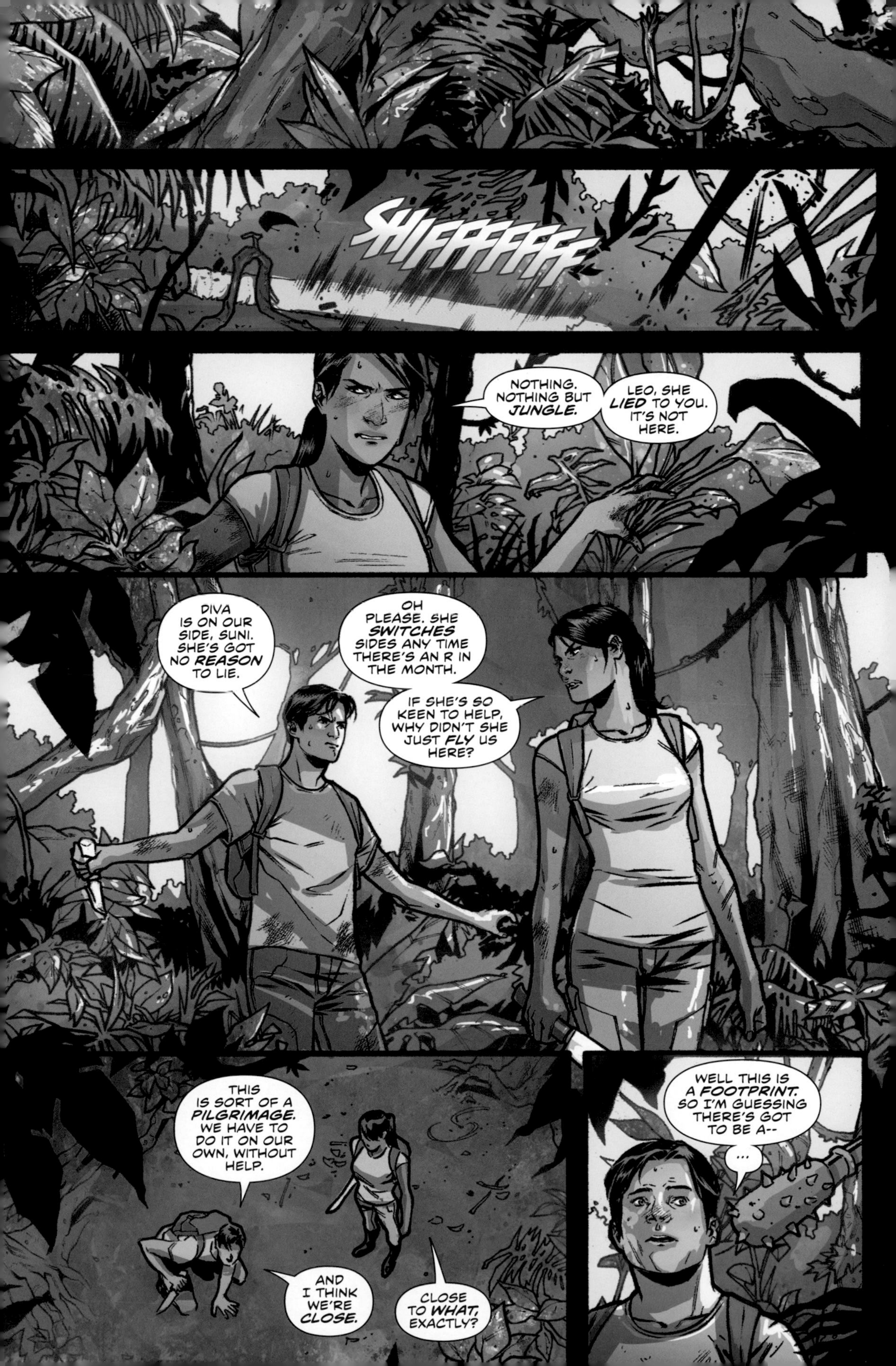
SHIFFFFFFF
NOTHING. NOTHING BUT JUNGLE.
LEO, SHE LIED TO YOU. IT'S NOT HERE.
DIVA IS ON OUR SIDE, SUNI. SHE'S GOT NO REASON TO LIE.
OH PLEASE. SHE SWITCHES SIDES ANY TIME THERE'S AN R IN THE MONTH.
IF SHE'S SO KEEN TO HELP, WHY DIDN'T SHE JUST FLY US HERE?
THIS IS SORT OF A PILGRIMAGE. WE HAVE TO DO IT ON OUR OWN, WITHOUT HELP.
AND I THINK WE'RE CLOSE.
CLOSE TO WHAT, EXACTLY?
WELL THIS IS A FOOTPRINT. SO I'M GUESSING THERE'S GOT TO BE A--
...

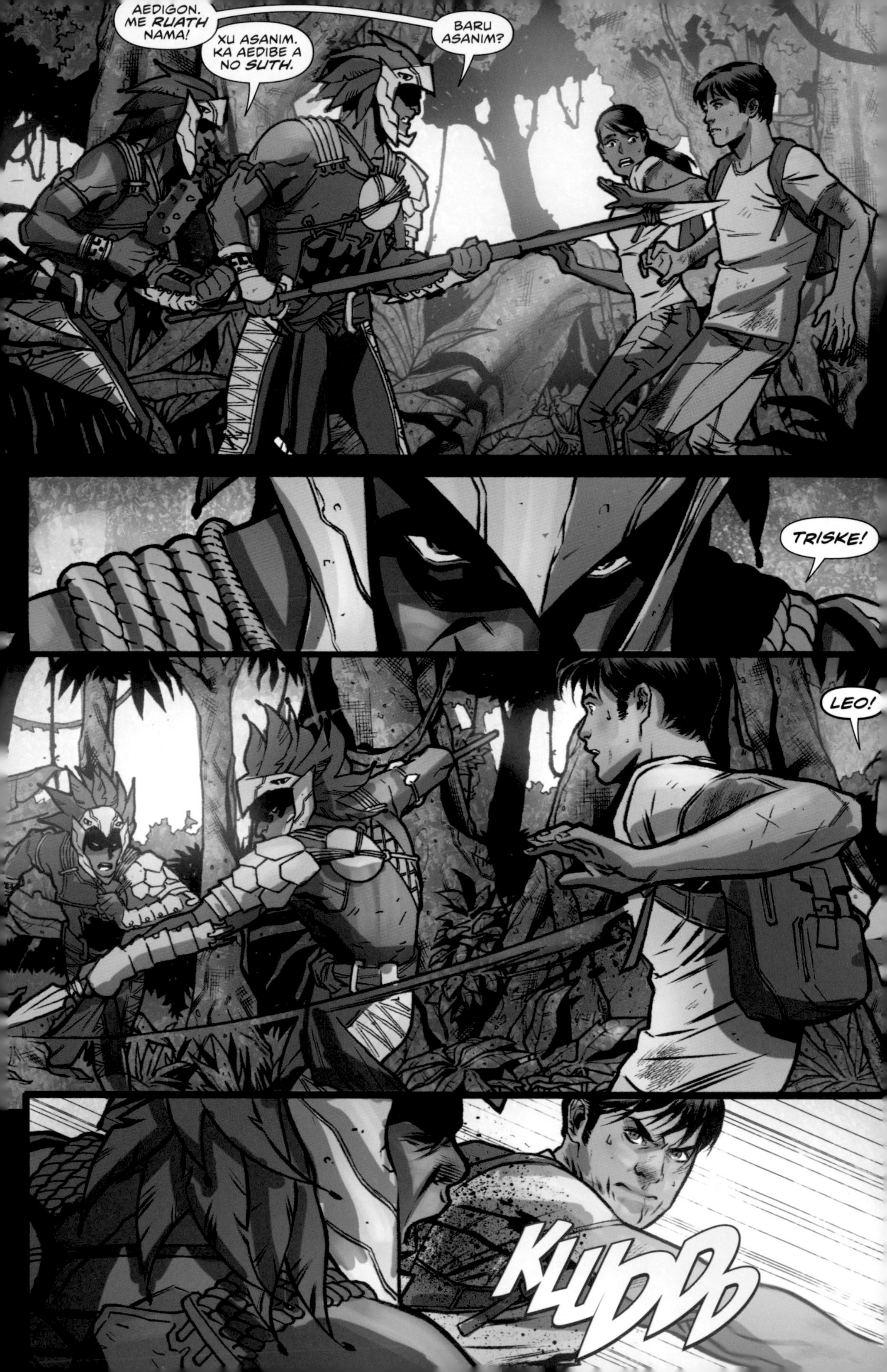
AEDIGON. ME RUATH NAMA!
XU ASANIM. KA AEDIBE A NO SUTH.
BARU ASANIM?
TRISKE!
LEO!
KUDOD

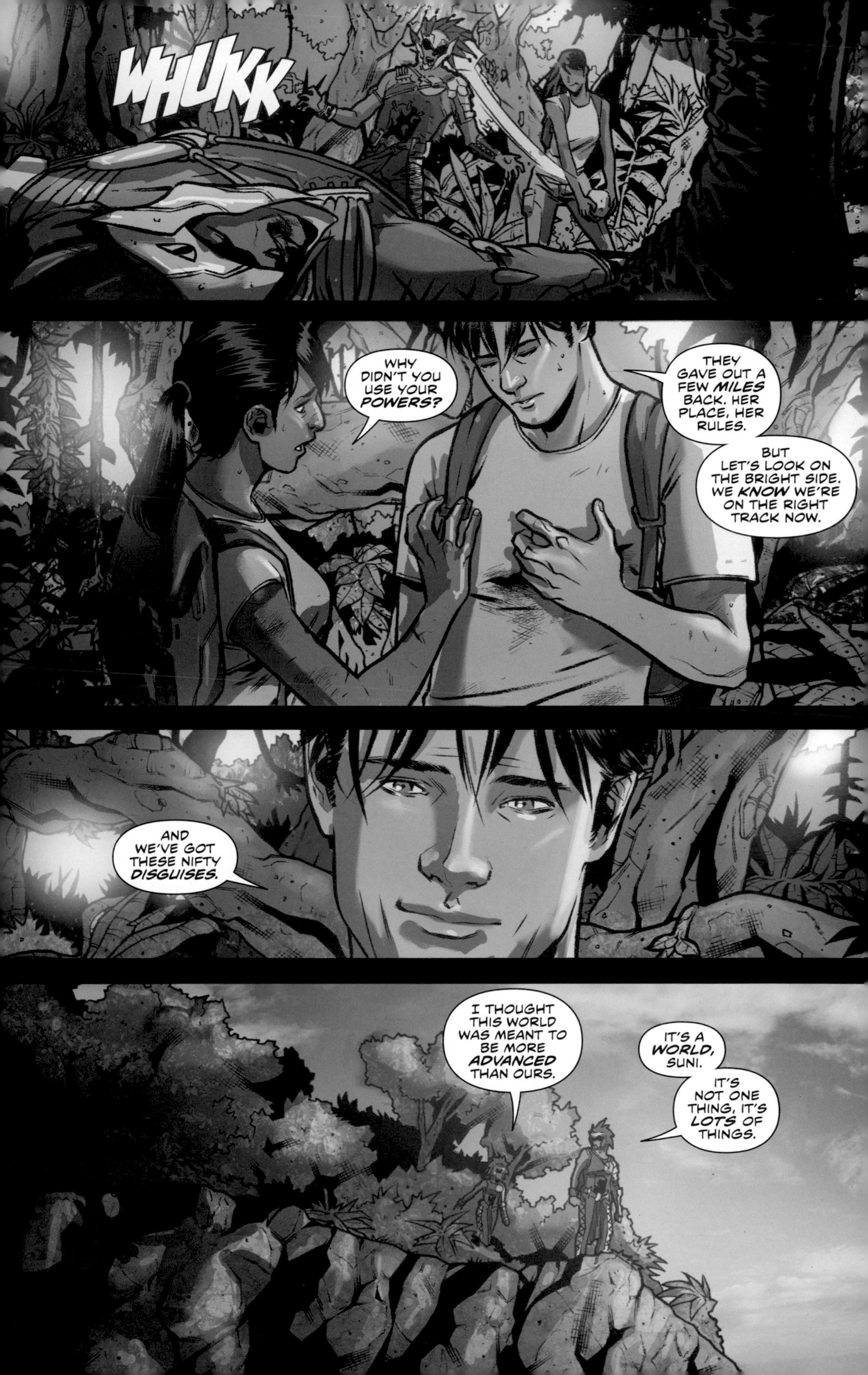
WHUKK
WHY DIDN'T YOU USE YOUR POWERS?
THEY GAVE OUT A FEW MILES BACK. HER PLACE, HER RULES.
BUT LET'S LOOK ON THE BRIGHT SIDE. WE KNOW WE'RE ON THE RIGHT TRACK NOW.
AND WE'VE GOT THESE NIFTY DISGUISES.
I THOUGHT THIS WORLD WAS MEANT TO BE MORE ADVANCED THAN OURS.
IT'S A WORLD, SUNI.
IT'S NOT ONE THING, IT'S LOTS OF THINGS.

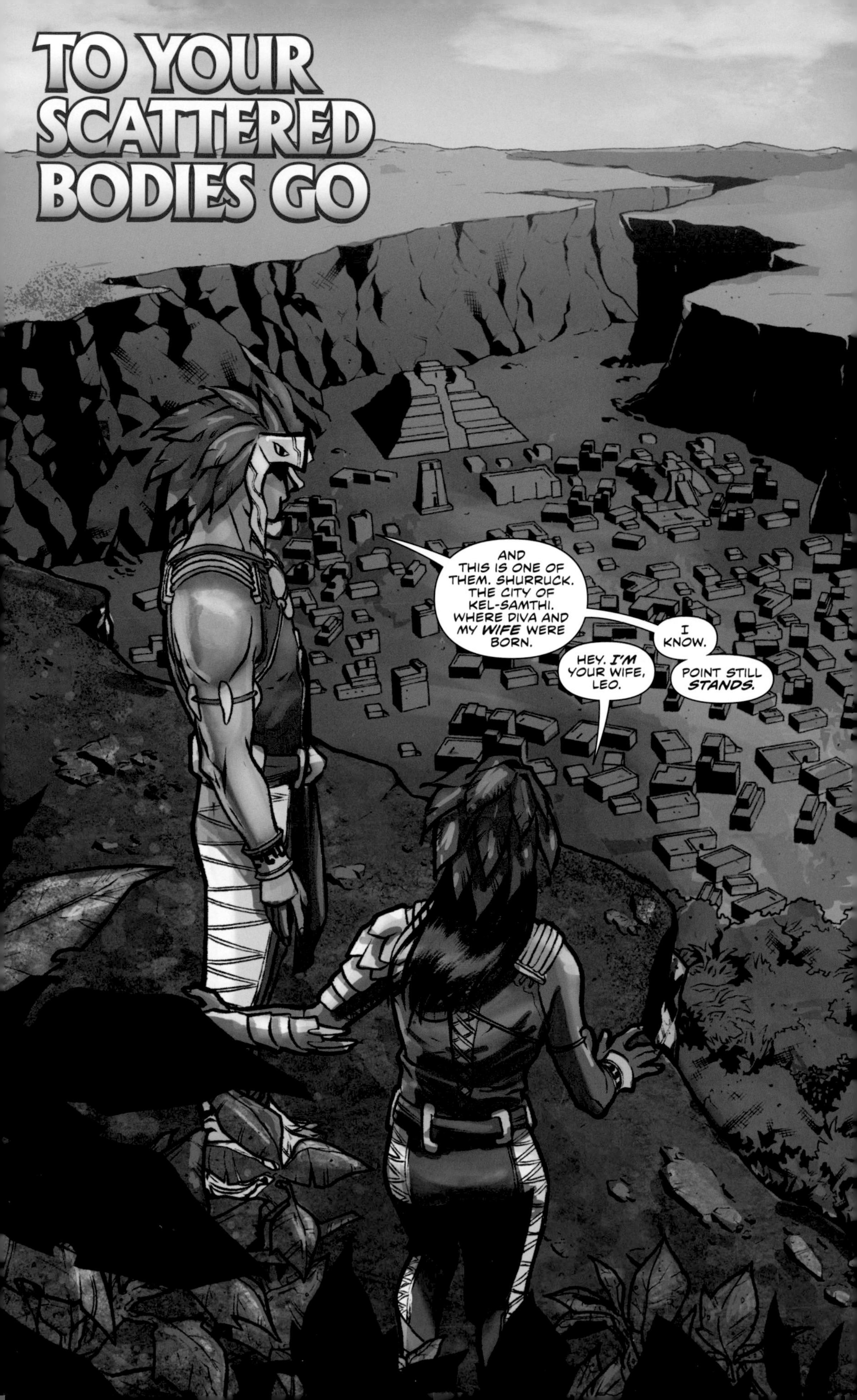
TO YOUR SCATTERED BODIES GO
AND THIS IS ONE OF THEM. SHURRUCK. THE CITY OF KEL-SAMTHI. WHERE DIVA AND MY WIFE WERE BORN.
HEY. I'M YOUR WIFE, LEO.
I KNOW.
POINT STILL STANDS.

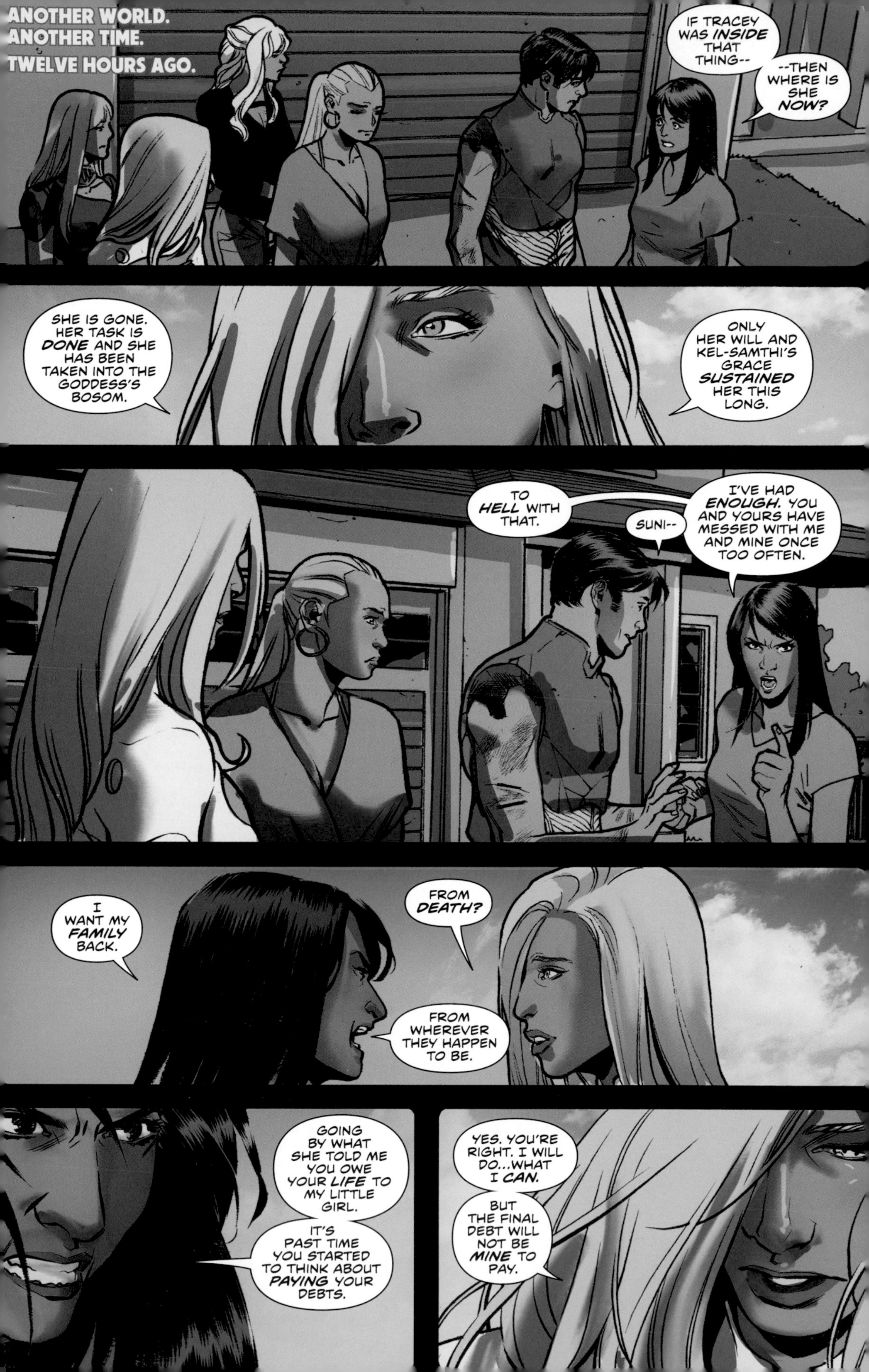
ANOTHER WORLD. ANOTHER TIME. TWELVE HOURS AGO.
IF TRACEY WAS INSIDE THAT THING--
--THEN WHERE IS SHE NOW?
SHE IS GONE. HER TASK IS DONE AND SHE HAS BEEN TAKEN INTO THE GODDESS'S BOSOM.
ONLY HER WILL AND KEL-SAMTHI'S GRACE SUSTAINED HER THIS LONG.
TO HELL WITH THAT.
SUNI--
I'VE HAD ENOUGH. YOU AND YOURS HAVE MESSED WITH ME AND MINE ONCE TOO OFTEN.
I WANT MY FAMILY BACK.
FROM DEATH?
FROM WHEREVER THEY HAPPEN TO BE.
GOING BY WHAT SHE TOLD ME YOU OWE YOUR LIFE TO MY LITTLE GIRL.
IT'S PAST TIME YOU STARTED TO THINK ABOUT PAYING YOUR DEBTS.
YES. YOU'RE RIGHT. I WILL DO...WHAT I CAN.
BUT THE FINAL DEBT WILL NOT BE MINE TO PAY.

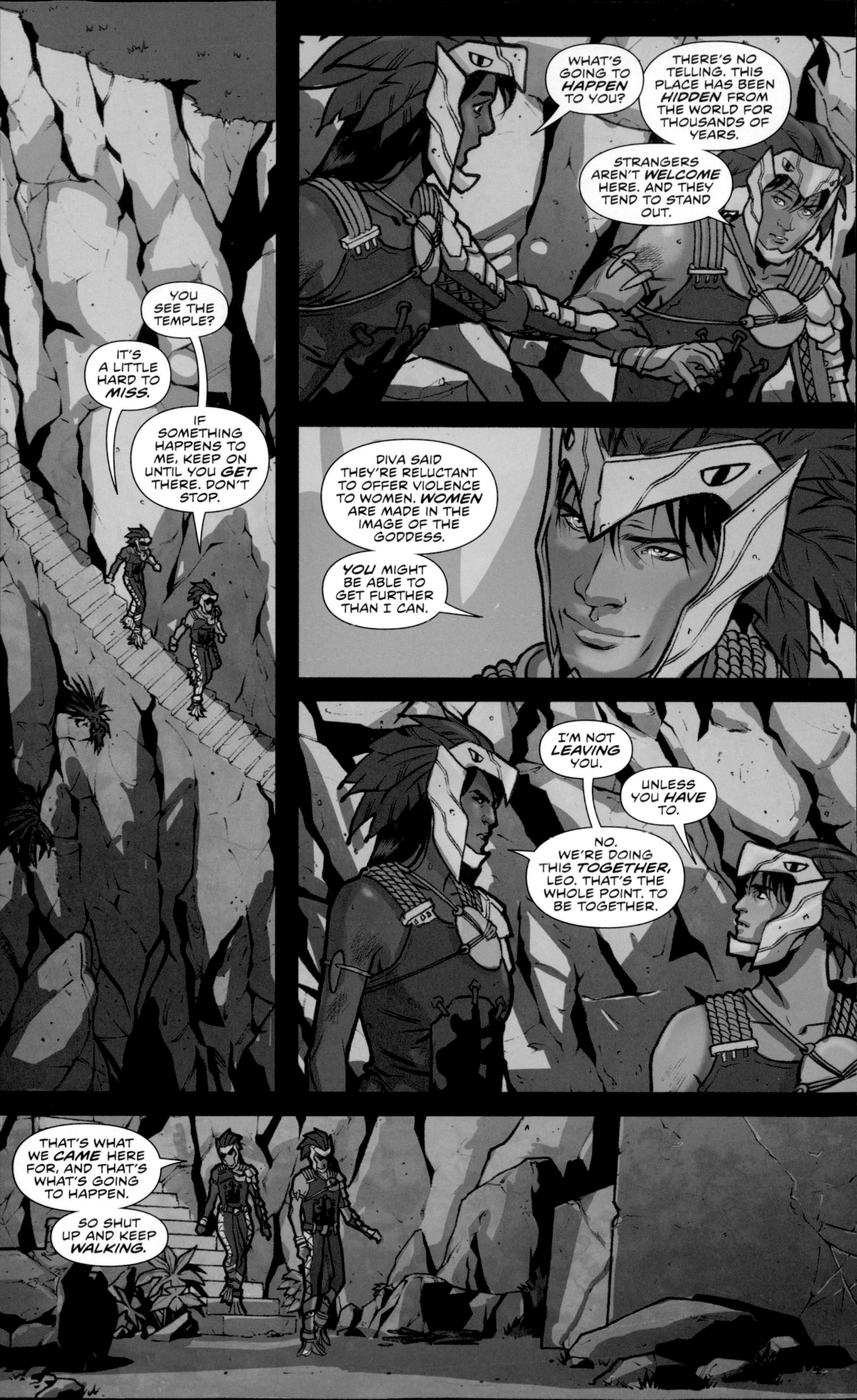
YOU SEE THE TEMPLE?
IT'S A LITTLE HARD TO ***MISS.***
IF SOMETHING HAPPENS TO ME, KEEP ON UNTIL YOU ***GET*** THERE. DON'T STOP.
WHAT'S GOING TO ***HAPPEN*** TO YOU?
THERE'S NO TELLING. THIS PLACE HAS BEEN ***HIDDEN*** FROM THE WORLD FOR THOUSANDS OF YEARS.
STRANGERS AREN'T ***WELCOME*** HERE. AND THEY TEND TO STAND OUT.
DIVA SAID THEY'RE RELUCTANT TO OFFER VIOLENCE TO WOMEN. ***WOMEN*** ARE MADE IN THE IMAGE OF THE GODDESS.
YOU MIGHT BE ABLE TO GET FURTHER THAN I CAN.
I'M NOT ***LEAVING*** YOU.
UNLESS YOU ***HAVE*** TO.
NO. WE'RE DOING THIS ***TOGETHER,*** LEO. THAT'S THE WHOLE POINT. TO BE TOGETHER.
THAT'S WHAT WE ***CAME*** HERE FOR, AND THAT'S WHAT'S GOING TO HAPPEN.
SO SHUT UP AND KEEP ***WALKING.***

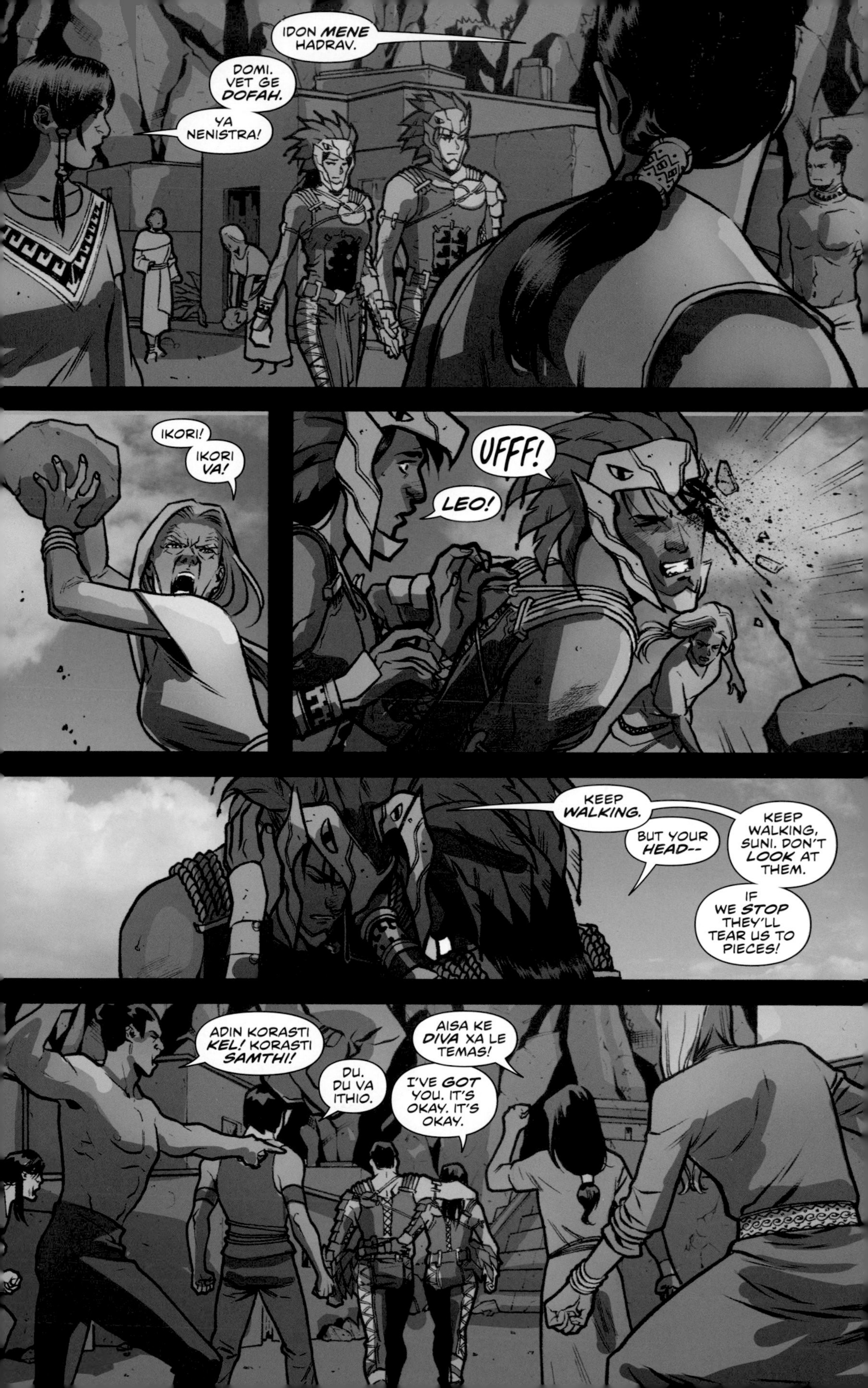
IDON MENE HADRAV.
DOMI. VET GE DOFAH.
YA NENISTRA!
IKORI! IKORI VA!
UFFF!
LEO!
KEEP WALKING.
BUT YOUR HEAD--
KEEP WALKING, SUNI. DON'T LOOK AT THEM.
IF WE STOP THEY'LL TEAR US TO PIECES!
ADIN KORASTI KEL! KORASTI SAMTHI!
DU. DU VA ITHIO.
AISA KE DIVA XA LE TEMAS!
I'VE GOT YOU. IT'S OKAY. IT'S OKAY.

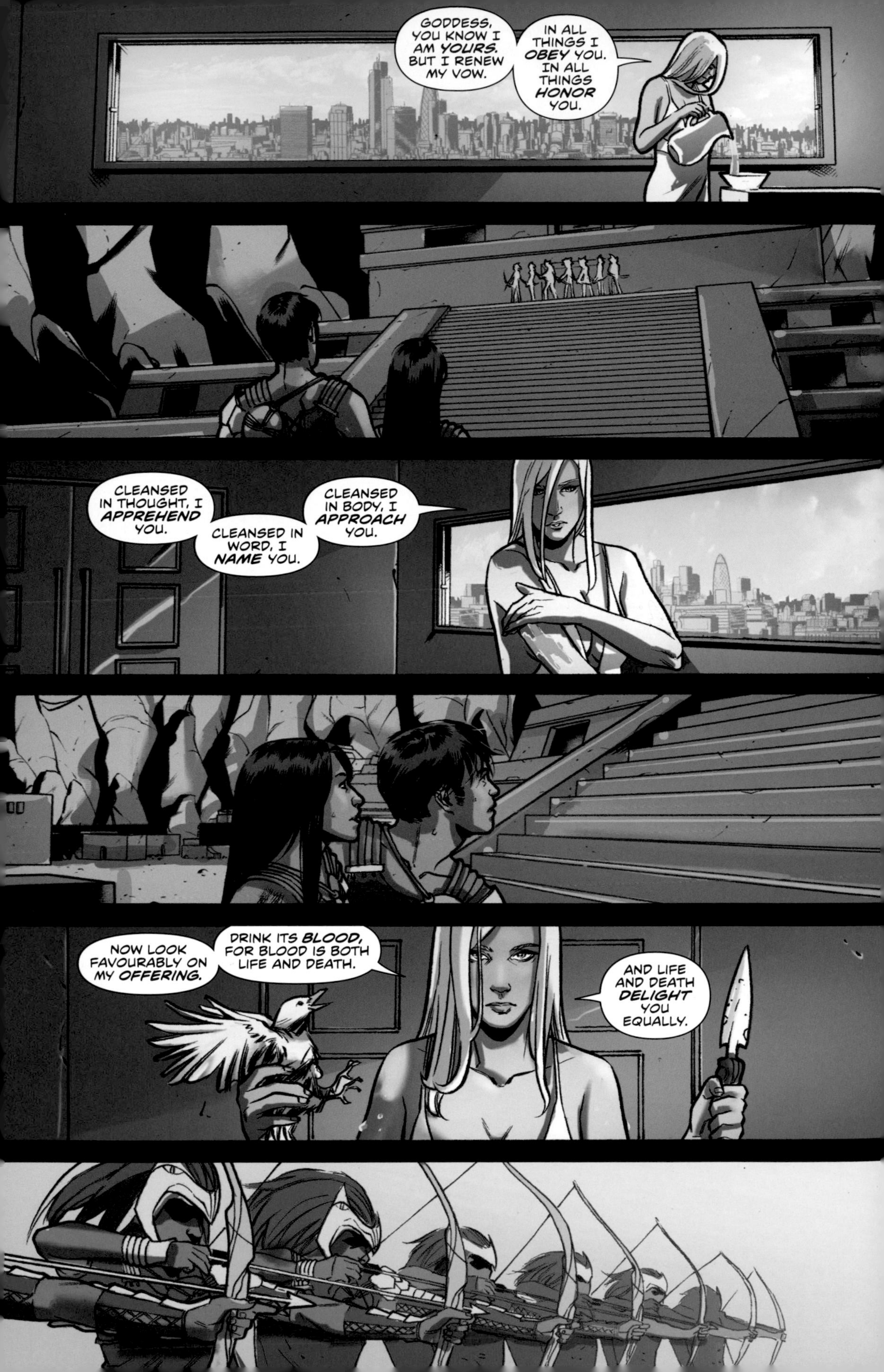

GODDESS, YOU KNOW I AM YOURS. BUT I RENEW MY VOW.
IN ALL THINGS I OBEY YOU. IN ALL THINGS HONOR YOU.
CLEANSED IN THOUGHT, I APPREHEND YOU.
CLEANSED IN WORD, I NAME YOU.
CLEANSED IN BODY, I APPROACH YOU.
NOW LOOK FAVOURABLY ON MY OFFERING.
DRINK ITS BLOOD, FOR BLOOD IS BOTH LIFE AND DEATH.
AND LIFE AND DEATH DELIGHT YOU EQUALLY.

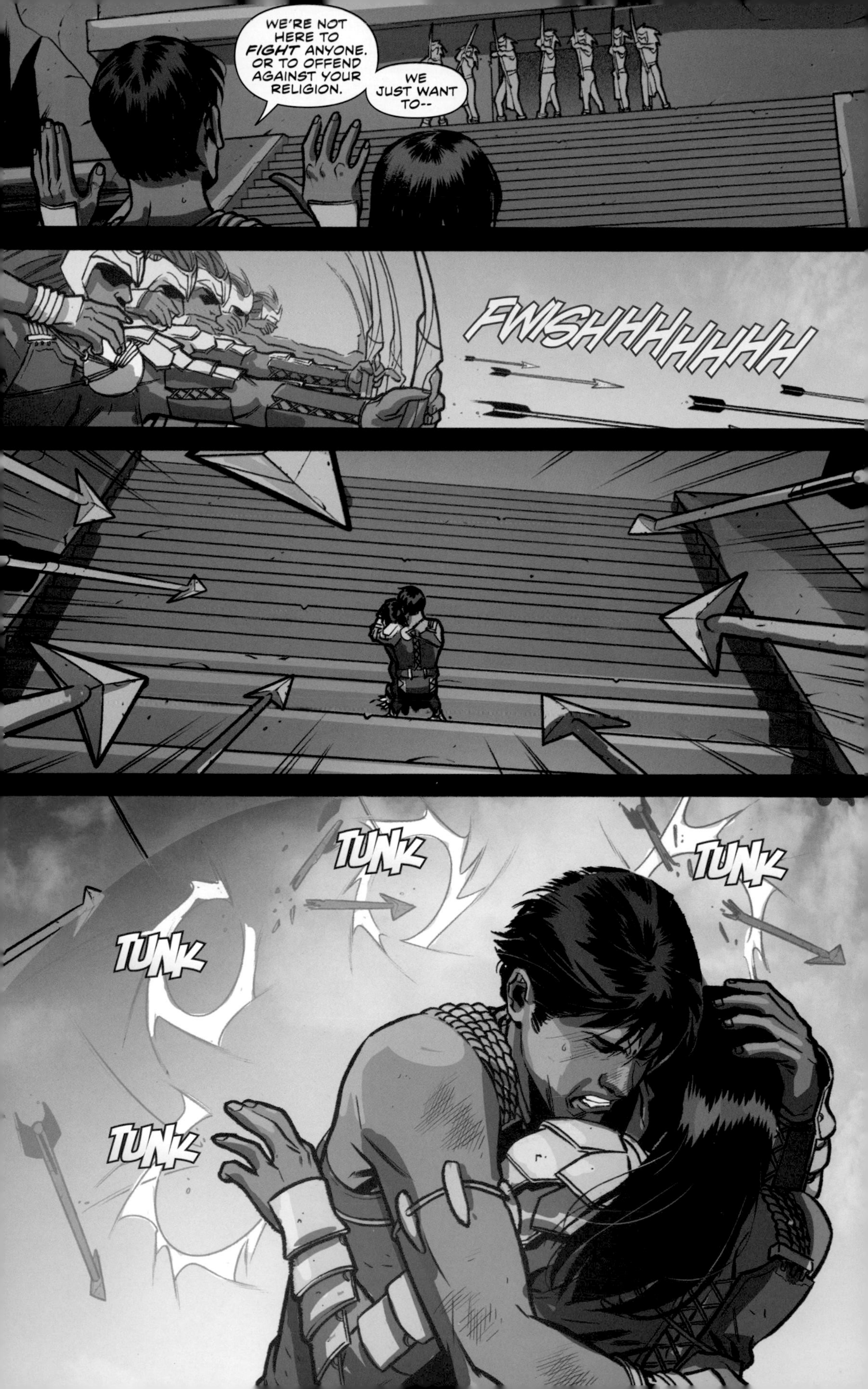
WE'RE NOT HERE TO FIGHT ANYONE. OR TO OFFEND AGAINST YOUR RELIGION.
WE JUST WANT TO--
FWISHHHHHHH
TUNK
TUNK
TUNK
TUNK

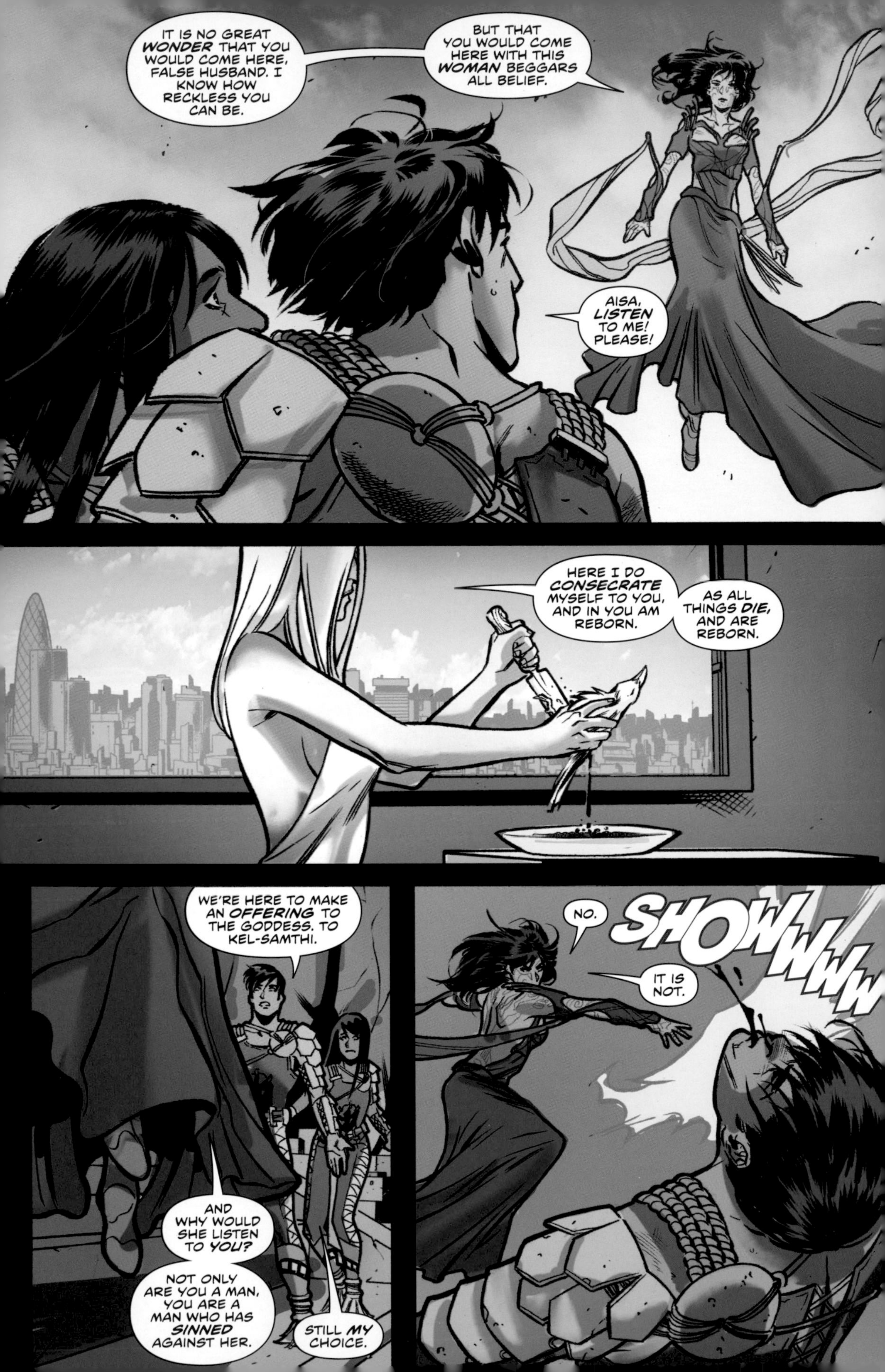
IT IS NO GREAT WONDER THAT YOU WOULD COME HERE, FALSE HUSBAND. I KNOW HOW RECKLESS YOU CAN BE.
BUT THAT YOU WOULD COME HERE WITH THIS WOMAN BEGGARS ALL BELIEF.
AISA, LISTEN TO ME! PLEASE!
HERE I DO CONSECRATE MYSELF TO YOU, AND IN YOU AM REBORN.
AS ALL THINGS DIE, AND ARE REBORN.
WE'RE HERE TO MAKE AN OFFERING TO THE GODDESS. TO KEL-SAMTHI.
AND WHY WOULD SHE LISTEN TO YOU?
NOT ONLY ARE YOU A MAN, YOU ARE A MAN WHO HAS SINNED AGAINST HER.
STILL MY CHOICE.
NO.
IT IS NOT.
SHOWWWW

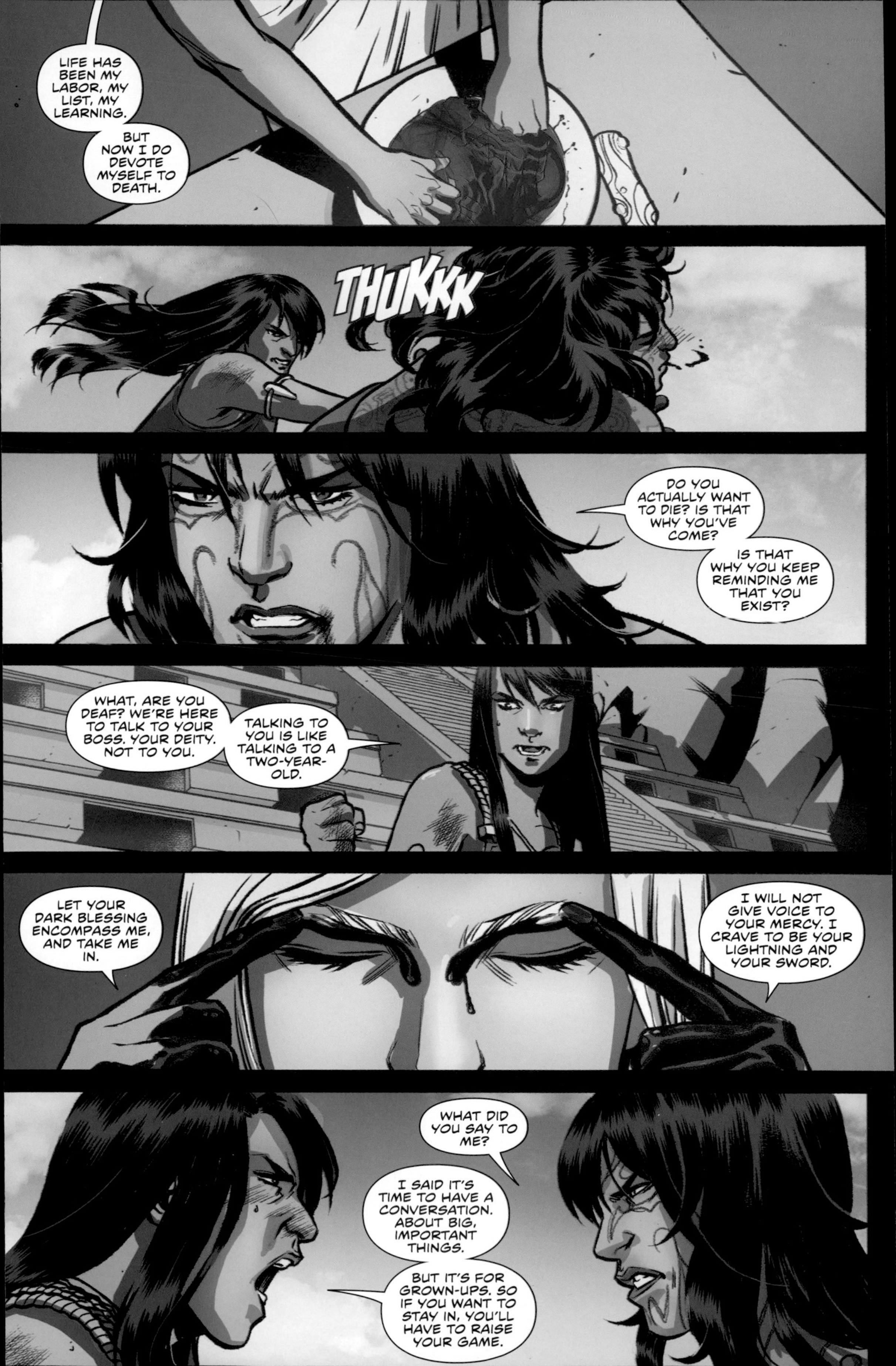
LIFE HAS BEEN MY LABOR, MY LIST, MY LEARNING.
BUT NOW I DO DEVOTE MYSELF TO DEATH.
THUKKK
DO YOU ACTUALLY WANT TO DIE? IS THAT WHY YOU'VE COME?
IS THAT WHY YOU KEEP REMINDING ME THAT YOU EXIST?
WHAT, ARE YOU DEAF? WE'RE HERE TO TALK TO YOUR BOSS. YOUR DEITY. NOT TO YOU.
TALKING TO YOU IS LIKE TALKING TO A TWO-YEAR-OLD.
LET YOUR DARK BLESSING ENCOMPASS ME, AND TAKE ME IN.
I WILL NOT GIVE VOICE TO YOUR MERCY. I CRAVE TO BE YOUR LIGHTNING AND YOUR SWORD.
WHAT DID YOU SAY TO ME?
I SAID IT'S TIME TO HAVE A CONVERSATION. ABOUT BIG, IMPORTANT THINGS.
BUT IT'S FOR GROWN-UPS. SO IF YOU WANT TO STAY IN, YOU'LL HAVE TO RAISE YOUR GAME.

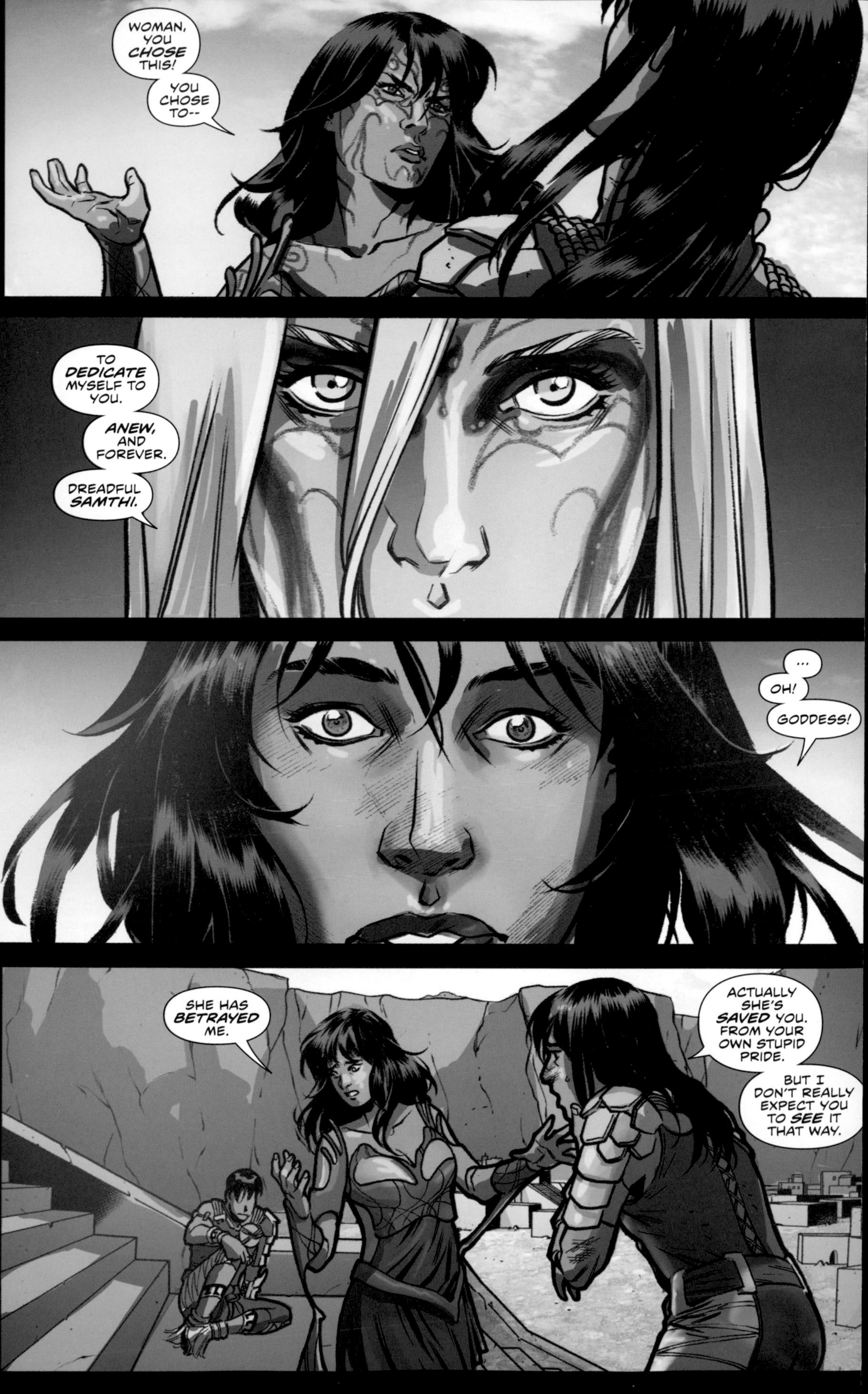
WOMAN, YOU *CHOSE* THIS!
YOU CHOSE TO--
TO *DEDICATE* MYSELF TO YOU.
ANEW, AND FOREVER.
DREADFUL *SAMTHI.*
...
OH!
GODDESS!
SHE HAS *BETRAYED* ME.
ACTUALLY SHE'S *SAVED* YOU. FROM YOUR OWN STUPID PRIDE.
BUT I DON'T REALLY EXPECT YOU TO *SEE* IT THAT WAY.

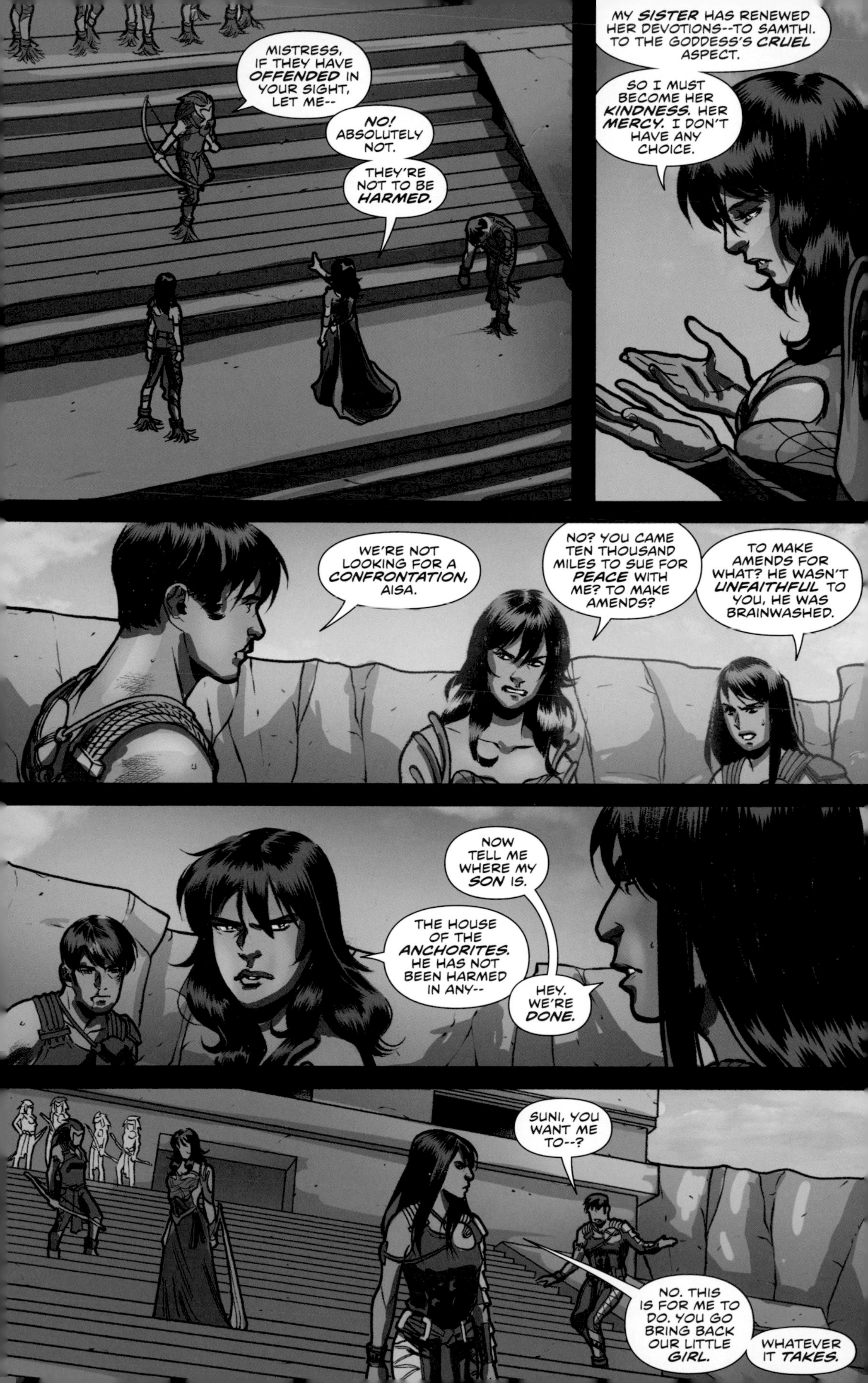
MISTRESS, IF THEY HAVE OFFENDED IN YOUR SIGHT, LET ME--
NO! ABSOLUTELY NOT.
THEY'RE NOT TO BE HARMED.
MY SISTER HAS RENEWED HER DEVOTIONS--TO SAMTHI. TO THE GODDESS'S CRUEL ASPECT.
SO I MUST BECOME HER KINDNESS. HER MERCY. I DON'T HAVE ANY CHOICE.
WE'RE NOT LOOKING FOR A CONFRONTATION, AISA.
NO? YOU CAME TEN THOUSAND MILES TO SUE FOR PEACE WITH ME? TO MAKE AMENDS?
TO MAKE AMENDS FOR WHAT? HE WASN'T UNFAITHFUL TO YOU, HE WAS BRAINWASHED.
NOW TELL ME WHERE MY SON IS.
THE HOUSE OF THE ANCHORITES. HE HAS NOT BEEN HARMED IN ANY--
HEY. WE'RE DONE.
SUNI, YOU WANT ME TO--?
NO. THIS IS FOR ME TO DO. YOU GO BRING BACK OUR LITTLE GIRL.
WHATEVER IT TAKES.

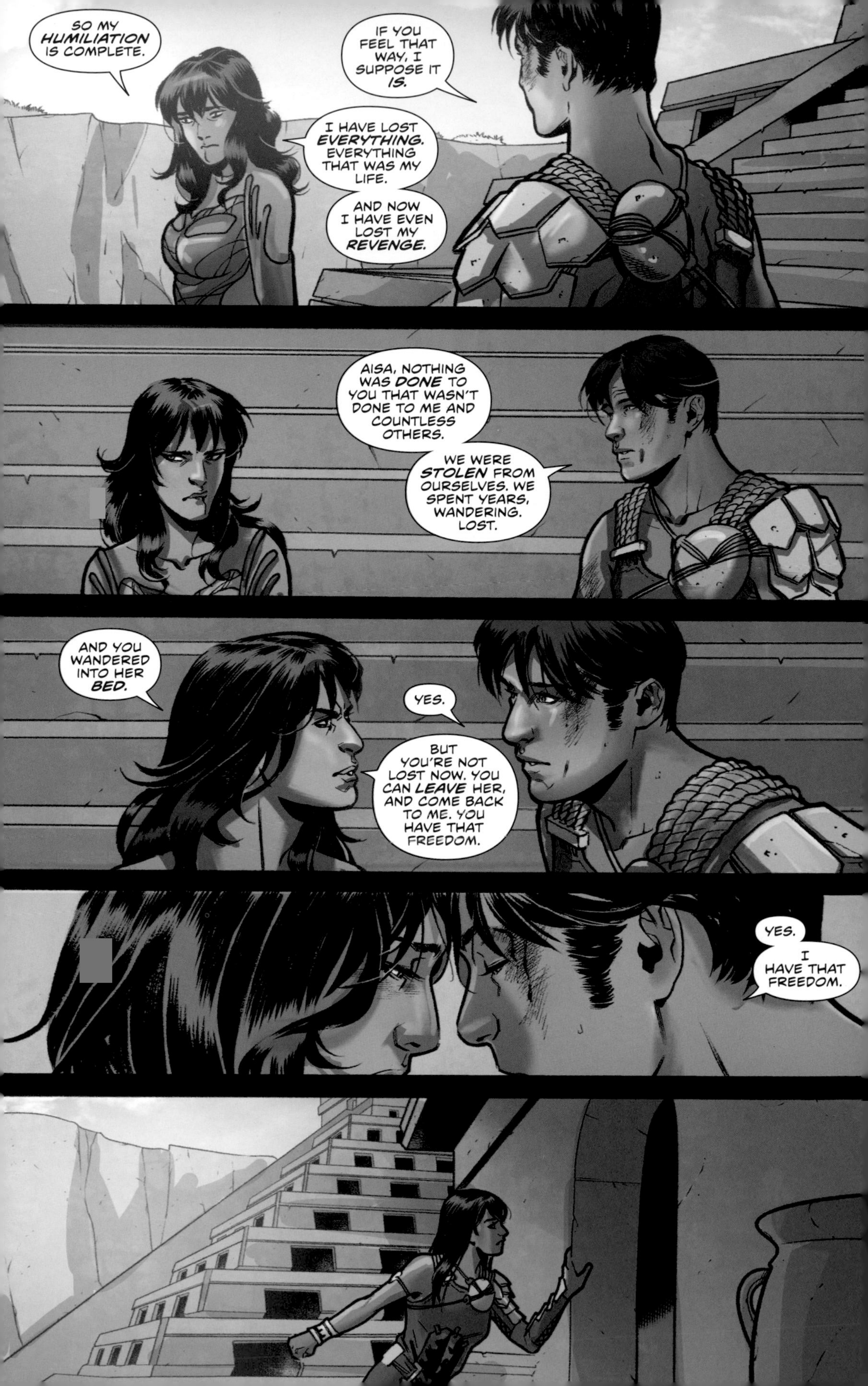
SO MY HUMILIATION IS COMPLETE.
IF YOU FEEL THAT WAY, I SUPPOSE IT IS.
I HAVE LOST EVERYTHING. EVERYTHING THAT WAS MY LIFE.
AND NOW I HAVE EVEN LOST MY REVENGE.
AISA, NOTHING WAS DONE TO YOU THAT WASN'T DONE TO ME AND COUNTLESS OTHERS.
WE WERE STOLEN FROM OURSELVES. WE SPENT YEARS, WANDERING. LOST.
AND YOU WANDERED INTO HER BED.
YES.
BUT YOU'RE NOT LOST NOW. YOU CAN LEAVE HER, AND COME BACK TO ME. YOU HAVE THAT FREEDOM.
YES.
I HAVE THAT FREEDOM.

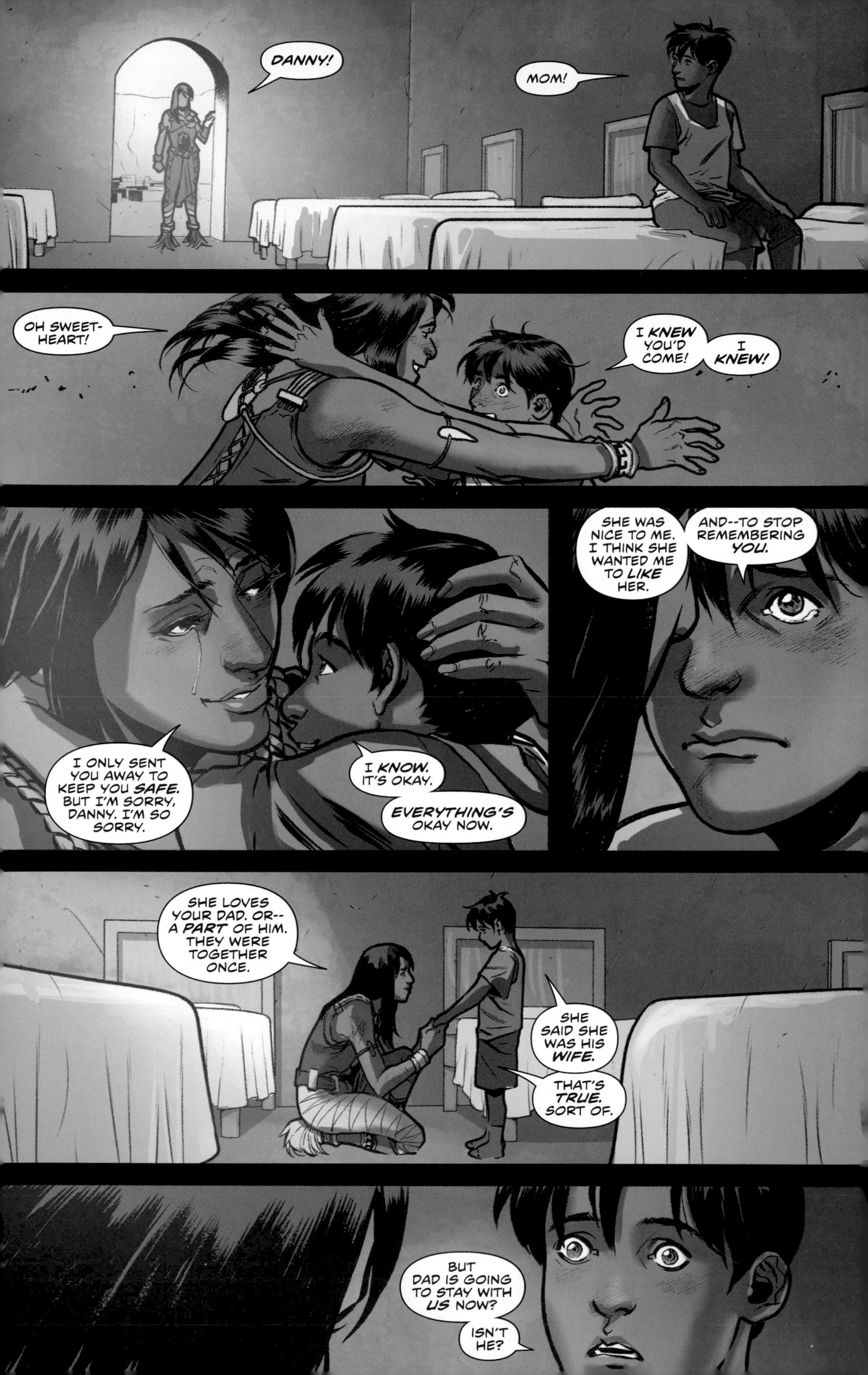
DANNY!
MOM!
OH SWEET-HEART!
I KNEW YOU'D COME!
I KNEW!
I ONLY SENT YOU AWAY TO KEEP YOU SAFE. BUT I'M SORRY, DANNY. I'M SO SORRY.
I KNOW. IT'S OKAY.
EVERYTHING'S OKAY NOW.
SHE WAS NICE TO ME. I THINK SHE WANTED ME TO LIKE HER.
AND--TO STOP REMEMBERING YOU.
SHE LOVES YOUR DAD. OR--A PART OF HIM. THEY WERE TOGETHER ONCE.
SHE SAID SHE WAS HIS WIFE.
THAT'S TRUE. SORT OF.
BUT DAD IS GOING TO STAY WITH US NOW?
ISN'T HE?

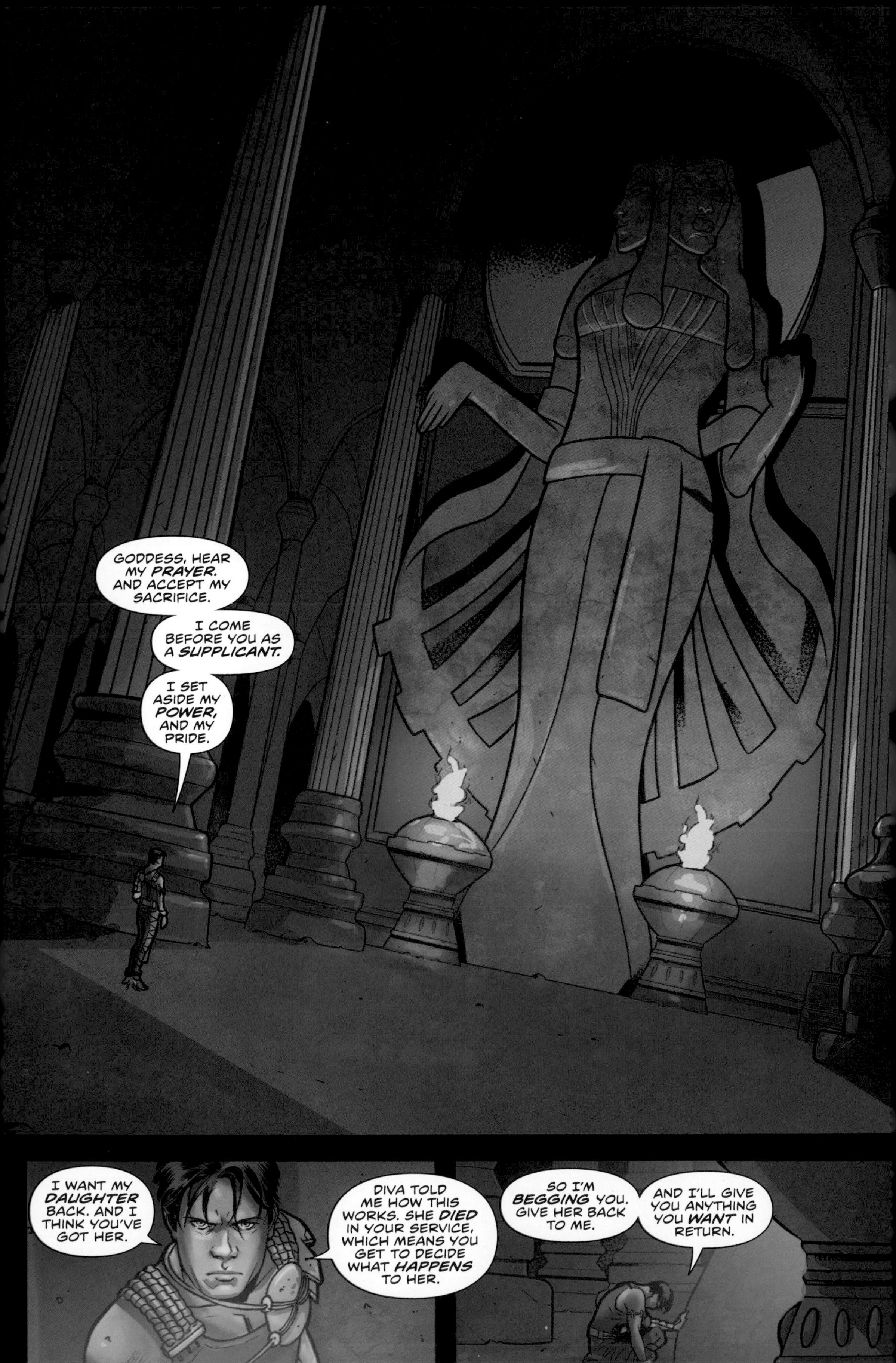
GODDESS, HEAR MY PRAYER. AND ACCEPT MY SACRIFICE.
I COME BEFORE YOU AS A SUPPLICANT.
I SET ASIDE MY POWER, AND MY PRIDE.
I WANT MY DAUGHTER BACK. AND I THINK YOU'VE GOT HER.
DIVA TOLD ME HOW THIS WORKS. SHE DIED IN YOUR SERVICE, WHICH MEANS YOU GET TO DECIDE WHAT HAPPENS TO HER.
SO I'M BEGGING YOU. GIVE HER BACK TO ME.
AND I'LL GIVE YOU ANYTHING YOU WANT IN RETURN.

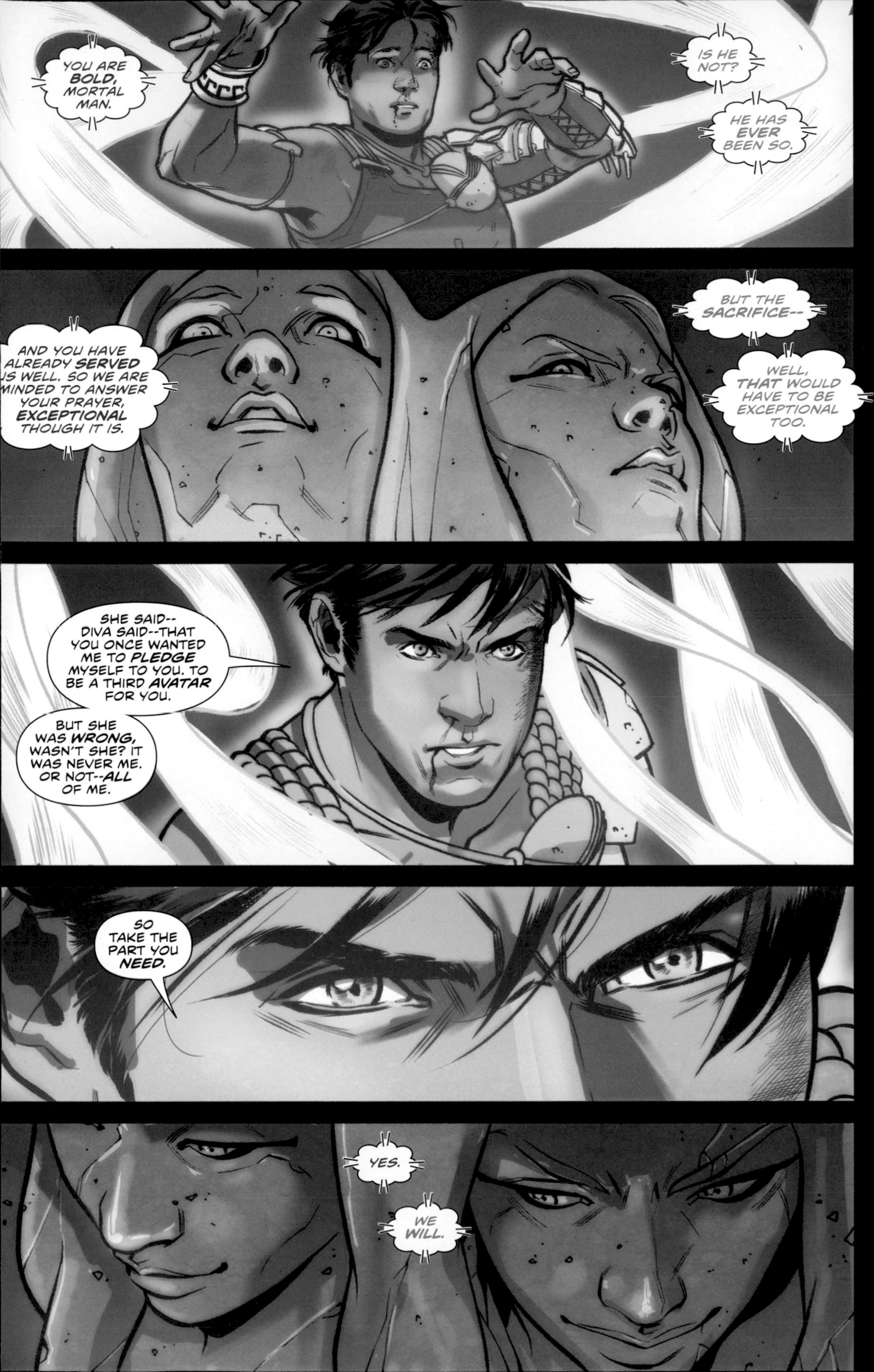
YOU ARE BOLD, MORTAL MAN.
IS HE NOT?
HE HAS EVER BEEN SO.
AND YOU HAVE ALREADY SERVED US WELL. SO WE ARE MINDED TO ANSWER YOUR PRAYER, EXCEPTIONAL THOUGH IT IS.
BUT THE SACRIFICE--
WELL, THAT WOULD HAVE TO BE EXCEPTIONAL TOO.
SHE SAID-- DIVA SAID--THAT YOU ONCE WANTED ME TO PLEDGE MYSELF TO YOU. TO BE A THIRD AVATAR FOR YOU.
BUT SHE WAS WRONG, WASN'T SHE? IT WAS NEVER ME. OR NOT--ALL OF ME.
SO TAKE THE PART YOU NEED.
YES.
WE WILL.

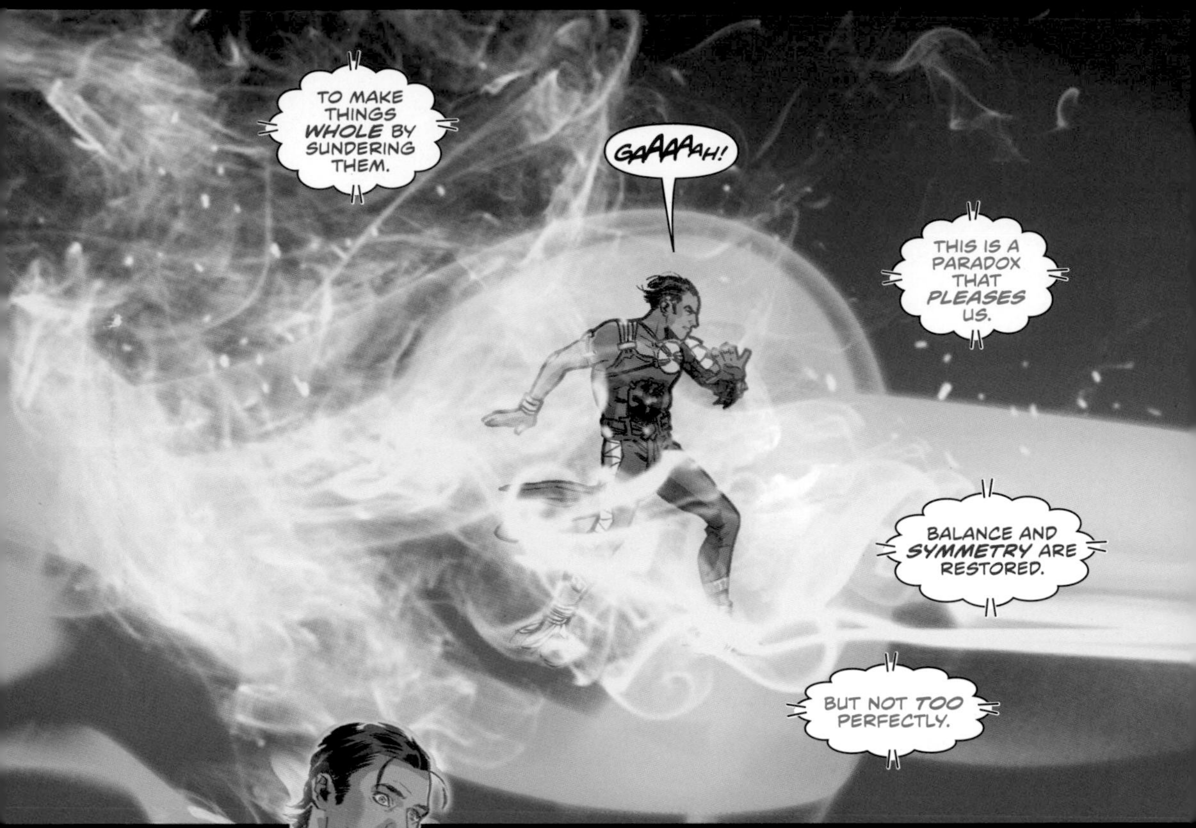
TO MAKE THINGS WHOLE BY SUNDERING THEM.
GAAAAAH!
THIS IS A PARADOX THAT PLEASES US.
BALANCE AND SYMMETRY ARE RESTORED.
BUT NOT TOO PERFECTLY.

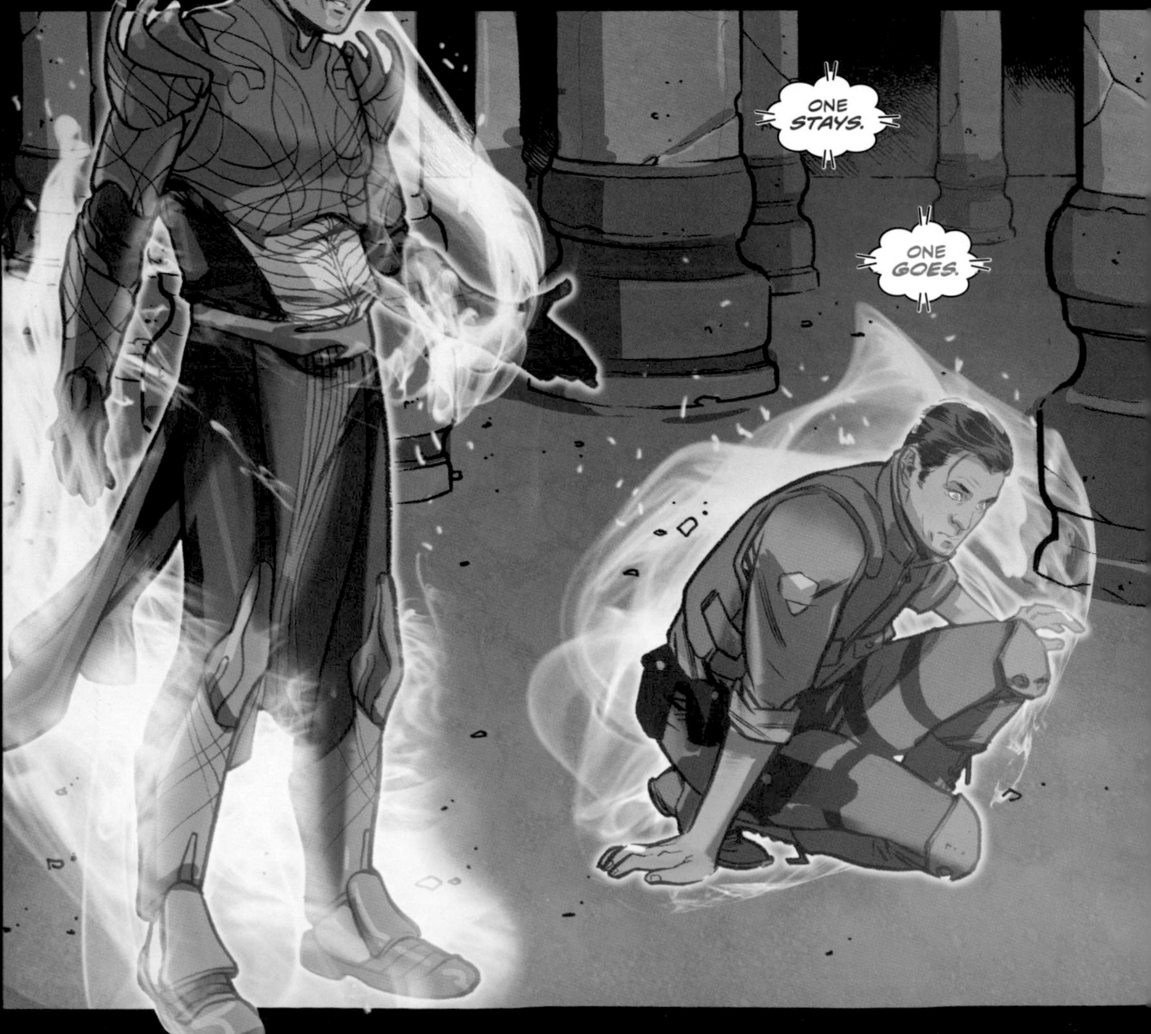
ONE STAYS.
ONE GOES.

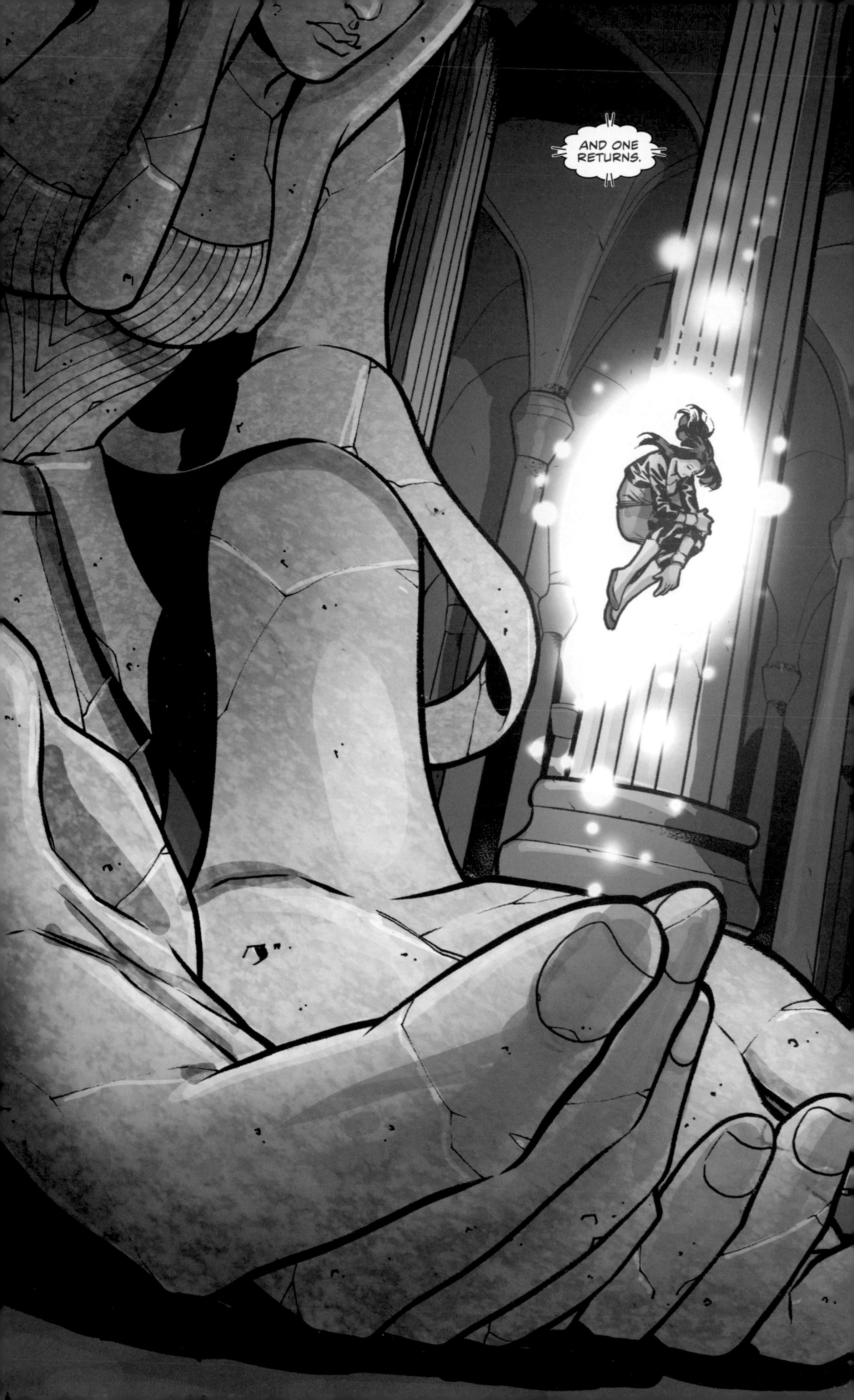
AND ONE RETURNS.

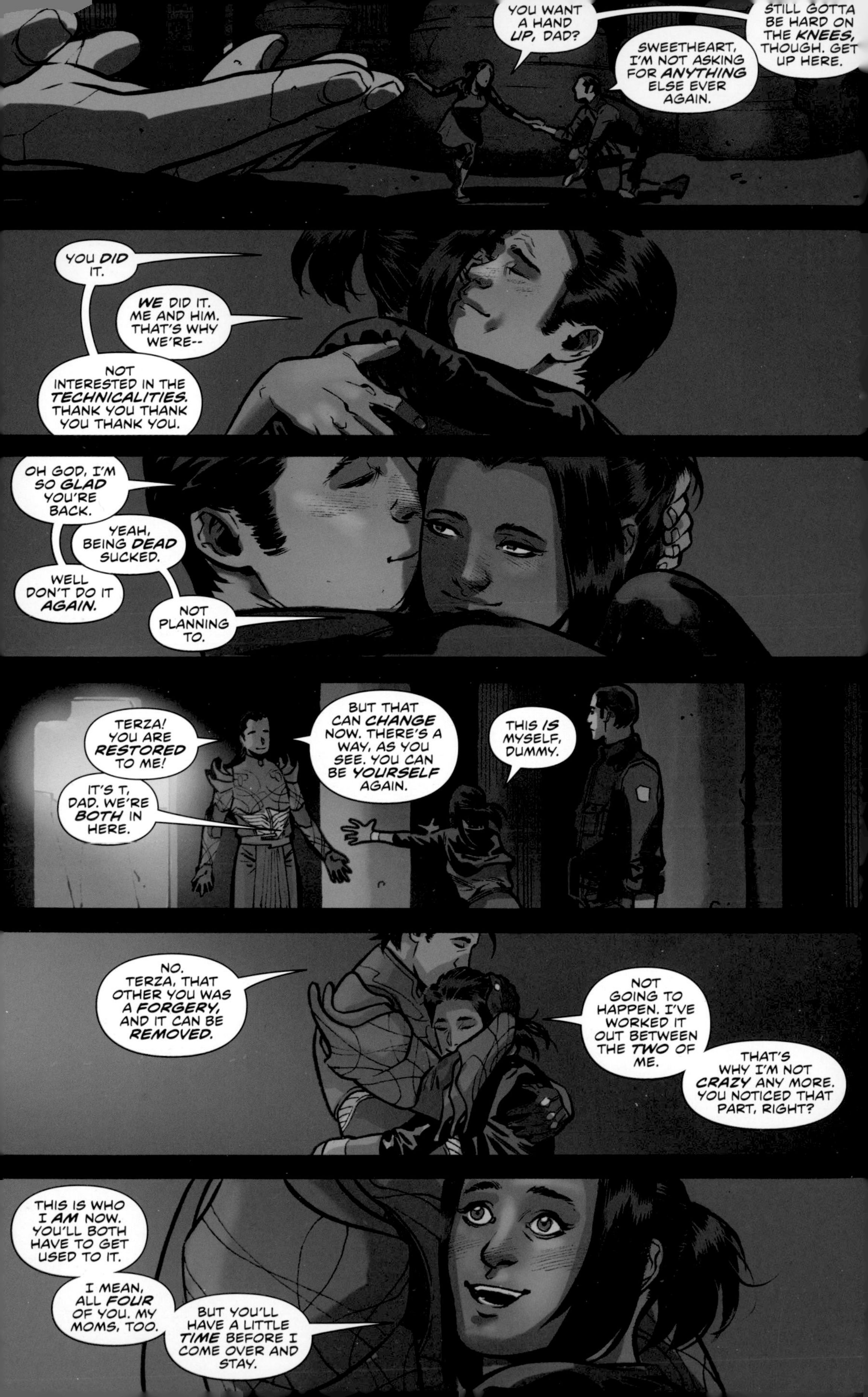
YOU WANT A HAND UP, DAD?
SWEETHEART, I'M NOT ASKING FOR ANYTHING ELSE EVER AGAIN.
STILL GOTTA BE HARD ON THE KNEES, THOUGH. GET UP HERE.
YOU DID IT.
WE DID IT. ME AND HIM. THAT'S WHY WE'RE--
NOT INTERESTED IN THE TECHNICALITIES. THANK YOU THANK YOU THANK YOU.
OH GOD, I'M SO GLAD YOU'RE BACK.
YEAH, BEING DEAD SUCKED.
WELL DON'T DO IT AGAIN.
NOT PLANNING TO.
TERZA! YOU ARE RESTORED TO ME!
IT'S T, DAD. WE'RE BOTH IN HERE.
BUT THAT CAN CHANGE NOW. THERE'S A WAY, AS YOU SEE. YOU CAN BE YOURSELF AGAIN.
THIS IS MYSELF, DUMMY.
NO. TERZA, THAT OTHER YOU WAS A FORGERY, AND IT CAN BE REMOVED.
NOT GOING TO HAPPEN. I'VE WORKED IT OUT BETWEEN THE TWO OF ME.
THAT'S WHY I'M NOT CRAZY ANY MORE. YOU NOTICED THAT PART, RIGHT?
THIS IS WHO I AM NOW. YOU'LL BOTH HAVE TO GET USED TO IT.
I MEAN, ALL FOUR OF YOU. MY MOMS, TOO.
BUT YOU'LL HAVE A LITTLE TIME BEFORE I COME OVER AND STAY.

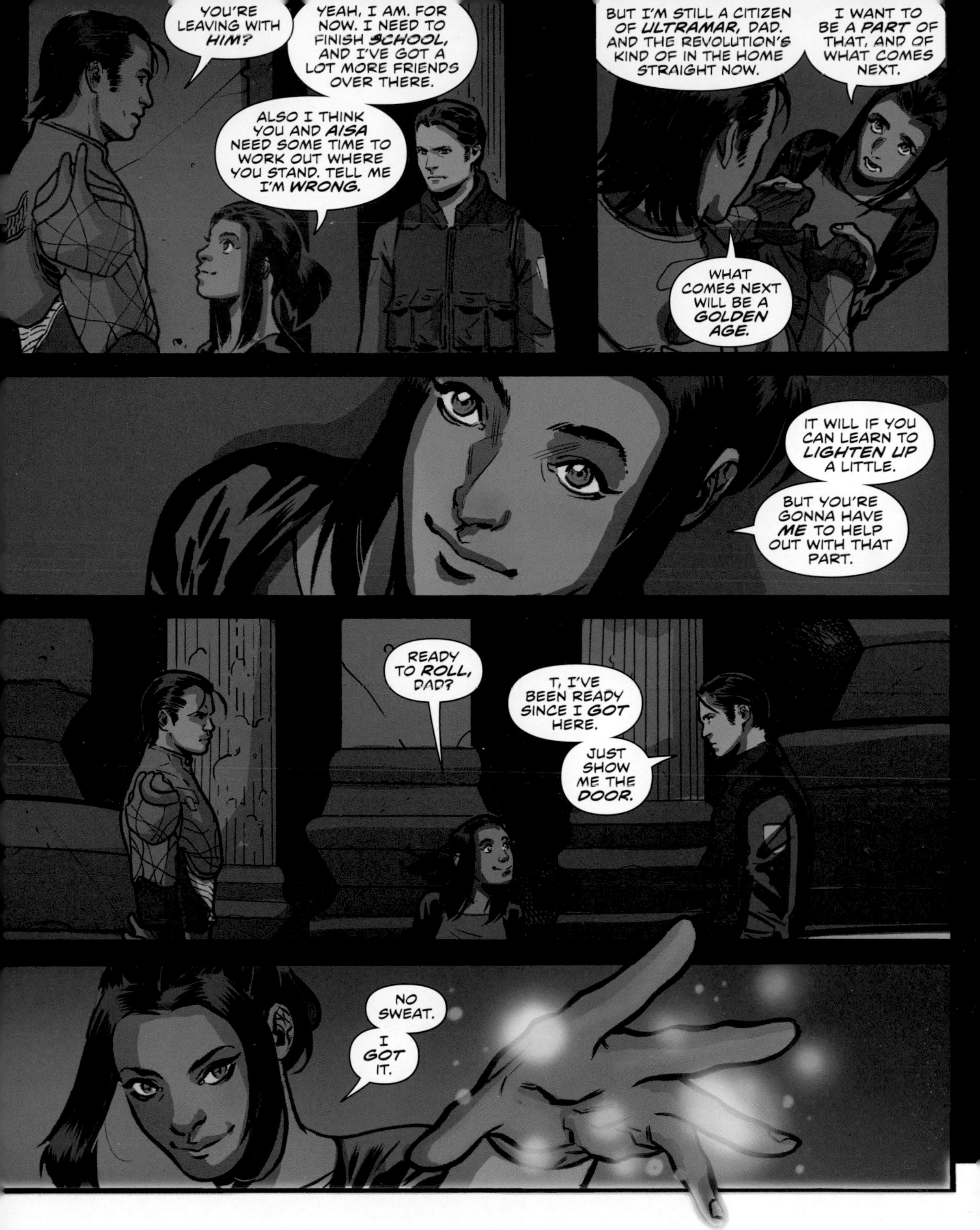
YOU'RE LEAVING WITH HIM?
YEAH, I AM. FOR NOW. I NEED TO FINISH SCHOOL, AND I'VE GOT A LOT MORE FRIENDS OVER THERE.
ALSO I THINK YOU AND AISA NEED SOME TIME TO WORK OUT WHERE YOU STAND. TELL ME I'M WRONG.
BUT I'M STILL A CITIZEN OF ULTRAMAR, DAD. AND THE REVOLUTION'S KIND OF IN THE HOME STRAIGHT NOW.
I WANT TO BE A PART OF THAT, AND OF WHAT COMES NEXT.
WHAT COMES NEXT WILL BE A GOLDEN AGE.
IT WILL IF YOU CAN LEARN TO LIGHTEN UP A LITTLE.
BUT YOU'RE GONNA HAVE ME TO HELP OUT WITH THAT PART.
READY TO ROLL, DAD?
T, I'VE BEEN READY SINCE I GOT HERE.
JUST SHOW ME THE DOOR.
NO SWEAT.
I GOT IT.

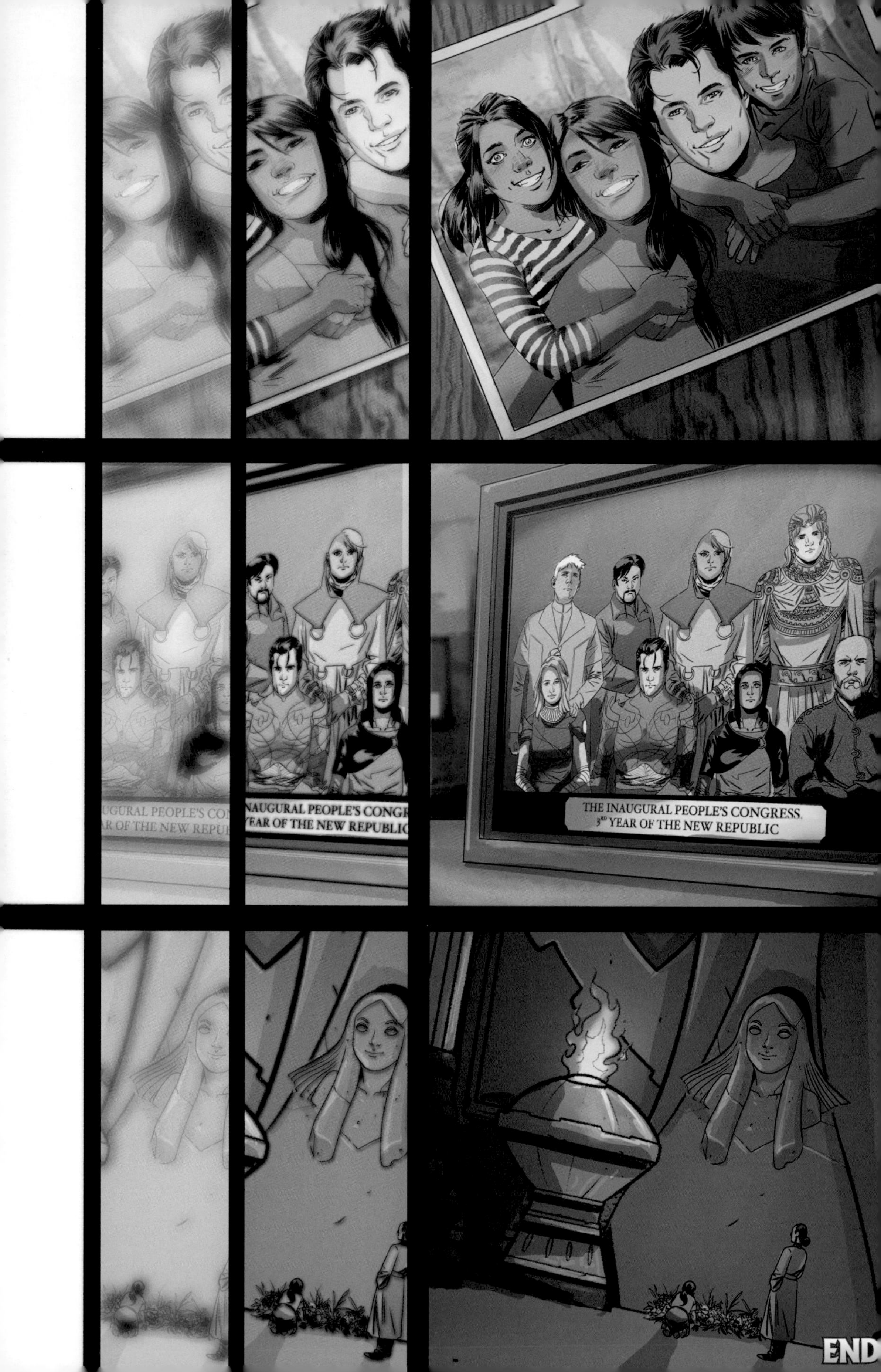

AUGURAL PEOPLE'S CONG
AR OF THE NEW REPU
NAUGURAL PEOPLE'S CONGR
YEAR OF THE NEW REPUBLIC
THE INAUGURAL PEOPLE'S CONGRESS,
3RD YEAR OF THE NEW REPUBLIC
END

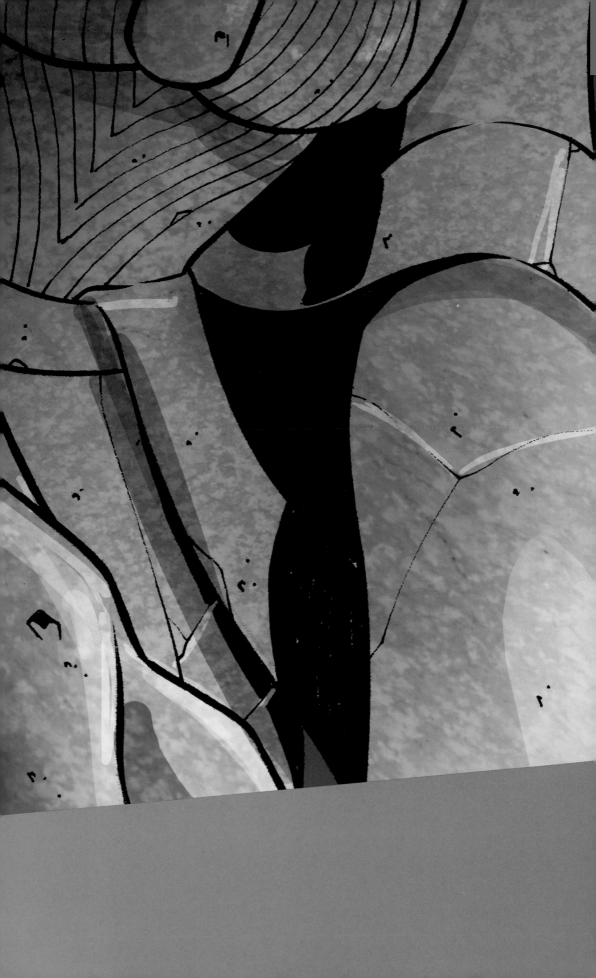

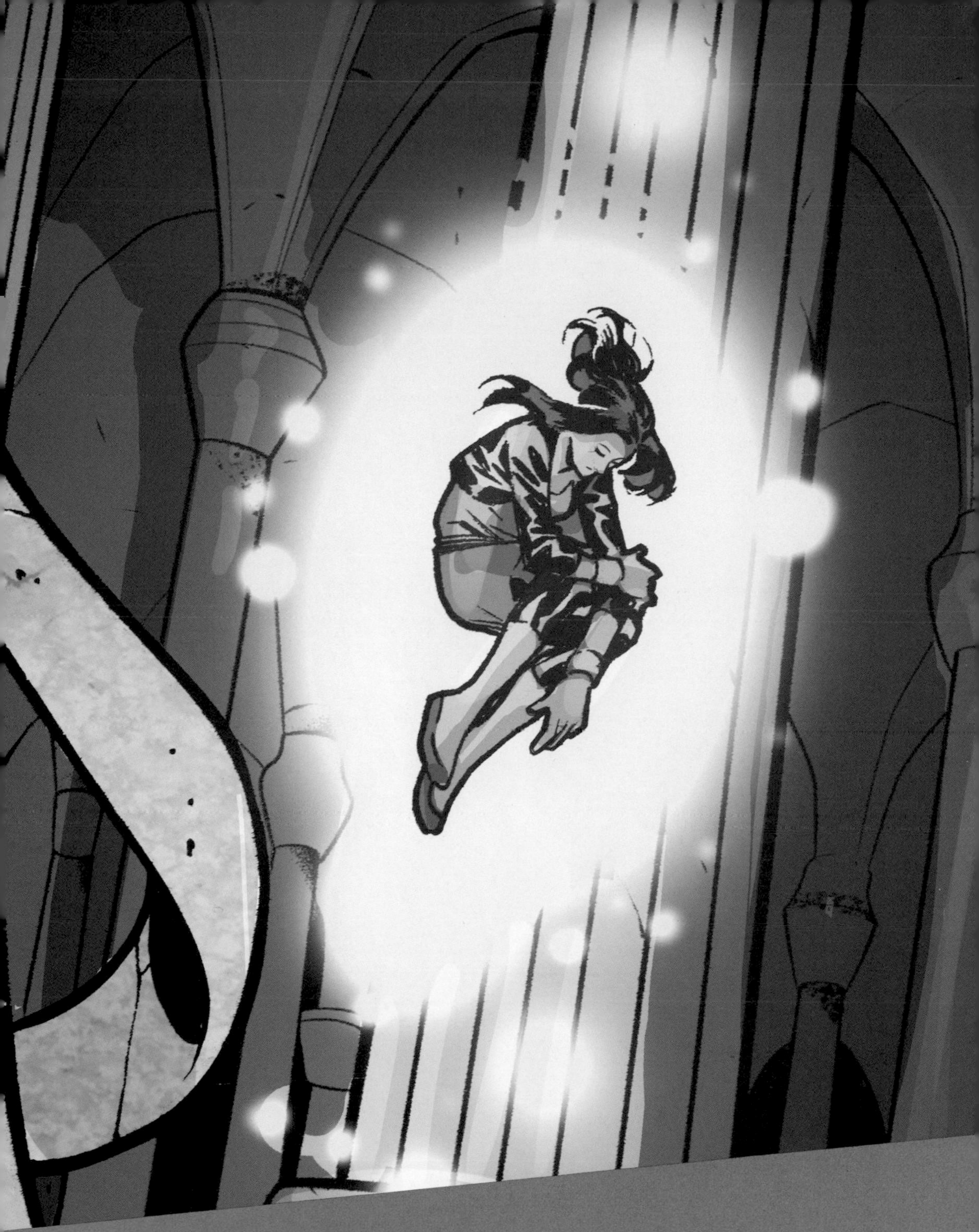

COVER **GALLERY**

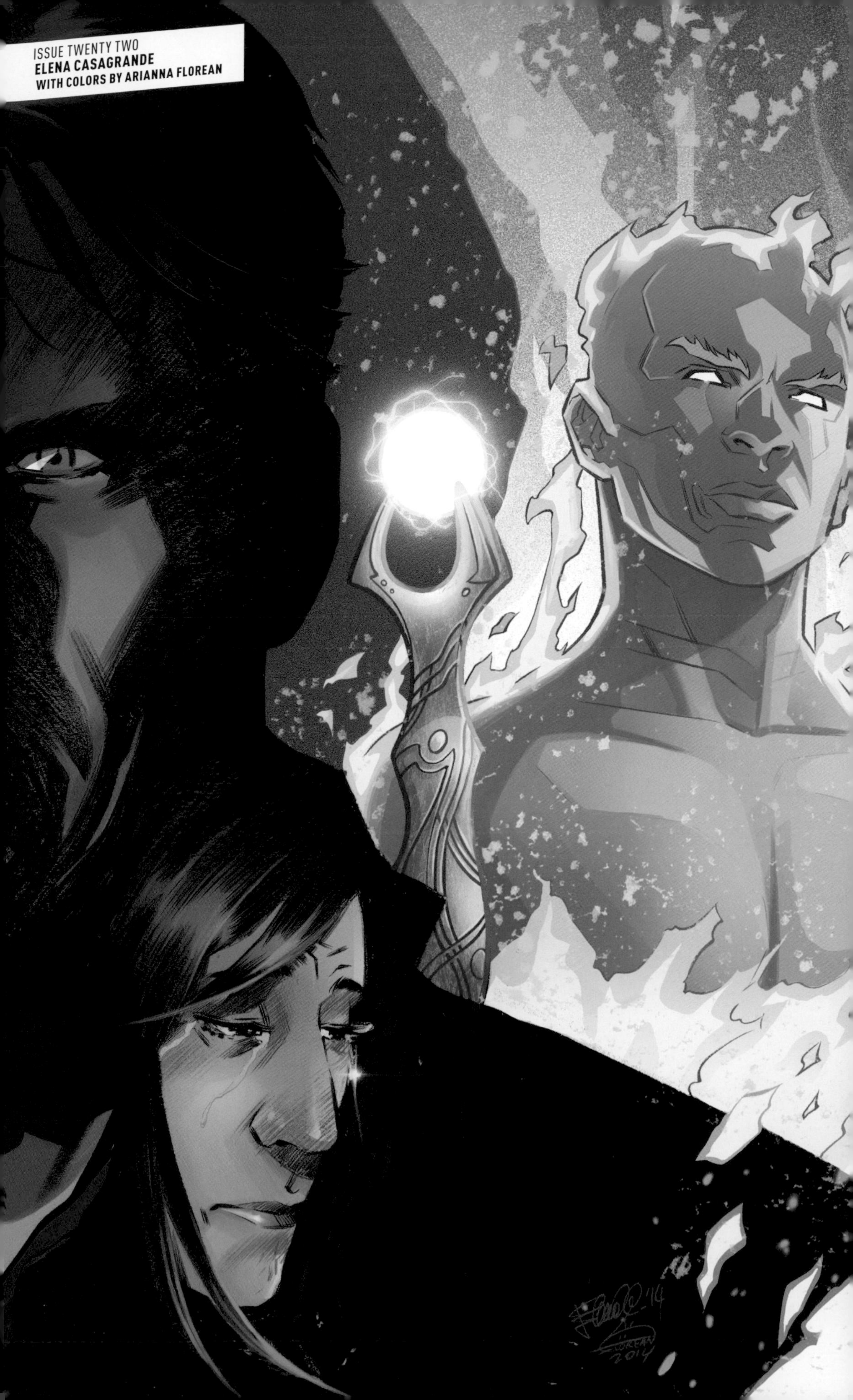

ISSUE TWENTY TWO
ELENA CASAGRANDE
WITH COLORS BY ARIANNA FLOREAN

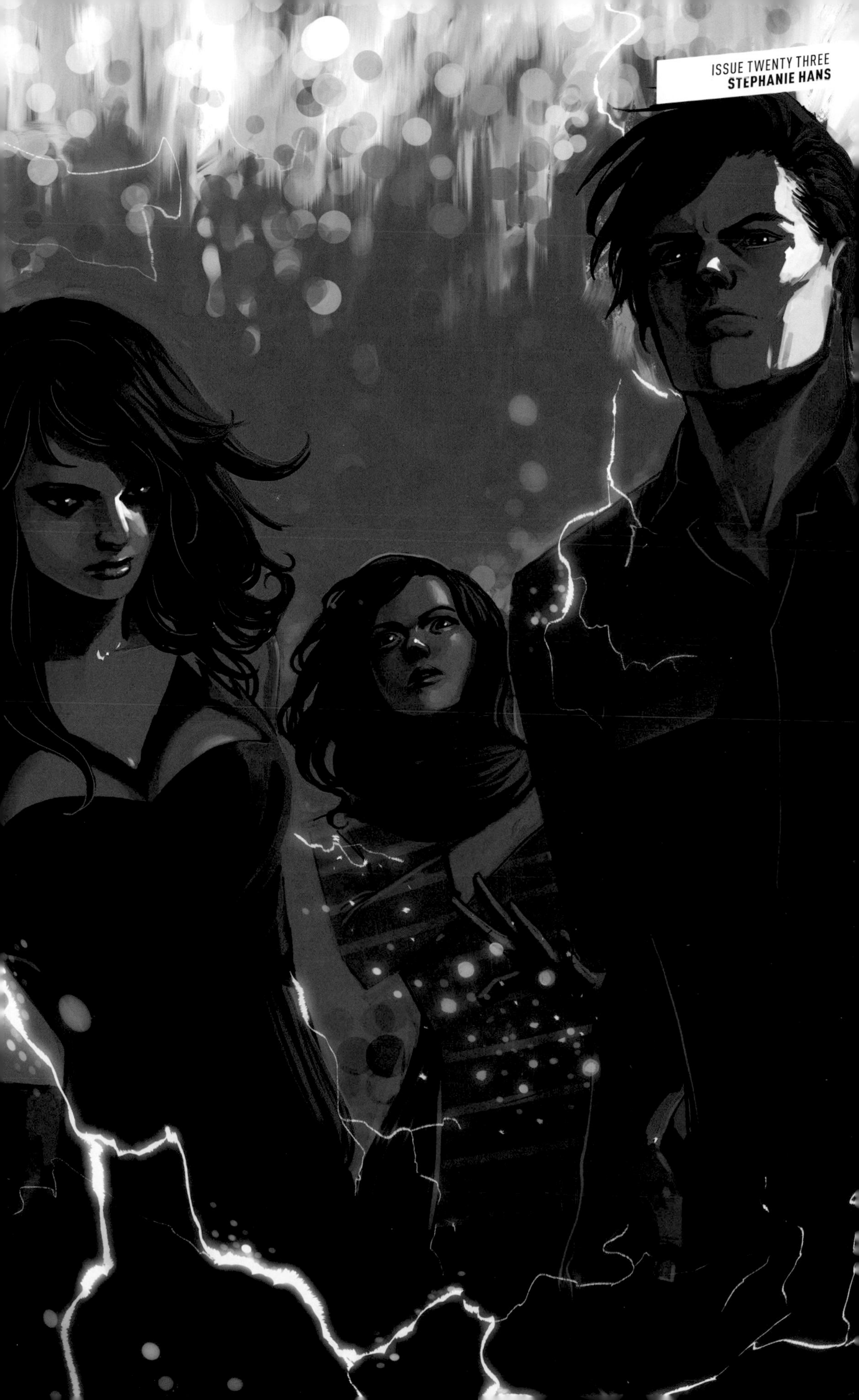

ISSUE TWENTY THREE
STEPHANIE HANS

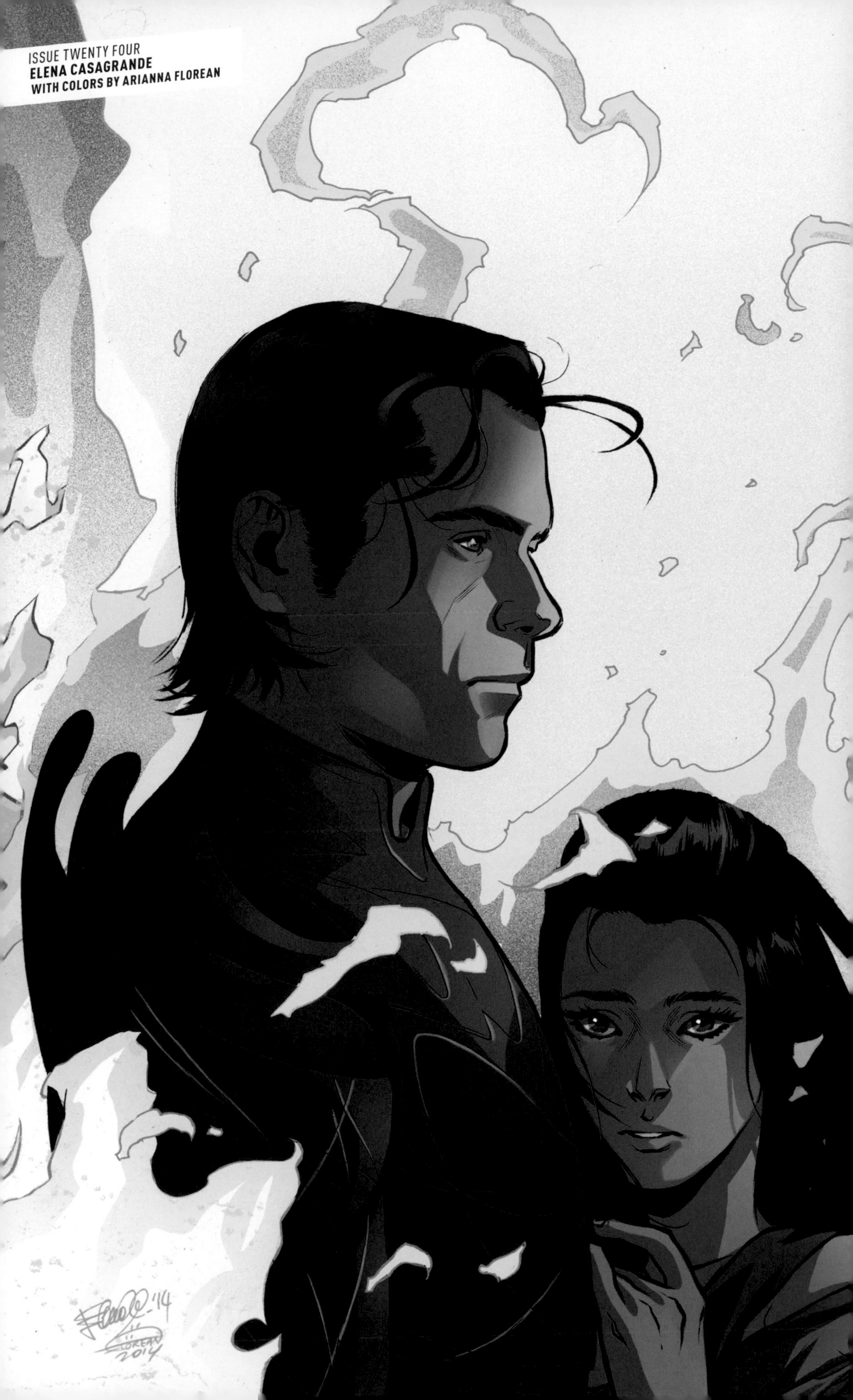

ISSUE TWENTY FOUR
ELENA CASAGRANDE
WITH COLORS BY ARIANNA FLOREAN

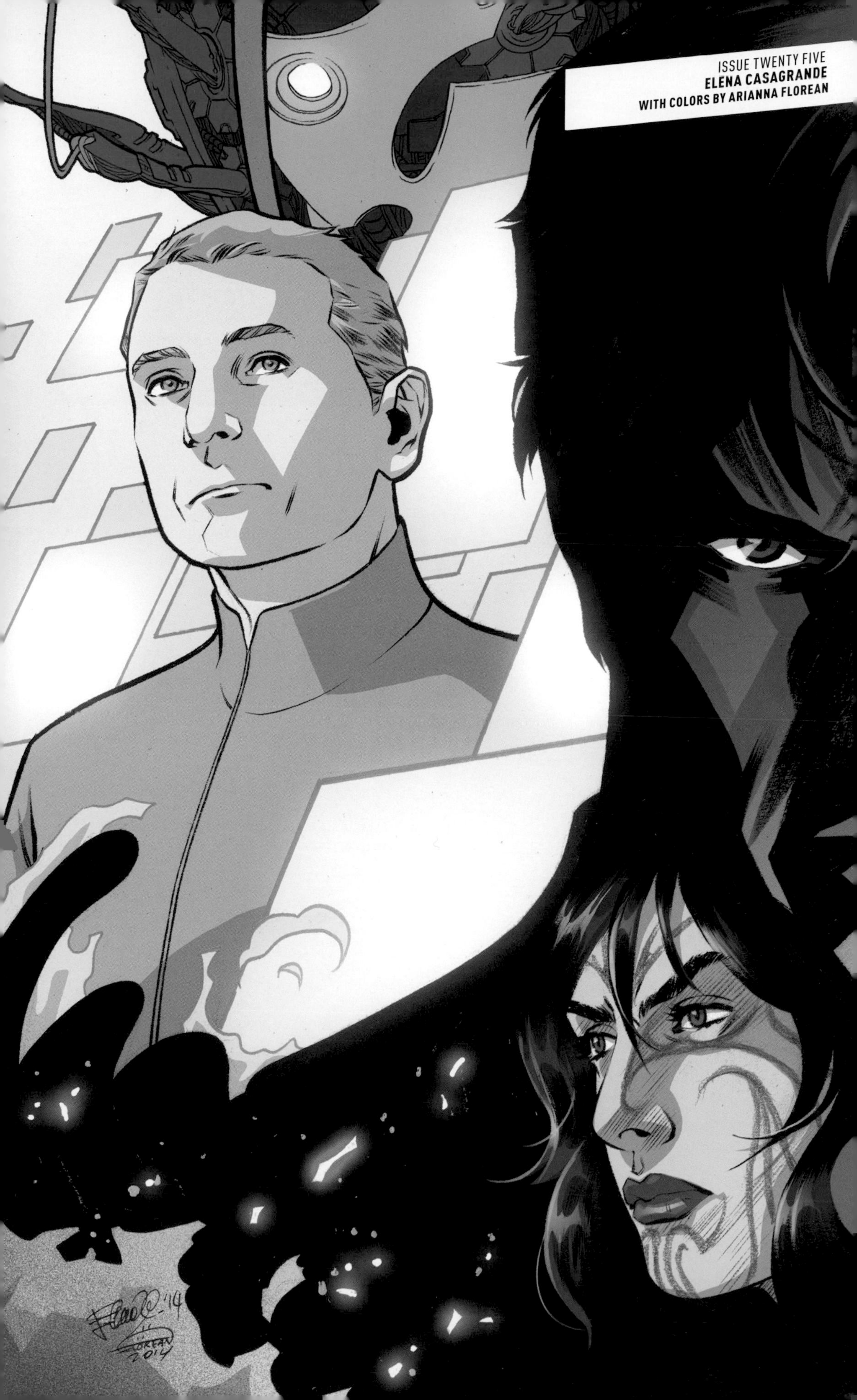

ISSUE TWENTY FIVE
ELENA CASAGRANDE
WITH COLORS BY ARIANNA FLOREAN

THE WINTERS FAMILY ALBUM

BY ELENA CASAGRANDE

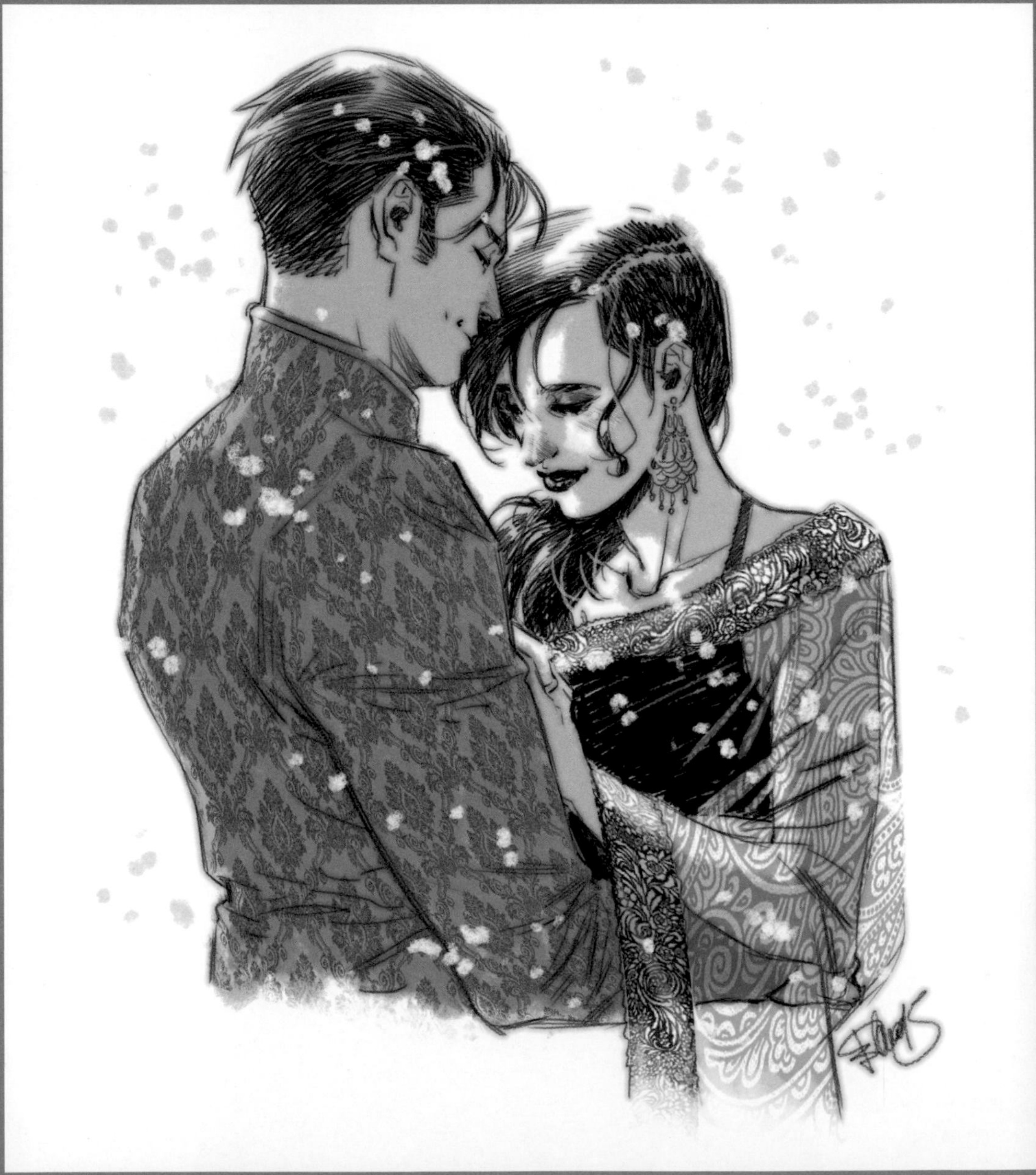

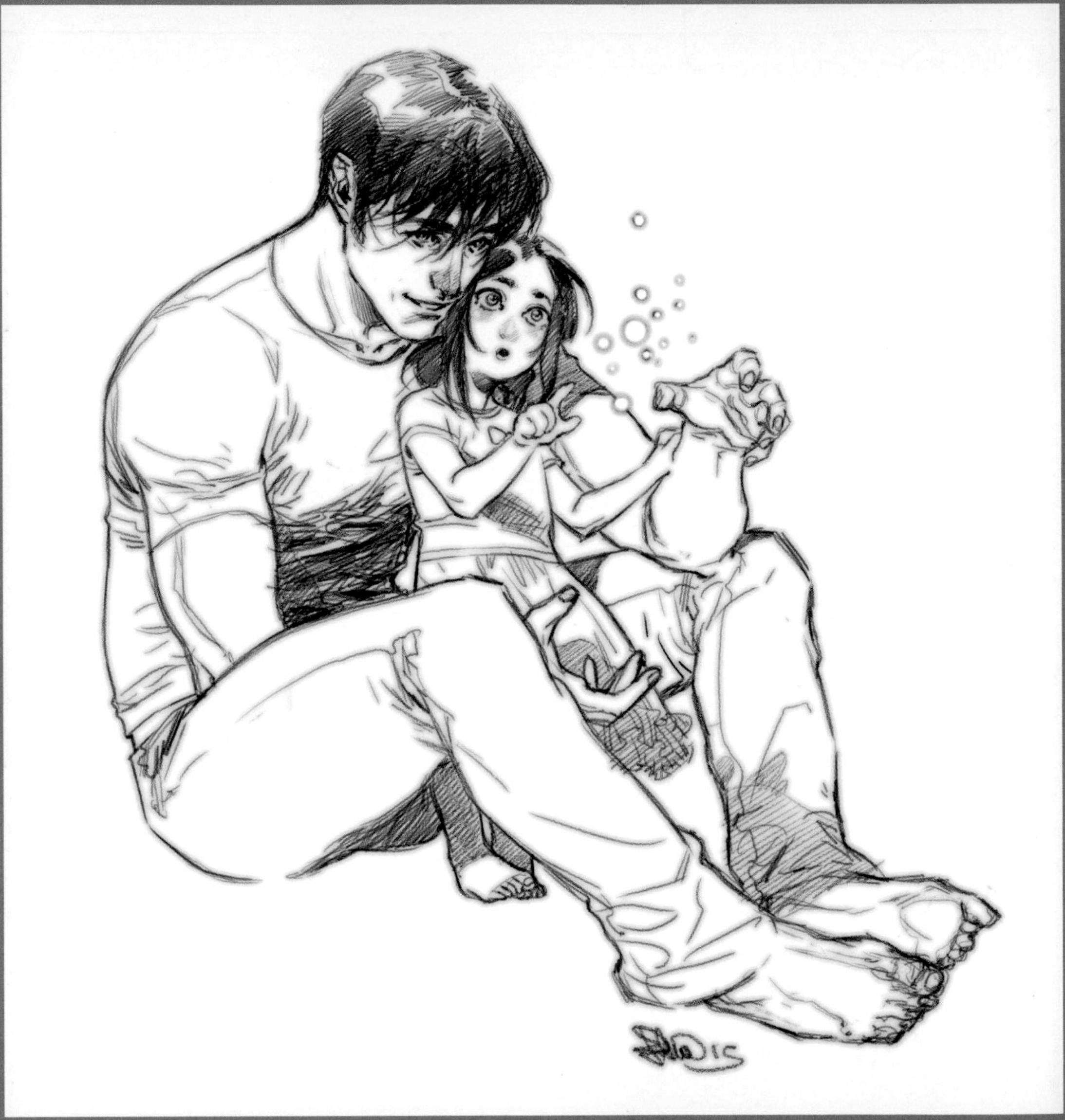

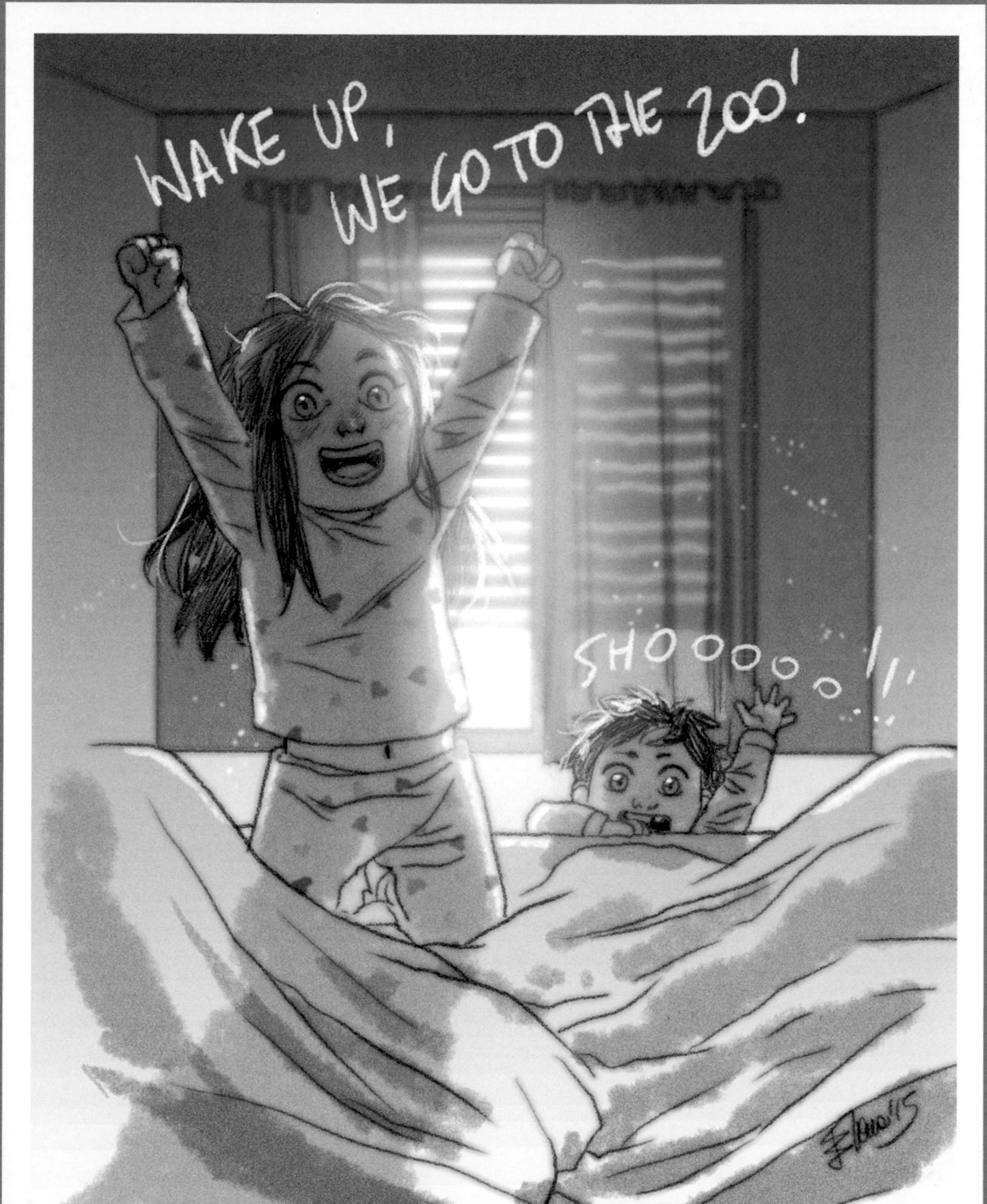
WAKE UP,
WE GO TO THE ZOO!
SHOOOOOO..!!!